FIELD
ETHNOGRAPHY

FIELD ETHNOGRAPHY

A Manual for Doing Cultural Anthropology

PAUL KUTSCHE

Professor Emeritus, Colorado College

PRENTICE HALL, Upper Saddle River, New Jersey 07458

Library of Congress Cataloging-in-Publication Data

KUTSCHE, PAUL
    Field ethnography: a manual for doing cultural anthropology/
    Paul Kutsche.
        p. cm.
    Includes bibliographical references (p.).
    ISBN 0-13-889452-3 (pbk.: alk. paper)
    1. Ethnology—Field work. I. Title.
    GN346.K86 1998
    305.8´00723—dc21   97-37716
                                                        CIP

Editorial director: Charlyce Jones Owen
Acquisitions editor: Nancy Roberts
Editorial/production supervision and interior design: Rob DeGeorge
Copyeditor: Anne Lesser
Buyer: Mary Ann Gloriande
Line art coordinator: Michele Giusti
Line art creation: Maria Piper
Marketing manager: Christopher DeJohn
Cover director: Jayne Conte
Editorial assistant: Maureen Diana

This book was set in 10/12 ITC New Baskerville by Oakland Publishing
Services, Inc., and was printed and bound by Courier Companies, Inc.
The cover was printed by Phoenix Color Corp.

©1998 by Prentice-Hall, Inc.
Upper Saddle River, New Jersey 07458

Printed in the United States of America

10   9

ISBN 0-13-889452-3

Prentice-Hall International (UK) Limited, *London*
Prentice-Hall of Australia Pty. Limited, *Sydney*
Prentice-Hall of Canada, Inc., *Toronto*
Prentice-Hall Hispanoamericana, S. A., *Mexico*
Prentice-Hall of India Private Limited, *New Delhi*
Prentice-Hall of Japan, Inc., *Tokyo*
Prentice-Hall Asia Pte. Ltd., *Singapore*
Editora Prentice-Hall do Brasil, Ltda., *Rio de Janeiro*

Some students grasp assignments as springboards rather than obstacles to their flights of imagination. To them I dedicate this book and my thirty-five years of teaching.

CONTENTS

TO INSTRUCTORS

The series of five field assignments in this book are the best learning tool I devised in my thirty-five years of teaching anthropology. The reason is at least twofold: Students had constant input as we developed the sequence and the wording of the text over a couple of decades. And learning anything by doing it is more effective than reading about what others have done. My newer colleagues in many fields, thirty and more years younger than I, are experimenting successfully with introducing subjects from politics to chemistry by constructing problems to solve rather than formulas to learn. This preface, then, contains both concrete advice on how to use the manual effectively and reflections on what I have learned from using it myself.

My journey along the path of student fieldwork accelerated when, after assigning ritual papers for almost twenty years and being pleased with the results but hungry for more, I jumped to adopt James Spradley and David McCurdy's revolutionary field manual, *The Cultural Experience,* when it came out in 1972. I think all American cultural anthropologists of the 1970s did the same. The resulting student excitement and commitment was gratifying, but soon the more perceptive students discovered that the Spradleyan assumption of cultural uniformity was out of whack with the disagreements about meaning which their own informants experienced in acting on their cultural stages. Jeff White's paper in 1975 on what are locally called the "Broadmoor Rent-a-Cops" broke the Procrustean bed and invited students to trust their judgment. (White's paper is the first in the illustrative section for big ethnographies.)

It took me a decade, however, to trust my own judgment enough to do without *The Cultural Experience* and to write a few tentative pages of instructions for the two assignments I then used—ritual and big ethnography. This modest handout increased in size and number of assignments year by year, and students critiqued it annually, until after about seven editions it assumed roughly the size and content before you.

This book, therefore, was more grown than built. I hope you will read it as a dialogue between one instructor and a succession of students. As it stands, it is designed to reach students of introductory cultural anthropology wherever they may be in their growing up, usually first-year students away from home for the first time, simultaneously trying to grasp new disciplines and to make the transition from childhood into more adult definitions of self. It seeks to hook them on field ethnography. The manual is both task- and student-centered. The tasks are scaled from dead simple to fairly complex and invite students to use their own lives as tools to understand various categories of culture. My experience, like that of many other teachers of anthropology, convinces me that ethnographic fieldwork does in fact stimulate students' interest, and frequently leads them to use ethnographic techniques as majors in anthropology or related fields.

Writing guides to ethnographic fieldwork became a popular occupation after James Spradley and David McCurdy published *The Cultural Experience* in 1972. Among their successors (I make no claim that this list is complete) are Julia Crane and Michael Angrosino, *Field Projects in Anthropology;* Robert Edgerton and L.L. Langness, *Methods and Styles in the Study of Culture;* and L.L. Langness, *The Study of Culture,* all published in 1974. Spradley followed up his and McCurdy's runaway success with *The Ethnographic Interview* in 1979. Conrad Kottak brought out *Researching American Culture* in 1982 based, like Spradley and McCurdy's 1972 book, on papers his students wrote for introductory cultural anthropology. David Fetterman published *Ethnography Step by Step* in 1989. Other guides, intended primarily for the advanced student or professional, have been used occasionally for introductory students. Oswald Werner and G.M. Schoepfle's *Systematic Fieldwork* (1987), Russell Bernard's *Research Methods in Cultural Anthropology* (1988), and Harry Wolcott's *The Art of Fieldwork* (1995) are well-known examples. Of the works just listed, everything by Spradley plus the Werner and Schoepfle book take the ethnoscience (also called ethnolinguistic) approach; Bernard's guide emphasizes quantitative methods and communication technology. To the best of my knowledge, all field guides up to the present are written only from the point of view of the discipline, offering road maps for the outsider who wants to become an insider. They almost entirely ignore the situation of the introductory student who seeks something more general from anthropology than an admission ticket.

My approach is deliberately low on theory, but not empty. The postmodern point of view, especially as it emphasizes reflexivity, not only engages students' minds, but invites them to tie the new adventure to other experiences they may be undergoing or have undergone, to make a bridge between the secondary school past and the more individuated college present. Having crossed over this bridge, students are ready to learn a variety of ethnographic methods in advanced courses. None of my students ever tackled a postmodern situation, which in this context I define as one characterized by interpenetration between two or more cultural universes. That would take more time, and perhaps a larger travel budget, than an undergraduate course allows.

Other considerations than ethnological theory or emotional need may influence students' choice of topics for their big ethnographies, and you will want to take into account the goals of your own students. For instance, students at Grand Valley State University in Michigan demand that their courses serve vocational aims directly, and they are impatient with the indirections of a classic liberal arts education. Some of them resisted when I urged them to move as far out of their past experience as possible, and they chose topics close to the careers they knew and had already chosen. One studied the employees of a store that sold the same sort of goods as her father; another interviewed middle managers in a factory similar to the one in which he wanted to work. I suggest that you experiment with your students, to help them find the cultural scenes that best serve the reasons they came to your college in the first place.

You can use this manual in any of several ways (plus of course others that may occur to you): (1) It can be a supplemental text for the introduction to cultural anthropology, the assignments as additions to tests on the main text. I used it this way at three colleges. (2) It would do equally well as the chief text for a course at the first- or second-year level on field methods, possibly supplemented by any one of a number of more positivist guides to fieldwork. (3) For a three-credit introductory course (mine at Colorado College was longer), you will probably want to use only the first four assignments, or assignments 1 through 3 plus 5. Students in community colleges, particularly, have a hard time finding time even for classroom courses, let alone the fieldwork for what I call a big ethnography.

If your own training in the discipline has been positivist and materialist, as mine was when I took courses from Leslie White, you may wonder whether this manual will permit you to maintain high standards of student performance. Do such exhortations as "stretch your envelopes" and "rules for breaking rules" actually mean "anything goes"? I don't think so—at least they need not. I find it useful to put an extra burden on those who prefer to write their own rules, asking them to demonstrate that they know what they are doing and urging them to explain why their methods of defining the situation and analyzing the data work better than those in the book. I require, for instance, that those who conflate presentation of data with analysis do a thorough job of probing for analytic meaning and demonstrate that their conflated papers are aesthetically superior to papers that separate the two. (Tony Muñoz in his private language and Josh Keilty in his ritual proved to my satisfaction that for their purposes conflation worked better than separation, which is one reason I included their papers.) Perhaps most important of all, I demand excellence in English composition. Since culture is symbolic behavior and words are the principal symbols which humans use, I have always felt that students of culture ought to speak and write their native languages (and ideally others) with precision. In short, good writing is not a bonus but essential to the task of understanding culture. Both concerning the quality of writing and other aspects of excellence, I follow the advice of my colleagues in writing programs and ask students to rewrite papers when that seems profitable and there is time. Few exercises return more learning per unit of effort than rewriting careless prose (which so often betrays sloppy thinking).

However you use this guide with your students, don't make the mistake of *substituting* it for class discussion of fieldwork. I did that the first year my text covered all the assignments, perhaps influenced by Carleton Coon's remark after he had published *Caravan:* "Everything I know about Moslem Africa is in that book, so I won't teach a course on it any more. If you want to learn Islam from me, read my book." The papers that year were dull, perfunctory. This text serves students best after they become excited about the work, and they do need road signs.

CHAPTER BY CHAPTER

Here are suggestions about what to watch for in each assignment, based on both my and my students' experience. The "Pitfalls to Avoid" sections near the beginning of each chapter describe the blind alleys we actually traveled, offered in the hope that your students will make original mistakes instead of repeating ours. (Students report that they like these sections particularly well.)

First, one general remark: The sequence in which students complete these assignments works well, but it is not cast in concrete. As I said earlier, you may find it necessary to choose among the projects because of time pressure. Or you may want to substitute a favorite project of your own for one of mine. Now for a review of the assignments one by one.

The Map

Students regularly question the worth of what they perceive as this busy-work assignment (mapping a block). But alumni of the course regularly report that the exercise helped them to focus on concrete place and time in the more interesting ethnographic assignments which follow; they did better jobs describing setting later on. A common error students make is to spend only an hour or two investigating their blocks, at only one time of day and/or week, and to dash off the assignment (especially the map itself) sloppily. Other frequent errors are to map a block they already know, using memory rather than a sharp fresh eye, and to ignore important features like alleys, yards, and cars. The best counter I have found is to urge them to find blocks that are new to them, mysterious, intriguing, and especially those which appear to be in flux. This assignment can be tied to reading about cultural ecology if that suits your strategy.

Private Language

Emphasize to the class that two kinds of nonstandard language are not appropriate: the technical terms of a vocation or avocation (in Colorado, the temptation is to get by with a list of skiing or camping terms, none of which in my experience has been invented by the student author), and common adolescent slang, which the individual had equally little to do with inventing.

Some students object that "I always use standard English, and never invented anything." You may find it useful to press their memories back to childhood, where virtually all human beings invented special terms in the process of mastering their native languages. When I broach this possibility to the class, faces squirm with a look that says, "Do you really want to embarrass us by demanding our baby talk?" I assure them that their papers will be read by no one but myself without permission, and the promise usually works to free their imaginations.

What students find exhilarating about this assignment is the chance to relive high jinx and high spirits, as in the Ximenes and Beall papers. You may find useful for class discussion their implicit critiques of male chauvinism about auto mechanics (Ximenes) and international hypocrisy (Beall), and they may stimulate discussion of other occult categories of culture. I suggest you use this exercise in connection with class reading about sociolinguistics and about the paradox between culture as the atmosphere one is born in and simply accepts, and culture as the creation of tradition to which each individual contributes his or her mite.

The most productive advice to students that I have discovered is to urge them to recreate the emotional context of the language and to remember their motives. Sometimes a bit of childish silliness has been a Proustian cake, hauling up from the subconscious a whole Christmas tradition, or the closeness of affection in a family.

Body Language

I invented this assignment late in my career, partly for fun. Students find it fun too. They also find it a tool to probe into discrepancies between verbal and nonverbal communication in the ritual assignment and the big ethnography. You can run some distance with this opportunity, as an exploration of deceit, irony, and outright lying as cultural regularities. The benefit to students of becoming aware of what bodies say almost always includes a sharper eye to the interactions between their informants when they work on more complex ethnographies. You may want to make nonverbal communication, à la Ned Hall or Ray Birdwhistell, a segment of your course.

Ritual

If I were to teach introductory students for another thirty-five years, I would revise and refine the section on ritual every year. It was the first field assignment I ever made, recommended to me in 1960 by the late Theodore Mc-Cown of Berkeley in answer to my plaint as a brand-new instructor that I hadn't found a way to make ethnography vivid to students. It was also McCown who recommended John Honigmann's functional definition of ritual as the symbolic expression of appropriate sentiments. You may have one you like better, but bear in mind that Honigmann's is broader than most, inviting students to find ritual in unlikely places rather than limiting themselves to obvious ceremonies.

Following the analytic outline in the text is not a difficult chore, although when it is performed minimally it becomes mechanical—checking items off a list. Nevertheless, I found it useful to insist that students follow instructions for this assignment more faithfully than they did for the other four, especially to defend that the described episode fit the definition. This protected them from the trap of mistaking mere habit and rote repetition for the symbolic expression of appropriate sentiments.

And then my students took over. They taught me the creative potential of imbuing ordinary behavior with symbolic import—that is to say, of ritualizing ordinary actions (the Keilty and Dunbar papers, for example, as well as Rosaldo's parody). As a result, I began to regard ritual as a key unlocking one's understanding of how particular cultures work in particular circumstances. Among its other virtues, the study of ritual extends a bridge from culture as techniques for survival of one species of mammal over to culture as art, as style, as flamboyance and color. By the same token, many students have made of the assignment a chance to conceive themselves as artists in the business of being human. Doing this exercise with enthusiasm has been liberating for quite a number of students. For some, the liberation has its humorous twist like Molière's bourgeois gentilhomme: "My God, I've been creating ritual all my life and didn't know it." As my own understanding of the power of ritual has expanded and as I have been able to present the assignment more and more enthusiastically, students have written more exciting papers and have reported in retrospect that exploring a ritual was more effective than any other single assignment in opening their understanding to how culture shapes human life.

Among the suggestions I made to students about the future study of ritual, three scholars treat it only as public and conservative—van Gennep, Leach, and Turner. Bakhtin and Reich see the culture-creating potential of ritual. Both approaches are equally valid, of course. Make sure that students see that they have these alternative ways of thinking about the assignment. (Among the student examples, Curtis and Stewart wrote conservative papers; the rest took more innovative paths.)

Big Ethnography

This assignment is labor intensive—so much so that I find colleagues who are convinced that (1) students don't have time to do it, and (2) faculty don't have time to guide it. The first objection I acknowledged earlier, by suggesting that if pressed for time you can assign either the first four exercises, or 1 through 3 plus 5. As for the second objection, student assistants can take most of the time burden off you. I regularly employ two assistants for a class of twenty-five students. Hiring both males and females gives students welcome alternatives in styles of communication. After the first year, I hired only assistants who had done big ethnographies themselves, so they empathized with the problems that students brought to them. Brilliant people are less effective as assistants than those who slogged through difficulties when they did their own ethnographies (so long as their final products were successful). I never had trouble finding money in a tight departmental budget to pay student assistants because they are used only for this one assignment and the total number of hours is not great.

After a certain amount of trial and error, my student staff and I arrived at a workable routine. I introduce the assistants to the class at the beginning of the semester (well before they would begin their fieldwork) with much fanfare. The assistants whip up enthusiasm for the project by offering autobiographical anecdotes focusing on why they chose their own projects and summarizing their own problems and triumphs. Members of the class often respond with enthusiasm edged by hysteria as they think ahead to what they fear and what they might dare in their own work, and they bombard the assistants with the sort of questions that students can more easily ask each other than they can ask a teacher. Practical information is given out on this occasion in the hope that students will make an early start finding their own cultural scenes—appointment schedules, local mail and e-mail addresses, phone numbers—with the invitation to start consulting at once.

It also helped at Colorado College, which is a residential liberal arts college, to retreat overnight with the class and the assistants to a mountain cabin just as work on the big ethnography was to begin. First-year students shared fears and hopes more easily over a campfire than they did in the classroom, and the unusual setting gave a boost to class morale. You may find that some variation on this device is appropriate to your class setting.

Teams or lone rangers? Both work; both have costs. My own approach is laissez-faire because some students work more happily one way, some the other. Schedule a discussion of these possibilities early in the course, so students can ponder their pros and cons.

In the beginning of the chapter on big ethnographies are instructions that read, "You will be expected to consult with the instructor or the assistants on or before a date to be announced." Students are encouraged to consult frequently, but required to do so at least on three stated occasions.

The first is to ensure that a cultural scene has been located, the permission of informants secured, and rapport is beginning to be established. It is essential to gain feedback at this point to assuage fears about intruding into strange spaces and to be sure the project doesn't violate the instructor's, the institution's, or the law's guidelines and has the prospect of success. I must reiterate that students typically feel freer to admit their feelings of inadequacy when talking with other students who have recently done field ethnography than they do with an instructor who seems entrenched behind degrees, authority, and (maybe) white hair. Ethnographic fieldwork is only in part an intellectual process; the rest of it is as much an emotional challenge as sailing one's first boat, fighting one's first bully, or making love for the first time. Peers are easier to talk with about intuitive experiences than authority figures are. Both instructor and assistants should use this occasion to reemphasize the importance of the discipline's code of ethics and to distinguish anthropology's sense of responsibility from those of other disciplines and occupations.

The second required consultation aims to ensure that data are being collected and the analysis begun. At this stage the staff help students find gaps in their data, suggest profitable lines of enquiry and ways of handling the usually inchoate mass of information, and reassure self-doubters.

The third consultation, a week or two before the due date for the paper, is usually shorter. It focuses on analysis, on writing problems, and on ways of saying goodbye that leave informants happy to have shared.

Throughout the consultation process, the staff must be receptive to the self-revelations and dismays that the demanding business of field ethnography awakens in all of us who get thoroughly involved in it. The cliché that ethnographers learn more about themselves and their own cultures than about informants and theirs, becomes a critical issue when the ethnographer is also a late adolescent whose most urgent life business is discovering a self which is separate from the family self she or he grew up with. In my opinion, only teachers willing to accept the responsibility to cope with whatever students discover about themselves as they discover the cultures of others can in good conscience include field assignments in their courses, at either the undergraduate or graduate level.

Student assistants can be insightful, dedicated, and creative. But they are still students themselves and thus need guidance. My staff and I worked out a way of providing it and of reviewing where the class is, which students have what problems and how they can be solved, and at the same time creating the paper trail to cover ourselves if that becomes necessary, as it did only once in twenty years. Assistants and instructor keep logs of all consultations, and the staff meets periodically for lunch, using the logs to go over the class one by one, to see problems that need attention. (I will have consulted myself with some of the students, either those who preferred to consult me or those referred earlier by assistants.) This technique is effective in ensuring that the odd quiet student doesn't slip through the net and come up empty on due date, and it has the added advantage of sharing perspectives on ways to handle field problems. The one time we needed to show documentation, we had a detailed record for the dean, demonstrating that a complaining student hadn't met consultation appointments, had been telephoned but hadn't responded.

A potential bonus: If the psychodynamics of the class have in general been good and if one or two students have become hyperenthusiastic about their fieldwork, give them time in class to share their delight and their problems. Andy Lewis took us through every new adventure he made into the world of homeless men. His enthusiasm was infectious, and his description of field and analysis problems incited a number of fruitful discussions about other students' problems. At least one other session started with hilarity and ended with useful sharing of field tips: A member of the class who ordinarily dressed in slovenly undergraduate fashion decided to study a stockbroker's office. Some of the other students reminded him that costuming is important to good rapport and not only gave him unsolicited advice as he assembled (and modeled) a field wardrobe, but loaned him essential items he didn't possess. Class members had great fun with what became a critical review of undergraduate dress codes, and they ended up becoming more sophisticated about dress as an aspect of the cultural scene that they should record and analyze.

I intended an ode when I compiled this manual over a couple of decades, but it turned to a sonnet (to paraphrase Austin Dobson's 1874 poem "Rose Leaves"). The "Rose" who "cross'd the road/In her latest new bonnet" was the response of students and alumni. My ode is first of all the graded assignments, designed so the student steadily acquires skills and concepts that will be useful for doing serious ethnography, practices those skills in assignments that increase little by little in complexity, and builds self-confidence to greet the big ethnographic project as a large but feasible challenge. Second, my ode is the presentation of a major ethnographic project in a way that invites the student to bring past experience to it, and to make of it an adventure and a dialogue rather than solely the application of a set of instructions about method. The ode took shape half-consciously over more than a decade. It turned into a sonnet *un*consciously as students began to say in many different ways that not only was the fieldwork the most interesting part of the course, but they learned and retained better when they were given wide scope on each assignment and when they could invest their own memories and dreams into an academic course. The impetus of what students learned in these assignments helped a number of them trust their judgment and creative powers in other courses and in their postcollege careers. I offer my fellow teachers both ode and sonnet and leave it to you to discover how each is useful to your students.

My colleague Paul Kuerbis in CC's Department of Education informs me that I reinvented the wheel: his discipline developed this approach some time ago, and gave it a label—*constructivism*. (See Brooks and Brooks, 1993, for a short readable description of theory and practice, and Airasian and Walsh, 1997, for a set of cautions that go far beyond the scope of our concerns here. The latter also note that constructivist learning is always labor intensive.) *Experiential learning* is almost synonymous. Many educationists believe that students of all ages learn, retain, and use concepts best when they take a creative part in the process, whatever the discipline. Memorizing is far less effective. Evidently I am less a patron of poetry than a bourgeois gentilhomme myself, having conducted a partly constructivist classroom for thirty-five years without knowing it.

If you are as self-confident as I was in the 1970s, you will convince yourself that your students are doing much better than mine, just as I was (and still am) sure mine did much better than Spradley's and McCurdy's. At the same time, if you are as fortunate as I have been in sharing with your introductory students a form of learning in which students become creators of the material along with the instructor, then you will find yourself, as I have year after year, revising your copy of this book as the method uncovers new layers of understanding of culture and of the contributions which students and faculty can make to their common tasks when both are free to bring a good deal of themselves to it. My 20-20 hindsight on what worked well and what worked ill in my own introductory course leaves me regretting that I never reworked all the material so as to present everything experientially, not just the field assignments. Satisfied students said consistently, "The fieldwork was the best part of the course"; disgruntled students said, "The fieldwork was fine, but the rest was boring."

I look forward to hearing from you about your discoveries. A letter addressed to Colorado College, Colorado Springs, CO 80903, will always reach me.

ACKNOWLEDGMENTS

Culture is social. Learning is social. Ethnographies are social. Writing books is a social process. This book is the result of social trials and errors in Introduction to Cultural Anthropology at Colorado College over a number of years, at Grand Valley State University in 1994, and at Pikes Peak Community College in 1996. Every student, good, bad, or indifferent, helped in his or her own way.

Special thanks go to the following former students who made suggestions and criticisms: Scott Bramwell, Arwyn Elden, Andrew Lewis, Laura Phillips, and Wendy Davis Pinger. Thanks also to students who permitted me to use their field reports for illustrations; they are enumerated in the table of contents. Lara Fedor and Wendy Powers reproduced charts and maps. My two secretaries, Alison Seyler and Suzanne Ridings, supported me generously during innumerable revisions for several editions of this field guide over several years. The staff of the Colorado College library supported my work superbly, as always. Beacon Press gave me permission to quote from Renato Rosaldo, *Culture and Truth.*

Among my colleagues, Alice Higman Reich has influenced me most in thinking about ethnography. She began as my student in the field in New Mexico and imperceptibly became my teacher. Her observation in 1968 about Hispanic village "rituals of hello and good-bye" helped me see ordinary social events as potentially ceremonial. Paul Kuerbis, Michael Nowak, and Laurel Watkins provided references in their specialties.

The following reviewers made helpful suggestions: Gregory Forth, University of Alberta; and Michael Warren, Iowa State University. At Prentice Hall, Rob DeGeorge did his best to transform an assembly line procedure into humane communication.

FIELD
ETHNOGRAPHY

INTRODUCTION

Doing field ethnography defines the American cultural anthropologist. The tradition, which began at the beginning of the twentieth century with Franz Boas and his students as a corrective to nineteenth-century armchair speculation, quickly became an initiation rite for anyone who wished to be admitted into the fraternity of professionals, and remains more often than not the high point of our careers. It is a demanding intellectual exercise and a deeply emotional encounter. It is frightening, exciting, and satisfying. It is a lot more fun than reading ethnographies that other people have written.

For beginning students of cultural anthropology, who are the intended users of this manual, ethnography is especially daunting, for you have little or no knowledge of the discipline, and probably have seldom or never ventured outside your own subculture. Therefore, this manual introduces fieldwork by steps, starting so simply that it may seem childish, ending with a real although small-scale challenge. By the time you finish this introductory course, you should no longer feel like a beginning student who has marked the squares on examinations about the concepts and data of cultural anthropology, but like a beginning ethnographer capable of judging the work of other ethnographers. You will understand both some of the powers of the technique of participant observation and some of its limitations and drawbacks. Although your work will be confined to what you can do close to the campus, and confined even more in the time you can spend in the field, you will use the classic methods that have marked field ethnography for a century.

Sequence of Field Assignments

1. Map of a block
2. Private language
3. Nonverbal communication
4. Ritual
5. The big ethnography

The five field exercises are graded in difficulty and in complexity. They proceed from the map, which requires nothing but a sharp eye for detail and systematic thoroughness, to a final assignment that requires ethnographers to step out of their skins enough to try seeing the world through the eyes of other people. Each exercise builds on the preceding, incorporating the skills learned and adding new ones. If you do all exercises with enthusiasm and care, you will find each new one only a reasonable challenge and all of them welcome additions to your intellectual power. The first four exercises prepare you for the big ethnography, for which you will go off campus, either alone or as part of a team, find a cultural scene different from anything you have yet experienced, immerse yourself in it as thoroughly as time permits, and write your mini-monograph.

TWO SPECIAL CAUTIONS

First, this book is not a textbook that you can absorb in a general way. It is a field manual, which, like a laboratory manual, is to be followed step by step. The most detailed instructions are in the sections on ritual and big ethnography. Read them especially carefully and follow them closely.

Second, if your big ethnography is to be successful, it will require a lot of preparation. Most of the fieldwork will be done in the second half of the course, but make contact with your sources as close to the beginning of the course as possible. Visit them from time to time so that when you begin serious work, your rapport will already be warm. The classic undergraduate last-minute attack and all-nighter writing are less likely to succeed with the big ethnography than with almost any other assignment you can think of.

RULES FOR BREAKING THE RULES

Anthropology is constantly reinventing itself, and new approaches to ethnography come into print faster than anyone can keep up. This manual contains explicit directions for completing every field assignment, but some students choose to bend the rules or go beyond them. For instance, Evan Hill's map goes well beyond the description of a block to speculate on its aesthetic relation to the physical and social structure of the city. Jen Sands's account of Dale House goes beyond that halfway house to connect it in her mind with the play she is acting in, and to speculate on structure and the lack of it in the lives of young people whose parents cannot cope. Josh Keilty didn't follow the procedure for writing up a ritual, but conflated description with analysis. I have deliberately included student papers that are not perfect, but chose each paper because of some element of intellectual excitement. You can learn from your elders' successes and also from their failures. The aim is to inspire you, not to intimidate or overwhelm you.

The rule for breaking the rule is that you must make it clear you understand what the rules are and why you are breaking them. The burden is on you. If you succeed, as the authors mentioned just did, you will have expanded the envelope of form and the range of acceptable work in ethnography. If you fail, you have merely done a bad job. *Caveat studens!*

A PHILOSOPHY OF ANTHROPOLOGY, AND OF LEARNING

This field manual has been more than thirty years in the making. It was intended simply as a how-to guide for students in introductory cultural anthropology. But conversations with my best alumni as I prepared revisions taught me that the field approach is actually an approach to learning in general: It stems from the conviction that the more involved students are in the work of the discipline, and the more involved they are in creating the structure of their education, the better the learning endures and the more useful that education is.

Anthropology (and probably every other discipline) is only in the broadest way what the textbook or the instructor says it is. Intimately, it is what students make it mean to them. If they are permitted and/or encouraged to help define the discipline from the very first course, then they are more likely to make original contributions in their doctoral dissertations and after, if they go that far. If they stop anywhere along the way, then practice in how to approach learning at once creatively and critically will spill over into every intellectual task they undertake.

That is, perhaps, little more than to say that anthropology is central to a liberal arts education, the aim of which is not in any large measure to impart information, but predominantly to help you develop the power of critical analytic thinking and to exercise and focus your creative powers.

Alice Reich, an anthropologist with whom I worked productively in the field in the 1960s, and who has inspired me ever since to think of my science as a humanity, expressed the philosophy that she and I share in a paper delivered at Colorado College in 1993, about the contradictions and ironies of anthropology. Here is a long excerpt from that paper:

Anthropology as Oxymoron

by Alice Reich
Regis University

I have been teaching anthropology for twenty-one years to students, most of whom will never have another anthropology class and virtually none of whom will become anthropologists. My entire context of teaching anthropology is in its contributory role in a liberal arts education. I continue to believe that anthropology is the quintessential liberal arts discipline because it is about meaningful human life, not as a set of answers, but as a series of engaged conversations.

In my cultural anthropology course, I ask students to enter into conversations among people of a different time and place, conversations between anthropologists and the people with whom they have lived, conversations among anthropologists who disagree about the people with whom they lived, and of course, those conversations the students themselves are creating. I ask students to bring openness and an ability to listen as well as a responsibility to contribute. I ask them to tolerate ambiguity, and to recognize the fundamental kinship that exists among human beings as well as the fundamental mystery that keeps us from knowing one another fully. I continually ask students to embrace a number of contradictions. (I am only slightly chagrined to admit that I have never abandoned as the central question of anthropology: What does it mean to be human? When a student said to me this semester, "How can we ever know the answer to that?" I congratulated her and welcomed her into the conversation.) Herewith my latest thoughts on the conversation.

FIELDWORK

In thinking about anthropology and the ways it contributes to a liberal arts education by shattering paradigms, I decided to look at all the ways I ask introductory-level students to accept contradictions. One of the first words the students learn is *oxymoron*—a rhetorical expression referring to a phrase that combines contradictory or incongruous terms. (Students know this, and offer their favorite examples, from business ethics to military music.) They often don't know the origin of the word, however. It comes from the Greek, from the roots *oxy*, meaning sharp, and *moros*, meaning foolish or dull, from, in fact, a Greek word meaning pointedly foolish. It usually appears on the chalkboard just above the two words *participant observation*. This, I explain, is the primary method of anthropology, a time-honored tradition of making a fool of oneself for a point. They will later read Yolanda and Robert Murphy's remark, "ethnography is conducted in good part through overcoming misunderstandings" (1985:60), and this will come to include not simply the misunderstandings one has of another culture, but of one's own. We discuss the contradictions between participating and observing, and the very major differences of this method of learning from that of the so-called objective observation they have been taught as the primary paradigm of Western knowledge. We discuss the fact that, far from being so-called research subjects (a phrase in which humans are turned into objects), the people anthropologists study are their teachers. This conversation leads directly into the basic epistemological issue of objectivity, and challenges, if it does not shatter, many students' view of what that means.

Within the first week they are asked to go into the field, into a setting which is probably very familiar to them, and to see the familiar as if it were strange. This is their next contradiction, and it is more difficult than it may seem. Many students, after a thirty-minute observation, will describe the people in their cultural scene in terms of social class, or in terms of their motivations or other personal qualities. "How do you know?" appears repeatedly in my comments on their field reports. Long before I had the vocabulary for it, I was asking them to deconstruct their own assumptions about the world around them, asking them to take apart their taken-for-granted knowledge and build new ways of seeing, hearing, and understanding the world. They do these by looking again and again at an ordinary scene in their culture. "How," one who had spent the semester in a pancake house asked oxymoronically, "could something so boring be so interesting?"

Another lesson from fieldwork is also another challenge to their paradigms. They have been taught that predictability is the primary purpose for studying humans. They want to observe an area of behavior about which they can make safe predictions and thus feel scientific. I suggest that what is most predictable about us is our unpredictability, or, as Manning Nash used to say to his students, "If you can think of it, somebody somewhere is doing it, has done it, or will do it someday." I ask them how they would respond if I predicted that they would all get up and leave at the time class ends. There have always been those students who resent being predicted, and assert they would leave early or stay late. This, to me, illustrates their existence as subjects rather than objects. And it is not difficult to translate the desire to be the true subject (as differentiated from the research subject) to other peo-ple like themselves. Seeing the people they are reading about or learning about from films and videos as subjects as well is more difficult. This takes me to ethnography in the sense of anthropological expositions of other cultures.

ETHNOGRAPHY

At the same time that I ask students to see their own social world as strange, I begin to ask them to see heretofore strange worlds as familiar. I ask them to see people who look like nothing they have ever seen before as their fel-low human beings, to see beyond their senses (and assumptions) into their shared humanity.

The primary contradictory concepts which I ask students to balance as they study what appear to them to be "other cultures" include that there is something we can identify with in every other human and at the same time there is fundamental mystery between us, something unknowable to us in every other human. We can use analogy with our own culture and our own lives as a bridge to understanding what at first appears incomprehensible, but once we have crossed that bridge, we must be willing to burn it and look into the unbridgeable chasm that is the mystery between us. No, they're re-ally not just like us only in costume. We begin here to understand the enig-matic fact that, as Clifford Geertz has told us (1973: Chapter 2), we can only be human in specific ways, ways that make us fundamentally different from each other.

Less profound, perhaps, but equally important to knowing, is the fact that we can know only in specific ways. I have given up a survey approach in favor of studying a few cultures in some more depth, taking the time to see the conflicts in various interpretations of, for example, the !Kung, talk-ing about the limits of our knowing, of anyone's knowing based on the knower's history and biography; talking, in fact, about something that con-temporary scholars call *standpoint*. Someone held the cameras, edited the film, wrote the narrative, chose the genre of romance, or tragedy, or com-edy to tell the story. Our task as learners is to know the tellers as well as the told.

CULTURE

I continue to value the concept of culture and to try to teach it. And the central contradiction here, though finally we would have to use the word *di-alectic* to comprehend what we are taking about, is the fact that as humans we are both the creatures and the creators of culture. Not only do I still explore through anthropology what it means to be human, but I suggest that it is to be simultaneously (or, more accurately, dialectically) the recipient of millions of years of culture and to be active as a creator of culture. The crucial awareness of ourselves and of all humans as culture makers as well as culture bearers is the strongest message anthropology has to offer in a liberal education. To be human is to have a voice that names the world in relation to one's own experience. To be human is to seize the right to one's own voice and to work for the rights of everyone to a voice.

The oxymorons, the contradictions, which we can embrace and by which we can be embraced, then, include:

    participant observation
    the subject object
    the strange familiar and the familiar strange
    the universal specificity of humankind
    culture/ourselves as creation and as created

These contradictions are central to anthropology, but also to our fully human participation in both knowing and constructing our world.

Ethics

The Statements on Ethics of the American Anthropological Association are being revised as this book goes to press. The new version, as it pertains to undergraduate fieldwork, will almost certainly stay very much the same. Here are the important principles for you to keep firmly in mind:

1. The interests of the informant come before all other considerations, even getting a high grade on an assignment. The informants' desires concerning whether they get copies of your paper, whether they are to be named or their identities hidden and whether certain things you learn can be included in your paper are paramount. Discuss these concerns with informants before you commit yourself to the particular scene you want to study. You are a guest on the scene. You have no rights vis-à-vis the informants' rights. Therefore, concentrate on kinds of information that informants want known.

2. Anthropologists do not misrepresent themselves to informants, and they never hide either their identities or their intentions. Scholars in certain other disciplines, under certain stated conditions, do mislead informants whom they label *subjects*. Anthropology does not criticize its sister disciplines for misrepresentation, but it holds itself aloof from imitating them. Our relation to our informants is that of students to teachers. They know their cultures; we go to learn those cultures.

To make sure my students understood how important these principles are, I warn them that violation of either principle will result in failing the course and the case being sent to the college's honor council. Consult your own instructors, and be sure you understand their policies regarding ethical fieldwork.

Once you abandon the CIA image of false identity, you will find that your collaboration with your informant/teachers to spread understanding about them is much more enjoyable and leads to close working relations with them. A small exception to entire openness: Infrequently, you may need supplemental information that can best be acquired by incidental participation. It is not necessary to carry a sign saying "I am an ethnographer" under these circumstances. For example, Andy Lewis's interest in a house for homeless people in Colorado Springs led him to spend a night in a Red Cross shelter in another part of town. He did not announce himself as a student doing a research project, and no one questioned him. If they had, he would have been obligated to identify himself correctly. In general, you may distinguish between impersonal behavior in public places and the relations of confidence with your principal informants.

The Zero

Zeros are socially and culturally important, although they are often overlooked both by professionals and by students. Anthropologists recognize zeros most easily in linguistics and in ritual: while the plural of dog is dogs, with the final /z/ the morpheme for plural, the plural of sheep is sheep, with the final zero the morpheme for plural (note that zeros can be tricky); a ritual of avoidance (see number 2 under "Miscellaneous Functions" in the section on ritual) is a communication made by avoiding doing something. Zeros are analogous to the white spaces on the Rorschach ink blots.

Do not confuse zero communications with the absence of communication. A social example of a zero would be an encounter between two professors on campus who would normally be expected to greet each other. If they do not, they are probably engaged in one of the petty quarrels which academics so delight in and are snubbing each other. An example of absence would be the child who neglects to write thank yous for Christmas presents. The observer may infer bad manners, but the child is not making the communication "I hate Grandma."

Look for zeros in all of the field assignments: the vacant lot, the (possibly pregnant) pause in a private communication, the dropped cues in nonverbal encounters, the things not said and words not spoken in rituals, the blanks in interaction between people who make up the cultural scene.

As you become skilled at recognizing zeros you will find them fun. They are like syncopated rhythms in Bach and in jazz. Keep them in mind as you analyze data.

A Final Introductory Word

This manual invites you to celebrate oxymorons. Good ethnography is, on the one hand, meticulous scholarship, which relies on close and accurate observation. It emphasizes crawling, insofar as possible, inside the skulls of your informants and seeing the world through their eyes. Good ethnographers listen to their informants and look at their cultural scenes very attentively, very quietly, to hear and see not what they want to hear and see, but what is important to informants. They must train themselves to be thorough, to probe, and to analyze as subtly as possible, leaving nothing unexplained.

On the other hand, good ethnography is creative and at its best poetic (look ahead at Muñoz's private language, at Keilty's and Muñoz's rituals, at Sands's big ethnography). The architecture of the reconstructions you make in this course is yours and can only be yours. Creative ethnography (actually, any ethnography at all that is sufficient to take seriously) imposes a responsibility on its author because by interpreting it changes reality. Look ahead to the ethnographic fragment by Renato Rosaldo in the ritual chapter: Rosaldo, by making the description he records there, "transformed a relatively spontaneous event into a generic cultural form" and "defamiliarize[d] the family breakfast." It was never the same again. As a scholar describing a part of your world, you must recognize your awesome power to become a magician changing that world.

Together, scholarly care and creative flights create scenes vivid enough that the reader can say, in Clifford Geertz's phrase, "I was there because you were there." Cultural anthropology is at once science and art.

Your fieldwork, in the five exercises that follow, will be severely limited in scope because of the pressures of time and space of a single semester with no subsidy for travel. But within those limitations you can make remarkable progress. You live in overlapping worlds full of complexity, contradiction (the oxymorons), and fine shades of meaning. While you cannot imitate Margaret Mead, whose first fieldwork put her on a boat for American Samoa, you can follow the lead of Henry David Thoreau, who "traveled widely in Concord." You can ring some of the changes on life in your own self-conscious society.

I do not go so far as some of my colleagues, to advocate abandoning the concept of culture in favor of the exclusive use of personal narratives (e.g., Abu-Lughod, 1991). Anthropology invented "Culture" in 1871 (p. 1 in Sir E.B. Tylor's *Primitive Culture*), has refined the definition numerous times since, and insists on it as the single behavioral characteristic that distinguishes *Homo sapiens* from the rest of the animal kingdom. We err hugely if we throw out our heritage for a mess of literary critical pottage. But, as the illustrative papers in this book make clear, it is possible and profitable to describe the culture (shared understandings) of a single scene while at the same time telling stories (narratives) about individuals in that scene, and keeping a reflexive log of one's own reactions as one overcomes culture shock and steadily moves beyond mere observation into active participation (see especially Sands's report on Dale House).

This is, in short, a somewhat eclectic approach, taking what I regard as the best of the modern and of the postmodern periods of ethnology in such a way as to permit you to discover the delights of ethnography in whatever fashion you find most compatible with your experience of life up to the point of taking the course.

THE SMALL FIELD ASSIGNMENTS

Instructions for each of the five field assignments make up the rest of this guide. In each case the how-to is followed by one or more examples of good results from students who have taken the course previously, reprinted with the students' permission. Some are shortened, and all have been copyedited for style and grammar.

✢

Map of a Block

Students often find this assignment childish and unproductive while they are doing it and recognize its value only when engaged in later more complex fieldwork. Two morals: The first is that the assignment, like spinach, is good for you; the second is that you can make it intrinsically interesting by selecting a block that has compelling features of architecture, layout, or spacing.

You may also object that you are learning far more than you care to know about the geography, the aesthetics, and the social nature of the place where you temporarily live. The intent is not to teach you about the town you live in, but to learn that ethnographic work is always located in time and place—the geographic parallel to Clifford Geertz's statement that people can only be human in specific ways, which Alice Reich cites in the Introduction. All of your own work must be at least as concretely located in its own time, place, and social situation as the blocks described here.

PURPOSE

This first bit of fieldwork is conceptually and procedurally easy, so you can proceed from small successes through larger ones. But the ease is deceptive because it requires you to observe closely and to see the familiar as if it were unfamiliar. Stripping away your preconceptions is not easy.

This assignment will help you experience a fundamental of ethnographic fieldwork: It is concrete as to time and to place and describes the relation between sociocultural behavior and physical environment. In subsequent assignments, what you have learned in this one becomes "the setting," which must always be given its due.

PROCEDURE

Find an interesting block. Find a block that is not merely convenient to campus, but one with something (building, landscaping, arrangement of features) sufficiently arresting to be worth rising out of the torpor customary for performing some classroom assignments. In the example that follows, Evan Hill made his eyes fresh so he could use poetic metaphor ironically, to peel scales from his eyes in order to see an ordinary city block as a social statement. Even if you don't use metaphor, you can select a block with an outstanding building.

The block may be defined either as a chunk of land bounded on four sides by streets, or as the two facing sides of one block of a single street plus the side street back to the alley (if any) on either side. *Without interviewing the people you encounter,* describe that block building by building, lot by lot. Don't neglect the alley. Draw a map of the block, annotating it as Heather Danielkiewicz does in the accompanying paper. Detail, detail, detail, but explain why the details you choose are worth noting.

Visit the block at different times of the day, to see how use differs. Some blocks change their character drastically from morning to evening.

PITFALLS TO AVOID

1. Do your best to describe without judging: "A warm inviting house," "pretty lawn chair," "ugly fence," "beautiful view," "cute child," "middle-class couple" (very few American adults describe themselves as anything other than "middle class"), "older car" (older than God? older than your father's Oldsmobile?), "pricey jewelry" (compared to what?). Above all, avoid the easy, meaningless adjective "nice." The trick is to go to the trouble of asking yourself what it is that makes the house inviting, the woman pretty or the man handsome, and so forth. Then, having done so, it is not only legitimate but compelling to say "on the basis of the foregoing description, I infer that the occupants must be wealthy," or the car student owned, or whatever it may be. You will find that acquiring skill in the game of avoiding judgment is surprisingly difficult. If you succeed, you will be practicing cultural relativism.

2. Nostalgia. This exercise is to sharpen your eyes, not your memory. (Field assignments 2 through 4 invite you to analyze "memory culture.") Don't describe a block you already know well. "I lived in this house for ten years. Across the street were Uncle Harry and Aunt Min, and the cousins played in all of the backyards" is a pleasant reminiscence that has nothing to do with the purpose of the map of a block. Use one sense organ only—your eye—and use it as sharply as you can.

FURTHER IN THE SAME DIRECTION

This first assignment was conceived to get you started almost painlessly in the adventure of field ethnography and to make the point that human events happen in particular places, weathers, times, and so forth. If you are intrigued, you will be pleased to know that what you are doing is a subdiscipline of anthropology called *cultural ecology*. Human interaction with the environment provides one of the best invitations to interdisciplinary work that anthropology has to offer. Graduate programs in regional and environmental studies welcome applicants who are well grounded in anthropology.

Ecology is about a century old as a concern in American anthropology. Clark Wissler of Harvard pioneered the field with his book *The Relation of Nature to Man in Aboriginal America* (1900), and Alfred Louis Kroeber of Berkeley published a study of Native American adaptations to North American environments that became a classic even before it was published in 1939. (The manuscript was completed in 1931, but publication was delayed because of the Great Depression.) Kroeber's contribution was already interdisciplinary: He lived across the street from the cultural geographer Carl Sauer, and the two of them exchanged both theory and method. A founding theoretical document was written by a student of Kroeber's, Julian Steward, who developed what he called "multilinear evolution"—the evolution of cultural traditions in relation to specific environments (Steward, 1955). Ecological approaches go in and out of fashion among ethnographers, but are always high priority with archeologists. The best entry into this complex field that I can recommend is Robert Netting's *Cultural Ecology* (1977), a short summary written with readers like you in mind.

A Changing Block in Standale

by Heather Danielkiewicz

This paper is a model of how to describe. It is thorough, the block chosen is interesting because its uses are changing, and the author explains how she reached her conclusions. Note "the mailbox . . . made me think the building was older . . .", "weeds are growing . . . indicating the building may not be as new as it looks.", and "One young girl. . . . By younger I mean less than 25 but older than 16." We cannot stress too much the importance of describing concretely and leading the reader through your process of deduction.

As a caution to readers, one flaw in writing style has been left uncorrected: overuse of "there is. . . ." Note how that phrase slows down the flow of sentences and decreases the reader's interest.

TIME OF DAY, 11:30–12:45

The block I chose is 8 miles east of Grand Valley State University on M-45 in Standale, Michigan. The block is surrounded on the south by Lake Michigan Dr., on the east by Parkside, on the north by Chesterfield, and on the west by St. Clair.

LAKE MICHIGAN DRIVE

4291—Standale Trading Company. One-story orange-red brick building in the style of a house. The roof is shaped like a pyramid and not flat like most buildings one sees in a city. There is a red wooden door frame and

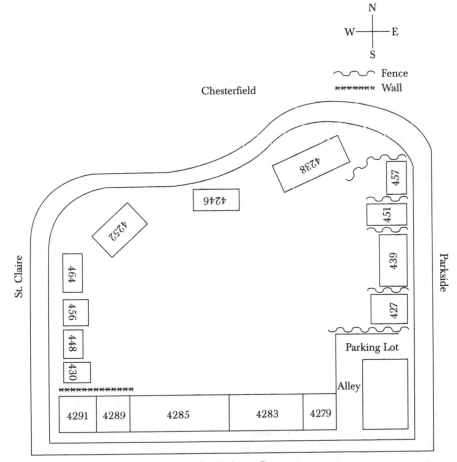

Lake Michigan Dr.

the address is painted on a sign above the door. This stood out because it seemed to add to the hominess of the building. The owners of the building appeared quite patriotic: There is an American flag hanging from the building and a flag draped across the inside of the window. A woman who looked to be in her 50s entered the store. She was wearing polyester pants and a blouse with a bow that tied around the neck. She drove a 1980s-model brick red Buick.

4289—The Cottage Pop Shop. This building shares a roof with the former building (4291). The roof looks fairly new as if it was redone to accommodate the business. The brick is of a slightly darker shade of red than 4291. It also has the same style door frame as 4291, but this one is white rather than red. There are a few green plants in the window, along with some woven baskets reflecting the cottage atmosphere being portrayed. On the outside of the building was an older style of mailbox. It was in the shape of a rectangle standing on its short end. This made me think the building was at least older than some of the others it was adjacent to.

4285—Creative Upholstery. One story white/coral brick building. This color scheme is seemingly more modern than the red brick of the building to the left. The building is square with a flat roof. There are two large windows separated by glass doors. One window reveals a bedroom set with a mirror behind. The bedspread contained a floral pattern with a shell-like headboard. This also made the building seem modern in comparison to the building to its left. Also in this room was a floral fabric chair, a brass lamp, and some old, unupholstered pillows on the right side of the room. Through the right window one could see the shop where the upholstering is done. The condition of the shop suggested that it is fairly new, while the sign out front contained just a metal rim, with no sign in it.

4283—Pearson-Cook Realtors. One-story brown brick building. The paneling and wood on the building appear new. There are no chips in it or weather-worn stains like the other adjacent buildings. I'm not sure what used to be here, but the sidewalk in front of the building is cracked in different places and weeds are growing out of the cracks indicating the building may not be as new as it looks. A man in a suit and tie walked out of the building and got in a clean white Grand Prix. This was a different clientele than was seen going into the Standale Trading Co.

4279—Standale Coin Laundry. The building is shared with the realtors mentioned above so the description is the same as far as the building goes. This laundromat is larger than the one that used to be across the street. I don't believe this one is opened yet for there were no lights on inside the building. The fact that the laundromat has expanded points to the fact that the town itself is growing. Perhaps it is growing because of students or beginning families who don't own washers and dryers.

Alley—Just gravel, with a big pothole probably from the delivery trucks which pass through it to deliver to the restaurant.

Johnny Notos Italian Ristorante—Brown brick building with patio out front. Newer looking brown roof. Truck loading in food to the restaurant. Few cars in the lot out front. Two business people walking into restaurant. Each wore a gray suit.

PARKSIDE

427—Two-story house with cream siding. Cement steps leading up to front door of the house look older than the rest of the house. Black railing on steps is loose and hanging on the left side. The paint is chipping on the bottom of the rim of the door. There is a red brick chimney attached to the side of the house. It obviously doesn't match the cream siding. This is a good indication that this siding is an addition to the house. There is an old white shed in the back whose paint is chipping and whose boards are loose. There are some summer chairs in the back of the house that don't coordinate with one another. The lawn is not well kept, meaning that it is quite long with several weeds throughout. There are lots of trees in the yard. There was a black Amigo in the drive and a gray Mustang with a broken left tail light. From the condition of the lawn and the cars in the drive, I assume the people living here are students or have an unstable income.

439—Rather large house (compared with the majority of them on the block) with gray siding. The siding looks new. The address is in brass letters. There is a gray roof darker than the siding with a matching brick to accent the siding. There is a pink door near the larger-than-two-car garage. A privacy fence surrounds the backyard. The lawn is cut closely and upon it sits a "welcome goose." Because of the crisp and clean appearance of the entire house, it appears to be new.

451—Two-story creamy yellow house. This house is small compared to the other three on the block. The cement step leading to the house is neat, but has a chip on the top step. The lawn and landscaping seem well groomed. There seems to be someone who stays at home living in this house, since the landscaping is kept up so well. The flowers don't have leaves stuck in their bed. There are two matching flower pots on the porch. There is a large greenish purple tree in the yard and a smaller tree on the right surrounded by flowers. A flower wreath is hung on the door. A Ford truck sits in the drive with supplies sticking out the back.

457—Ranch-style home with white siding and red brick in the front. Country blue shutters envelop the windows. The privacy fence is of a few different colors: gray, country blue, and brick red. The lawn is well kept with shrubs scattered throughout, but not as many flowers are contained in this landscape as at 451. There is a scene of a deer in the woods on the mailbox. This makes me think the person(s) living here like to hunt.

CHESTERFIELD

4238—Ranch-style home larger than most on Parkside. Gray siding with gray shutters. Steps are made of cement, but no cracks. The style of the door looks older than the outside of the house. Perhaps the house has been newly redone and the door has been left for a later time. The lawn is extremely green and different kinds of shrubs surround the house with tall purple flowers. The garage is closed and no cars are outside.

4246—This ranch looks much older than the other houses on the street because of its color scheme. The colors look as if they were chosen in the 1970s. The brick is light brown with yellow tint. The front door is a chocolate brown with dark yellow squares placed vertically down the center. The one-car garage is also a chocolate brown with dark yellow diamonds on it. There are two huge pine trees in the front yard. They appear to be several years old due to the fact that they are about 25 feet tall. There is a huge tree on the right side of the lawn providing shade for most of the lawn. It appears the occupants of this home like privacy. When looking at the house straight on, all one can see is the front door and part of the window on the right.

4252—Large yellow ranch home. Wooden garage is painted yellow with white squares. Two 1980s-model Chrysler and Plymouth minivans were in the drive. The steps are weathered while the lawn is well kept. Some dead cut grass is lying in it.

ST. CLAIR

464—This yellow ranch is on the long side. The shutters are black. There are purple flowers hanging from the lamppost. It appears as if a family lives here. There is a basketball net on the roof. A rusty dark blue Tempo was parked in the street along with a blue truck. A stone deer sits on the well-kept lawn.

456—A stout dark brown brick home. Beige garage and beige siding. Clean steps with a cut lawn. No cars in the drive.

448—Gray ranch recently (last 10 yrs.) remodeled. New garage. Two bay windows, one large and one small. Well-kept lawn. Two older cars in drive, rusting, along with a new model Jeep Cherokee.

430—Two-story home. Brown brick with cream siding and brick-red shutters. Country style. Flowers in barrels. Green heart wreath on door. The wooden garage looks like an addition because the material doesn't flow with the brick house. Wooden privacy fence. Several large trees in yard including five tall pine trees. Recycling container in the drive. A brick-colored Buick was parked in front of the house.

TIME OF DAY

Wed. 11:05–11:55 A.M. This is a very busy time on Lake Michigan Dr. It was a warm sunny day. Two women could be seen pushing young children in strollers. Both women were dressed simply in T-shirts and either jeans or shorts. A young girl(14–17) was seen riding a three-speed bicycle down Lake Mich. Dr. There were a few cars in the parking lot. Around 11:20 a.m., activity seemed to pick up in front of the Standale Trading Post. Two rather worn cars pulled up. The first car was a rusty orange car. It was a 1970s model and the driver of the car appeared gruff looking with a dark beard and curly brown 1970s-style hair. The next car that came was a 1980s-model Ford that was quite dirty. The owner may live out in the country and have to drive daily on dirt roads. Even in this small section of businesses there appeared a range of clientele, from country looking to suit and tie. This shows that Standale isn't at a standstill. Businesses are moving in, yet there are many farmers and blue-collar workers in the area.

Wed. 6:55–7:10 P.M. During this time the lights were out in the upholstery shop and the cottage shop. Parked in front of the Trading Co. were a newer model truck (1990s), a new sporty green Honda Civic, and a mobile traveler. The realtor was open and a few cars were parked in the front. At Johnny Notos there was a full parking lot. Many different style cars occupied the lot but almost all were made since 1980. The back door was open, revealing the kitchen inside. A few kids rode through the parking lot on bikes. One young girl was walking by. By younger I mean less than 25 but older than 16. She appeared to be a student. She was carrying a Mexican-style bag, wore baggy jeans with a more fitting shirt and had her hair in a bun. Several of the houses had additional cars parked in the driveway or the street. Front doors were opened in a few of the houses. To my delight the houses on St. Clair had Avon bags hanging from their mailboxes. I'm assuming women live in those houses. Obviously, these people are gone during the day, probably working 9–5.

Conclusion: The street has definitely changed throughout the years as indicated by the buildings on Lake Michigan Drive. What used to perhaps be residential is now expanding into businesses. The area is also building up residentially as indicated by the expanding laundromat. The neighborhood appears to be middle class. There is time to keep up a lawn and money to redo a house. In the future, I see Standale growing as a business community and continuing to grow residentially as well. It seems like a place people can move to who are just starting out. With the Grand Valley campus growing as it is, Standale could become increasingly populated.

In the Cracks

by Evan Hill

Although the purpose of this first assignment is to improve your eye, to record accurately what you see, there is no rule against seeing with a poetic eye, as this author does in describing a block in Colorado Springs that seems to have fallen into the cracks.

Walking was really the only way I know how to get to the block I studied. It is bounded by the railroad tracks, the creek, and two overpasses—walking to get there somehow fit.

I had first seen this block when I was about to hop a freight train, and the block fascinated me. It seemed to have fallen into a crack and taken root.

This crack appeared as a crack in the context of the city. The context that most of us are used to is that of the car. A place in a city is someplace you can drive to by car. Roads and cars constitute our framework of understanding space in the city. We are baffled when someone on foot walks under an overpass and disappears. Where did they go? There are no roads there! Hence, the implication that because you don't drive there, there really is nothing—merely a crack.

This is where I found the block. Of course you can drive there, but it really seems to belong more to the world of hopping trains and walking. The spatial context is that of a person on foot. This is because the block has fallen between the two overpasses where Colorado and Cimarron cross Monument Creek and the railroad tracks. There is much greater access to this area on foot. In the context of roads and cars there is only one entrance and in a car you cannot travel to many parts of this area. On foot, a much greater integration with the surrounding area and city is possible. You can walk onto either overpass, down into the creek bed, and across the railroad yard to get to the rest of the city. Thus, I find it easier to place this area within the contextual framework of a person on foot than the contextual framework of roads and cars. In the world of road and cars, this place is in a crack.

Enough reflexive contemplation. A more objective look at the composition of this area follows:

1. General contractor—This lot consists of a building and a chain-link enclosure topped with barbed wire. Architecturally speaking, the building is a typical American rectangular block topped with a sloped roof. The facing is stucco. In front of the building are low evergreen bushes. The windows are barred. The materials within the enclosure are neatly arranged. These materials consist, among other things, of a handful of old travel trailers and some dressed logs. There are also two piles of dressed logs outside.

2. Private residence—This building is a very nondescript house built in the "rectangular block" style. The siding is typical wood siding that used to be green but is now quite weather beaten. There is a waist-high chain-link fence in front and, 2 feet behind that, a 6-foot privacy fence that conceals most of the house.

3. "Sales"—This cinder-block building is very squared off, with a flat roof, but it is not just one rectangle. It is painted green with big black letters

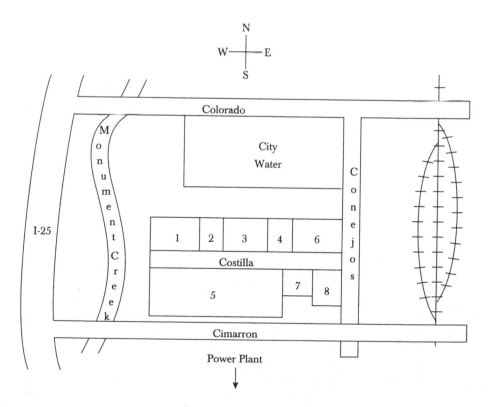

on the front—A.P. HARLEY SALES. The primary commodity dealt with seems to be tires. There are tires, among other things, piled in the fenced-in barbed wire enclosure around the building. There are also some old gas pumps. Like the general contractor enclosure, this one has shrubbery in front, barred windows, and a general neatness.

4. Private residence—This is a rectangular box, slope-roofed house that is quite weather-beaten. The old sedan parked out front has mud tires in back. The backyard resembles a junkyard with the main constituent being piles of wood.

5. Empty lot—The sign says NO DUMPING OR TRESPASSING and this rule seems to have been followed. This is a well-cared-for vacant lot. On the front edge of the lot is parked an International pickup in excellent shape and a trailer. This vacant lot is across from the first four buildings.

6. Susie Perkins cottages/apts. for rent—This is a lot entirely composed of various houses. At one end are several identical bungalow cottage type buildings quite close together. Toward the other end, the bungalows become less similar and are arranged in a different pattern. The final building is a two-story house with some windows boarded up in pale green plywood. A high cinder-block fence connected to two buildings creates a courtyard that is somehow part of all the other buildings in the lot. There is an old picket fence around the whole shebang. The cars parked out front are all large, old, and American.

7. Private residence—This is a brown stucco house in excellent repair. The yard is filled with various types of junk all of which are useful and in good repair (e.g., fairly new tires and a stack of firewood covered with a tarp). There are four cars parked out front, all of which are fairly new (within ten years). There are two foreign pickups (the only foreign cars on the block). There are four dogs in the yard as well.

8. Church—This church was built in the style of a Catholic mission, but quite recently and very stylized. All of the elements that are supposed to be there are, but the building is obviously a copy. It is labeled simply "Chadbourn." The windows are lead stained glass covered with screens, and there is a recent construction on the back that hasn't been painted, although the stucco has been applied.

My visit was in the late afternoon on a Sunday and I saw three groups of Chicanos—one group of females and two of males—on foot walking along the roads. They all appeared to be under 30. One truck did arrive at the brown stucco house. In it were two middle-aged white males dressed in work clothes and carrying a lunch cooler. Otherwise, there were a couple of cars driving along the road. The clothing of those people that I did see indicated a blue-collar, working-class lifestyle.

The only speculation I have as to the development of the neighborhood is that the businesses might be family businesses owned by people who live nearby. The residences and businesses both were clearly built for the purposes they are being used for, and none look like they were built in the last twenty years. The vacant lot might indicate future development.

Unless more roads are built, however, this will continue to be a block in the cracks of the road and car context of the city.

The Block of Española

· *by Adán Trujillo*

Despite the general instructions for this assignment to put away cultural and personal bias in favor of literal seeing with the literal eye, no one can entirely succeed. The author of this description is a native of Northern New Mexico, where except in the mountains the landscape is dry and brown, a good-sized tree or an emerald field is a sure sign of an irrigation ditch, and every house is built of real or fake adobes. Española, New Mexico, grew haphazardly around a railroad terminus, unlike Colorado Springs, which was platted in the 1870s by its founder, William Jackson Palmer—hence the emphasis on the "feeling of social order" in the latter. Trujillo whimsically chooses a street in Colorado Springs with the same name as his hometown. What to him is a "great abundance of trees" in this old and affluent section of town that has been irrigated for over a century would seem a bit scanty to a student from the eastern woodlands.

Only the first section of this paper is reproduced, because Trujillo's house-by-house description is similar to that in Heather Danielkiewicz's paper.

In 1983, my family moved from El Rito, New Mexico, to a house in Española, New Mexico. Although I had previously lived in Chimayo to the age of 5, and Chimayo is where some of my extended family in the past is from, my home is in Española, about 7 miles away. I felt an immediate connection when I came across Española Street. Many ironies arose in conjunction with the name *Española*. The fact that this block is an example of a style of architecture not found in Española or all of Northern New Mexico to my knowledge, made me think about how a common name can draw unconscious comparisons instantaneously. You will have to pardon my ignorance on the topic of bourgeois architecture, for I didn't grow up around any such buildings. I don't know their style, and I'm not familiar with their construction. I couldn't help thinking how this block was polarly distant from my home, yet they share the same name. Not a "deep" thought, or a profound one either, just a thought coincidental enough to make this block special to me. Now I have two Españolas, one as my home and one as my assignment.

I noticed that this block has a great abundance of trees. On all sides, the houses on this block are set away from the street with a small, grassy strip of lawn, then a sidewalk, then the houses' yards and then the houses themselves. On every strip of lawn, there is a column of trees surrounding the block. Most houses on this block have at least one tree in their yards. Everything is neat, with orderly patterns, and symmetry is everywhere. This all gives the unconscious impression of "city beautiful" and establishes a strong feeling of social order.

✥

Private Language

PURPOSE

For the species *Homo sapiens,* culture is a survival technique, just as the speed of the jaguar, the hide of the rhinoceros, or the cunning of the weasel are for those species. Changing environment dictates changing survival strategies, so culture has to make frequent changes. Here lies one of the many paradoxes of human existence: Culture is a straitjacket, but culture also provides the means for us to get out of our straitjackets.

This assignment focuses on the creative aspect of culture and on your own part (whether large or small) in creating it. Since culture is for the most part language behavior, you are asked to discover your cultural-innovative capacity by recording some language item(s) that you helped invent. Although you invented new words and may have invented new morphemes, you will probably discover that you used the phonemes of your own or another standard language. In private languages, culture is simultaneously straitjacket and facilitator of innovation.

PROCEDURE

Record a segment of private language. Narrative form usually works best. Set down a dialogue (or other speech) in which the invented terms are used. Having done that, in a separate section analyze the segment. That is, discuss briefly how the private language came to be invented, what the social, cultural, and emotional circumstances of the invention were. Did the segment persist or not, and why? As you did in the first assignment, describe the setting concretely. Your paper may be very short, perhaps two or three pages in all.

Since it is harder to invent new language than not, after you have recorded your segment and before you write the analysis, reflect on the following critical question: "Why did we bother to invent new terms instead of using standard language for the same meaning?" The answer to that question may reveal a good deal about the circumstances surrounding the social moment or social unit.

PITFALLS TO AVOID

1. Total passivity. Most slang, for instance, is used so widely that it is *only* a straitjacket for you, and you invented none of it personally. Make sure your sample of language bears your own stamp.

2. Technical terms. Most vocations and avocations rely on nonstandard technical terminology. Such terms serve a different purpose and are not inventive for the individual who uses them (except the cultural innovator who made them up in the first place). Avoid technical terms.

FURTHER IN THE SAME DIRECTION

Linguistics is the most rigorous and sophisticated subdiscipline of cultural anthropology. Much of it, called *structural linguistics,* is highly technical, focusing on phonetics, phonemics, morphemics, and grammar. The portion of the field called anthropological linguistics, however, is usually presented in straightforward English and can be understood without special training. It studies how language is formed in social situations. Donald Brenneis and Ronald Macaulay (eds.), *The Matrix of Language* (1996), provide an introduction to such topics as (to quote its subheadings) "Learning Language, Learning Culture," "Gender, Power and Discourse," "Genre, Style, Performance," and "Language as Social Practice." The articles in this collection lead in turn to folklore, politics, and other cultural topics. Another useful book, reviewing the history of anthropological linguistics, is Ben Blount (ed.), *Language, Culture, and Society* (1995).

Tree Huggers

by Jenny Irving

This paper accomplishes the assignment neatly and concisely. Presentation of data is minimal but sufficient. Motivation for creating the language is crystal clear. The ori-

gin and growth of the language is spelled out. The satisfaction to the creators is emphasized. And the author wastes no words.

DATA

Two girls (Susie and Jane) are on a bus and they have the following conversation:

Susie: That's a tree.
Jane: Yeah, but the tree next to it is better.
    S: But it's just a sapling.
    J: Better than the oldgrowth you're talking about!
    S: I like the one on the left—it has great leaves.
    J: There sure are a lot of trees around here!

ANALYSIS

Although not the usual way of talking about nature and trees in particular, our "tree talk" was very meaningful to us. It all began my senior year in high school, but the effects have extended right up to the present. Its use continues today with a new group of people and with even more variations.

    The jealousy of boyfriends whenever one of my friends or I would comment on the looks of another male is what led to the creation of our tree code. It began as a simple way of expressing to each other the merits of an attractive male and quickly grew into a whole secret language that long outlasted the boyfriends.

    At the very basis of the language is "tree," or in other words a good-looking male. "Tree" is the code word because they are such common objects and the mention of one would not attract much attention. In the beginning, a tree stood for any male we thought of as "cute." Eventually this expanded into a much more elaborate system.

    Tree then came to mean a "cute guy" of approximately our age. Saplings are younger boys, while oldgrowth are those who seem much older than us. Along the way tree has gained negative as well as positive connotations. These were used especially for cases of mistaken identity. Deadwood, waterlogged, and snag are examples. Leaves stand for hair, bark for skin, and branches for body build. We also have ways of expressing availability. A tree's girlfriend or what appears to be a girlfriend is called lichen, while a girl who is only a friend is moss. We also play with common terms such as "tree hugging," which normally is reserved for environmentalists. We apply it in the obvious way.

Not long after the coining of the original word, a large group of us came to use it. It was passed from girl to girl, and everyone was careful not to overuse it or give its secrets away. From the original four inventors, eventually about fifteen of my friends became knowledgeable about it. At the end of senior year the word was still in common usage and was written in many yearbooks. The language did not die out with our separation to college. I have passed it on to my new friends in college, who have readily adopted it and helped to expand it.

Creation of terms for members of the opposite sex such as "babe," "chick," "stud," and so on, has always been a common form of teenage slang. The fun part of our language is the part we all had in creating it. The use of these terms created a separation between males and females, but more importantly and positively it created a bond between females, especially between me and my friends. The fact that our language has lasted so long is amazing and rewarding. It has become very common for us and a part of our everyday lives.

A Study of Automobile Terminology

by Colleen Ximenes

This paper is also classic in form: The data come first, succinctly but clearly, then the analysis. Ximenes explains competently why the private language developed and why it persisted. What is fun about the paper is that these modest data are handled lightly and gracefully. They capture a moment in the changing lives of young people that cannot be returned to and continues to live only in such memories as these. But don't miss the social criticism implied in paragraph 2 of the analysis. Part of the author's fun is satirizing the misogynist belief that women know nothing about cars.

THE CHARACTERS

Stephanie, Chris, Robyn, Colleen, Mr. Murdock (a truck driver), and Buffalo (his dog).

SETTING

Four stranded young woman receive a ride to the nearest gas station from a friendly truck driver and his dog. In this truck cab a new set of terminology for the standard car is formed.

DIALOGUE

Mr. Murdock:	What seems to be the matter with your car?
Chris:	I'm not sure but I think something is wrong with that big silver-mabob thing that holds all the water for the car.
	(Snickers from the occupants of the cab)
Mr. Murdock:	The radiator?
Chris:	I guess, I mean how am I supposed to know?
	(Snickers turn into laughter)
Stephanie:	Maybe you have a problem with your cylinderadoodad and the air is not circulating properly?
Robyn:	(Laughing) No, I think it is definitely has to be that rubberband-eight-doerthing!
Mr. Murdock:	Please tell me you mean the fan belt?
Colleen:	I still think we should have checked the air in the plastotubular modes when we left!
Stephanie:	No, no, it was the rainomatic swipers that caused the whole problem.
Mr. Murdock:	(with a look of relief) For a moment I thought you all were serious.
	(More laughter)
Chris:	You guys, this is not funny!

ANALYSIS

During the summer break of my senior year of high school, several friends and I decided to take a trip from Colorado Springs to Beaver Creek. The four of us, Stephanie, Chris, Robyn, and myself, piled into Chris's Toyota Corolla. About an hour away from Beaver Creek we began to smell smoke and then eventually began to see it coming out from under the hood. We decided to press on, figuring that we only had a little way to go until we arrived. The car had other intentions, however, and stalled about two minutes later. There we were, stuck on the side of the interstate with no clue as to what was wrong with the car. Checking under the hood did not help. It only made us smell like smoke and illustrated quite clearly our ignorance of the finer points of car repair. A truck driver named Mr. Murdock accompanied by his dog Buffalo pulled over and offered assistance by taking us to the nearest gas station. We all climbed in and began to tell him what we felt was wrong with the car. Hence came the amusing and in retrospect interesting terms in relation to automobiles.

Socially and culturally speaking, we all belonged to the "youth" culture. Outside of school we often boggled our parents with new and unique twists of the English language by using such words as "dude" or "Spooby." In those cases we either received strange looks or a lecture on the proper use of the English language. The use of these words had a great effect on our own new terminology. We even spoke in a pseudo-valley girl voice for emphasis. Another social and cultural influence on the language was the stereotypical view that women do not know a thing about cars. True, we would not have been hired by Goodyear, but three of the four of us knew what the radiator was and the idea of playing out this stereotype made the game more enjoyable. Up until we started talking about the tires and the windshield wipers, I honestly believe that Mr. Murdock thought we were being serious about our lack of knowledge about car parts.

Emotionally speaking, the language terms were invented out of total amusement and humor, except for Chris who was genuinely distraught over her car. Once she described the radiator, the rest was easy. We had, after all, just graduated from high school and that euphoric feeling of freedom had taken over. We no longer had to deal with principals, teachers, or hall passes. Final exams were over, our college plans had been finalized, and most importantly, we had no adult supervision. Once we realized how typical the situation was (that is, a group of women being stranded on the road), the words and descriptions seemed to become a game to see how stupid or weird we could appear.

As to whether the language has persisted the answer is an unequivocal yes! The radiator is still the silvermabob that holds water, we still put air in our plastotublar modes, and often our rainomatic swipers do not work too well in a storm. We only use these terms with one another, for with anybody who was not there the humor would be lost. I even called Stephanie about this assignment and we laughed all over again. I believe these terms have lasted because they remind us all of a wonderful time in our lives. It was a time between youth and adult responsibilities when it was OK to be a little silly and not have anyone criticize our actions. In a sense, our language "liberated" us from the constraints of the practical and technical world we at the time thought we were entering.

"Oh American"

by Brad Beall

*Beall's lighthearted paper has several messages for us. First is that a memorable seg-
ment of private language almost always arises from events that are charged with emotion, thus heightened for the cultural inventors. Second, private languages often arise
by chance, with a sense of shock. Third, as terms spread, their meanings change to
fit new situations and new speakers. Finally, no correlation exists between linguistic
invention and liberal or politically correct behavior.*

*The author will probably have to watch his tongue in the future, for after grad-
uating with honors in anthropology, Beall is applying to law school.*

This private language originated on my trip to the Soviet Union back in the
summer of 1988. I had not thought about the incident from which it came
for several years, but after reflecting upon it again, I realized it mushroomed
from a tiny phrase to somewhat of a cult language.

Soviet citizens, particularly the youth, are in love with Western goods.
They want anything from blue jeans to tennis shoes, shirts, tapes of music,
or whatever they categorize as "Western." There is an immense black market for these things. A pair of old Levis can go for as much as $100. Since
these things are not legally available to the Soviet public, their only outlet
to get them is Western tourists. But because of the serious implications for
anyone caught dealing on the black market, we had been warned not to accept money in exchange for anything. If we wanted to exchange things, we
were told that we could trade. Trading was borderline black market, but it
probably would not get us into trouble.

DATA

My best friend Brian and three others from our group had invited two Soviet youth up to their hotel room in Moscow to trade things. It was a no-no
for the Soviets to come up to any private rooms for reasons of security, and
when our chaperone saw that they had gone upstairs, she asked me to go
up and be there to even the sides out in case a fight or other bad situation
arose. When I got there, I opened the door to find the two Soviets flinging
clothes out of suitcases trying to find things to trade for. I discovered that
Brian had already made a trade when I saw one of the young Soviets was
wearing Brian's Risky Business sunglasses, and Brian was wearing a Soviet
Army officer's coat that was covered with medals. Now I knew that this pair

of sunglasses had a huge spiderweb crack in the left lens, but when you have them on, you can't see the crack because they are so dark. We had often joked about this junky pair of sunglasses between ourselves. I caught Brian's attention and mouthed the words, "Does he know that those sunglasses are broken?" He swallowed hard and shook his head. Meanwhile, the two young Soviets were wrapping up their whirlwind search of the suitcases.

Finally they decided that they all had what they wanted to trade for. Brian and the two others from our group were decked out in Soviet military uniforms holding an armful of Soviet flags, hockey jerseys, and other knick-knacks. The two Soviets had two concert T-shirts, a couple of tapes, an armload of blue jeans, and a pair of broken (as yet undiscovered) sunglasses. As they were turning to leave, the one who was wearing the sunglasses took them off to be sure that he had not forgotten anything. Then it happened; he saw the crack in the lens. His eyes grew to the size of baseballs, his mouth dropped open and with a constipated moan he blurted, "Oh, oh American, you f—— me! You f—— me and give me s—— sunglasses!" His tone was of a genuine feeling of betrayal. That, compounded with his panicked expression and his attempt to relate to Americans on our level by using our language made for one of the most culturally hilarious moments I have ever experienced. While the two others in our group were scared to death at this development, trying to blend into the wallpaper, Brian and I were clutching our sides from laughing so hard. Being the quick-witted diplomat that he is, Brian went on to explain that cracked lenses were a new style in American sunglasses and that all of the real ones had cracks. The young Soviet was skeptical about it, but when Brian offered to revoke the trade for something else, he decided that he had found a treasure and he and his friend both made a quick exit.

So the base phrase of this new private language was, "Oh American, you f—— me!" As word of the incident spread through our group, the phrase picked up momentum and came to be used and changed to fit particular situations. For example, if someone got cheated on a trade, a sympathetic friend might say, "Oh American, he f—— you! He give you s——ty sunglasses!" Or, if someone had gotten drunk over the course of the evening, with head in toilet, someone might tell them, "Oh American, you f—— yourself!" Always the phrase would be repeated with the same tone of constipated urgency in a mimicked Russian accent.

The real fun started when school began in the fall. Brian and I were still charged from our trip to Europe, exchanging memories of it as often as we saw each other, and greeting each other with an amused, "Oh, oh American, you f—— me!" It wasn't a month before both of us began hearing this phrase and offshoots of it all around our high school. People had heard us saying it to each other, and not knowing what it meant, began to repeat it in various other ways. I happened to overhear two freshmen talking at their locker one day about an uncompleted homework assignment. One turned to the other and said in a southwest Missouri accent, "Oh American, we are both screwed!" The phrase grew in popularity so much that everyone had at least heard it, and half the student body used it regularly. The acclaim that it gained was totally unintentional, and only Brian and I knew exactly what it meant and where it had come from.

ANALYSIS

The private language originated from a cultural faux pas. The young Soviet man who inadvertently set the whole thing off was trying to relate to us on our level. For many of the Soviet youth, Western culture is looked at with a sense of awe and desire. It seems to me that by trying to mimic our language and expressions, he was attempting to be as "Western" as he could. But since he was not accustomed to the Western ways of expressing feeling, and moreover the appropriate use of U.S. profanity, his reaction to the broken sunglasses was very amusing to us. He was confused as to why we had found his reaction so funny, but there was no way for us to explain our cross-cultural differences in a way that would have made sense.

As it started, "Oh American, you f—— me" was a private inside joke between Brian and me. Then we began to take its meaning in different directions, which we applied to our own funny situations. Those around us in our group picked up on it and changed the phrase in a number of different ways to apply to themselves. They, however, could understand its original meaning more than our friends back in high school, for they had been in the same setting and could understand its humor. Our friends in high school were totally removed from the cultural setting from which it came, and to them, it was just another funny way to create profanity. So its evolution began with a panicked reaction to a broken pair of sunglasses by a young Soviet man, and ended as one funny saying among a field of others in an American high school.

Fighting the Bear

by Tony Muñoz

Muñoz's paper starts out as lightheartedly as those of Ximenes and Beall. It ends as a serious battle cry between young Chicano knights about to fight for their places in the world. Note the paradox in the last sentence: It was sharing rather than keeping private that made this private language worth remembering. Like some other stu-dents, Muñoz fails to separate data from analysis. The paper is strong and clear nevertheless.

Instead of becoming a professional writer or ethnologist, Muñoz chose the law.

This private language developed during a youth work trip to a village in Northern Mexico during the summer of 1989. About sixty teenagers gathered in Tempe, Arizona, preparatory to proceeding to Mexico. We were all from the Christian youth group known as Young Life. We had gathered from the far reaches of Colorado—Denver, Pueblo, Steamboat Springs, and the small towns of Brush, Delta, Cedaredge, Durango, Saguache. Few of us were fluent in Spanish and many knew no Spanish at all.

DATA

Not long after arriving in Tempe, we from Delta decided that we were sick of each other's company for the day and struck out to introduce ourselves to people from other groups. I quickly met Dave and Paco, both from Denver South High School. Dave was a tall lanky Caucasian who wore "Glacier" sunglasses because he complained of the sand and the wind drying out his contact lenses. Paco was a short wiry Hispanic who was always smiling and always had something comical to say. They later introduced me to the rest of the Denver group, and during dinner we began to find out more about one another.

After dinner we decided to play volleyball. Dave grabbed a boom box from his van and soon the air was filled with thumping bass and screaming lyrics. Between games Dave would change CDs and soon Paco asked if he had any by the rap group Public Enemy. Dave replied "No," and Paco exclaimed, "What, no Public Enemy? Then you must fight the bear!" Since Dave had not changed CDs, laughter rang out from the volleyball field. I stood there with a bewildered look on my face and said, "What the hell is so damn funny?"

The others from Denver explained to me that on the most recent episode of *Saturday Night Live* a take was made about a business executive coming home to his family and finding a bear on his doorstep—actually a stuntman in a bear suit. The commentator explained, "now the executive must fight the bear." So the executive boxes and wrestles this "bear" until the bear decides he has had enough and scampers away. Those six words, "Now you must fight the bear," in their various meanings, changed the course of communication between the groups for the next six days in Mexico.

The new phrase grew in acceptance until all the U.S. students were using it. For example, one member from Pueblo drank some unpurified water and was suffering from diarrhea. When asked how she was doing, she replied, "The bear is winning." A more somber use occurred when three large football players from Steamboat Springs staggered into camp late one evening. Their clothing was torn, and the dried blood on their lips and knuckles told their story: they had encountered unfriendly locals in a town about 5 miles away. When asked what had happened, they triumphantly stated, "We have fought the bear."

One night as we sang songs with Mexicans of the village around the campfire and shared the day's experiences, one of us repeated the phrase, to which everyone else smiled and laughed. One of the Mexicans asked, "*Qué es el chiste?*" (What's the joke?) I translated the phrase literally and his eyes widened with fear and he looked around. I explained that it was from a television show, which calmed him down. When I finished, he shook his head and said "*Qué mentiras!*" (What lies!) I asked him to explain, but he simply shook his head again and smiled. I shared the conversation with my group and we all began to ponder what we had been saying for the past week.

By the end of our trip the phrase was on its last legs, but everyone still got a grin out of it when we said our good-byes. Paco used it when we got ready to leave—he to Denver, I to Delta. We had become good friends and had many similarities in our lives, in our beliefs. We had often stayed up late to talk about sports and life in general. As we parted Paco hugged me and said, "Be strong, for you are yet to encounter your bear."

What started out as a humorous scolding had evolved, at least for Paco and me, into deep communication. Emotionally, it could relay everything from pity to joy, conditioned by the tone of voice and manner in which it was spoken. Socially, the phrase became somewhat like a Lego block—very universal, because you could attach many other "pieces," types of phrases and expressions, to it. Its active use was shared only by the U.S. visitors, yet it was understood by our Mexican friends. I no longer use this phrase but, surprisingly, I remember the emotion and meaning of it very clearly. The best part was that everyone used it; if we had had sole access to it, then maybe it wouldn't have been so special.

Body Language

All animals—and, some argue, plants—communicate. Human animals use symbols (especially speech), but they still use the nonsymbolic ways of communicating that the species inherited. We have recognized body language explicitly for centuries; when Julius Caesar said, "Yon Cassius hath a lean and hungry look," Shakespeare's audience was presumably as accustomed as we are to a remark about body-as-statement. Today the formal study of nonverbal communication is a staple of all of the behavioral sciences, including biology.

PURPOSE

Body language is an extensive and complex topic, but the purpose of the present assignment is modest: to provide a brief introduction and to heighten your awareness of the extent to which people communicate with their bodies. This awareness will make you a better student of ritual and of the ethnographic scene in the two final assignments.

PROCEDURE

Either (1) record a communication exchange between two or more people that does not involve words, or (2) record the nonverbal portion of a communication exchange which does involve words. As before, in a separate section of your paper, clearly marked off from the first, analyze the communication including its social, cultural, and emotional context. You may want to entertain the question, "To what extent was this nonverbal communication culturally mediated? To what extent is it identical or very similar to communication among nonhuman animals?" And also, "To what extent did the participants invent the communication, to what extent is it culturally stereotypical?" This paper is also short, from three to five pages.

PITFALLS TO AVOID

1. Sign languages are nonoral but not nonverbal. They are gesture substitutes for words, hence verbal communications that don't happen to use the aural-oral channel. We're seeking genuinely nonverbal communications, including zeros (i.e., the significance of not communicating when a communication would normally be expected). You may want to look at physical distance between people who are communicating: for example, lovers and Latins and Arabs stand closer, haters and Puritans and other Northern Europeans stand farther apart.

2. Contact sports don't usually work well for this assignment, although they fit the definition. Most communication in a fast-moving game is nonverbal, but one cannot see subtleties from the audience. The spectators, in contrast, provide material for observation as their interest waxes and wanes, focuses on the playing field or on their neighbors, and so on.

3. Avoid overconfidence in your analysis. Gesture is less specific than words and easily misinterpreted. One student decided that the body language a client of her employer used meant dissatisfaction with the service a clerk was giving him, only to discover later that he was describing a baseball player he didn't like. A paper describing misunderstandings of body language would be an interesting way to do this assignment.

FURTHER IN THE SAME DIRECTION

Not many professional anthropologists specialize in nonverbal communication, although all of us are sufficiently aware of it to note it as we do our ethnographic work, and its formal study is a staple of several behavioral sciences. Two who have devoted themselves to the topic are Edward T. Hall and Ray L. Birdwhistell. The former invented the term *proxemics,* or the study of cultural systems of using space, including interpersonal distance, and the latter invented *kinesics,* which is the study of cultural systems of body movement (see Hall, 1959, 1966, 1974, 1976, 1983, and Birdwhistell, 1952, 1970). Hall has had more influence than Birdwhistell, in part because he usually avoids technical discussion and writes for lay audiences. Both cite works by ethologists in biology and psychology, thus establishing connections between human and nonhuman communication without words. More recently, feminist scholars have focused on the gender of body language;

two such reports by psychologists are Clara Mayo and Nancy Henley (eds.), *Gender and Nonverbal Behavior* (1981), and Judith Hall, *Nonverbal Sex Differences* (1984).

Isolation and the Pickup

by Chris Lawler

This example of nonverbal communication is notable in two respects beyond the inherent interest of the topic. First, each actor on the stage is described concretely, and the setting comes vividly to life. The author wastes few words on the description, but his few words tell. Second, in the analysis section he teases out varieties of meaning concerning the situation developing between Mary and Joe, and also the resolution of Jack's relation to the other two. Initially we suspect that Jack may have been the catalyst who brought Mary and Joe together, but then we find him to be a considerate friend who realizes when he is one too many. The author discovers that he understands this social encounter almost better without hearing words than if he had eavesdropped.

Lawler is sensitive enough to body language to have promise as a trial attorney, but he decided to give up politics for medicine.

DATA

The nonverbal exchange described here occurred at the FIJI house on April 2, 1991, around 11:30 P.M. Three participants were involved, two males and a female. The first male, whom we'll call Joe, was wearing a black and blue thin-striped mock turtleneck with the sleeves rolled up, tan cotton pants rolled up at the ankles, and brown moccasins. Joe's brown hair was short on the sides and spiked on the top (about an inch high). Jack, the second male, was wearing a black v-neck sweater, madras shorts that came to his knees, and white sneakers with fluorescent stripes (Nike cross-trainers, I believe). On Jack's head was a white baseball cap with Mountain Chalet printed on it. Mary, the female, was wearing a white buttondown shirt tucked into a pair of black knee-length shorts. On her feet she wore black flats. The only makeup she had on appeared to be pink lipstick. Mary had her shoulder-length black hair pulled back in a ponytail, which was fastened by a red bow.

Mary, Jack, and Joe were standing behind a big table against a wall. The table was laden with potato chips and punch. Loud dance music could be heard filtering up from the basement. Mary, Jack, and Joe all had brightly colored 8-ounce cups in their hands that presumably held beer. The din of other students talking/partying combined with the music made it impossible for me to hear the three subjects' conversation. However, this made it easier to pay attention to their body language.

Joe—leaning against the wall with one leg propped up on a chair, looking directly and intently at Mary, with thumbs inside of pants and hands resting over pants pockets.

Mary—standing about 2½ feet away from Joe. Hands are on hips. Mary is smiling, and looks animated. She is sticking her chest out. Her body is turned toward Joe.

Jack—standing about 4½ feet away from both Mary and Joe. Jack is swaying back and forth on his feet, his hands are in his pockets and there is a smirk on his face.

Mary, Jack, and Joe are engaged in conversation with each other, probably something funny, since they're all laughing.

Joe—brings eyebrows down, stops smiling, and looks down at his shoes (a look of bewilderment crosses Jack's and Mary's faces). Joe looks up quickly and bursts out laughing (Mary and Joe look relieved and start smiling).

Jack—looks around, then looks at Mary and Joe. Jack then says something, reaches out and shakes Joe's hand, then gives a short wave to Mary (Mary smiles and gives a quick wave back). Jack walks away. As he leaves he looks back at Joe and gives him a big cheese-eating grin and the "thumbs-up" signal (Mary doesn't see any of this).

Joe—looks at Jack as he walks away and frowns at him, then smiles and looks back at Mary. Joe puffs his chest out a little.

Mary—reaches behind her head, undoes her ponytail, and shakes her head back and forth. She then moves about a foot and a half closer to Joe and puts her hand on his thigh.

ANALYSIS

The segment of nonverbal communication just described contains many different gestures. Some of these gestures carry symbolic meaning, such as Jack's thumbs-up sign, which means good luck. However, most of these gestures are postures that carry nonsymbolic meaning. In the segment there are two things I would like to take a look at: the "pickup" and the "isolation."

The "pickup" occurs between Joe and Mary. In my mind, most pickups are usually males coming on to females. But in this case the female was coming on to the male. To begin with, look at Mary's posture—hands on hips, chest stuck out, and she is facing Joe. The hands on the hips to me appears to be an aggressive stance, as if Mary is saying, "Here I am. Come look at me . . . but beware. I'm going to stand my ground." The fact that her chest is stuck out makes this sexual aggression, almost as if Mary is saying, "These are my breasts. Look at them." Personally, if I'm talking to a female and she is thrusting her chest out, I tend to look at her chest. Sooner or later "typical male" thoughts cross my mind (like I'd rather be doing something with these female breasts other than having a conversation with them). The expansion of a female chest could be interpreted by males as a mating call. Furthermore, Mary is facing Joe, instead of facing Joe and Jack. This shows she is paying attention to Joe and wants Joe to pay attention to her.

Joe responds to Mary's body language by semireclining against a wall and looking intently at Mary. By reclining, Joe shows that he is relaxed and not threatened by Mary's sexual aggressiveness. Furthermore, Joe shows Mary that he is interested in her because he is looking her in the eyes as she speaks and apparently paying attention to what she is saying. These postures indicate to me (and probably to Mary) that Joe is interested in Mary, but for the moment is not willing to respond to Mary's sexual aggression, and is making her do all the work. But these attitudes begin to change as time passes.

When Joe frowns and looks down at his shoes, he is playing coy and showing that he feels hurt by what was just said. However, since he looks back up and bursts out laughing he shows that he was only joking. After Jack leaves, Joe puffs his chest. This gesture directed at Mary shows he is a strong and virile male. This is not unlike some male birds who puff their chest out in mating season to show their colors.

The last part of the pickup takes place after Jack leaves. Mary, not having to worry about two males, moves in for the kill. To start with, Mary unfastens her hair and shakes it about. This is a very sexy gesture. It implies that "I'm unburdened, loosened up (sort of like undressing) and ready to relax." The release of her hair also suggests to me a lowering of her guard. Mary then moves in closer to talk to Joe ("Latins and lovers stand closer together"). Finally, Mary places her hand on Joe's thigh. Touching someone is not necessarily sexual. However, in this instance, putting her hand on Joe's thigh (so near his groin) is most definitely sexual.

The second segment I would like to describe is the "isolation." Jack is the one who is being isolated. Although Jack may be friends with both Joe and Mary, his presence is annoying to Mary, who wishes to focus on Joe. Jack's isolation is imposed by himself as well as by Joe and Mary. Joe and Mary isolate Jack by looking at each other and not him; Mary further isolates Jack by turning her body toward Joe instead of facing both Jack and Joe. Not having seen the beginning of the conversation, one could speculate that Jack walked up to and interrupted Mary and Joe. Once Jack realized that Mary was stalking Joe, Jack began to isolate himself so he could leave the conversation and avoid making a faux pas. Jack isolated himself by standing farther away from Joe and Mary than they were from each other.

By swaying back and forth, Jack showed that he was either drunk or un-comfortable and felt the need to move. Feeling it was time to leave (being isolated pointed this out to him), Jack looked around to see if there was any-one else he could talk to and left.

Not having heard the conversation, I find it amazing how much one can deduce from watching the body language and gestures of people. Body language added a whole dimension to Joe, Jack, and Mary's conversation. If there had been no posturing in the episode, things might have turned out differently. For instance, Jack might not have taken the clues to get lost. Per-haps Mary would have had to tell Joe outright that she was attracted to him and wished to copulate. Maybe she would have said, "Take me to bed or lose me forever."

A Drug Buy

by Paul Thompson

At least three aspects of this paper are noteworthy: first, the author's keen observation of an exchange which is not only nonverbal but also somewhat hidden; second, his explicit consideration of cultural mediation and stereotype; third, his speculative discussion of the cultural significance of what he has just described. In an exchange lasting only a minute or two, he sees a good part of the power tension between young whites and blacks.

The nonverbal exchange described here occurred in the spring of my junior year at Evanston Township High School. My friends and I witnessed the event from Gee's, a hamburger joint across the street from school. It is in a lower-middle-class, predominantly black neighborhood on the border between Chicago and Skokie. The participants are a white teenage male with long bushy black hair, wearing blue jeans and a Slayer T-shirt, and a black teenage male wearing a full-length Charlotte Hornets' winter jacket, blue jeans, and a pair of Air Jordans.

INCIDENT

White male—walks slowly up the sidewalk, gradually slowing down as he gets closer to the black male. He makes eye contact several times.

Black male—glances at the white male, does a quick check of the surrounding area. He then looks back at the white male and reaches up, touching his own left nostril.

White male—nods, glances around quickly, stops walking, and stands
next to the black male. He then reaches into his pocket, pulls out a closed
fist, and stretches his arm out to the black male.

Black male—glances around again, sticks his palm out, receives what's
in the white male's fist, and closes his fist around it. He then turns his palm
toward himself, opens it briefly, then puts it in his pocket. He then reaches
in another pocket, glances around again, and extends his closed fist to the
white male.

White male—extends palm and closes fist on object offered by the
black male. He then glances around, looks at the object, appears to fiddle
with it, and then sticks his pinky finger in his mouth. Then he smiles and
gives the peace sign with his hand to the black male and continues down
the block.

Black male—nods and grins at the white male, walks in the other direction for about 30 yards, and then stops to lean against a lamppost.

ANALYSIS

The segment of nonverbal communication just described contains a variety
of gestures. Some of these gestures have a very specific meaning (such as
the touching of the nostril to ask "you want cocaine?"); others are just the
effects of the situation on the individuals (such as the constant glances
around for police), which tend to communicate the nature of the situation
to the observer.

In a way, the black male begins the interaction and the nonverbal communication simply by wearing a full-length Charlotte Hornets' winter jacket
in the middle of spring, and standing around idly. In the neighborhood my
high school was in (partly just because the school is there), this communi-
cated the fact that one had something illegal to sell. The white male receives
this communication and communicates his interest in making a purchase by
slowing down his walking speed as he nears the black male. The black male
then attempts to get the white male to stop and buy drugs from him by
touching his nostril. The white male then confirms he wished to purchase
cocaine by nodding.

The next few steps of the exchange contain nonverbal communication,
but not between the two participants. The fact that they exchange fistfuls of
objects (one presumably cocaine and the other cash), being careful not to
let them be seen, and the fact that they look around constantly, communicates to anyone watching them that they are engaging in illegal activity. For

the drug dealer, however, this communication to those around him is a benefit, as long as there are no police officers nearby. That way he can communicate to others that he is the man to buy drugs from.

The final communication from the white male is when he tastes the cocaine with his pinky finger and nods. This shows that he is happy with the purchase he made. (The method of discovery of the potency of cocaine is taste. If it numbs your tongue, it is supposedly very good.) The final communication from the black male is the grin and the nod, which shows he is also happy with the exchange, and seems to say, "I'll be around if you need more."

Although some parts of our society are becoming more liberal toward some drugs that are currently illegal, you will not find many who will stipulate that cocaine doesn't kill. This situation is of special concern for many in the United States because the sale is happening at lunchtime across the street from a school. As a result of the highly illegal nature of the interaction, the white male's and the black male's communication was done in different emotional contexts. The white male's communication was motivated by the fear of getting arrested. The black male's communication was motivated by the fear of getting arrested, plus the emotional need to appear unafraid of getting arrested to those around him.

The nonverbal communication in this situation is definitely culturally mediated. One aspect of the cultural mediation is the fact that cocaine is illegal and frowned upon. The communication is sneaky and speeds up the process by not having to speak. Another way in which the communication is culturally mediated is the fact that our culture has in many ways forced young black teenagers into the position where they have to sell drugs in order to keep up the lifestyle they think they must have. Somehow material goods, such as the $400 Hornets' jacket and the $150 Air Jordan basketball shoes, have become a necessity for them, so much so that they will kill each other for a pair of shoes, or sell drugs to someone else, and kill them. Although society can't be completely responsible, it does deserve some of the blame.

The individuals involved in this communication didn't invent it by any means. It is rather the "official" nonverbal communication of the drug dealer. All over the city you can see glimpses of drug deals going down in which symbols similar to those I saw that day are used. As for the question of stereotypical communication, I don't think I could have picked an incident more so. One of the strongest stereotypes in our society is the one that all young, black male teenagers in the city are drug dealers. Sadly, the way things are going today it doesn't look as if that stereotype will ever die out.

Eyes to Heaven

by Gay Boyer

This eye blink of communication is used both by the older and the younger genera-
tions of one family. The author occupies the middle generation and sees "the look"
both up and down the family tree. Boyer is a nontraditional student at Grand Val-
ley State University in Michigan; her paper demonstrates that what preoccupies late
teenagers is different from what grandparents see and take note of.

There is a "look," which includes raised eyebrows and eyes rolled to the sky, that seems to be used to communicate various messages, such as disbelief, disrespect, and boredom. Sometimes it denotes ridicule.

This "look" is often in evidence when persons of different generations are gathered together. For example: Grandmother is enthroned at the festive holiday table. Seated also around the table are her children and grandchildren. Someone always says, "I can't eat another bite . . . I'm stuffed!" The grandmother (who tips the scales at close to 300 lbs.) agrees, but then as the children are clearing away the remains of the feast to facilitate presentation of dessert, the grandmother says, "I believe I'll have a bit more of that dressing . . . just a dab." Out of her line of vision, two or more of the older children exchange the "look": Eyebrows are raised and eyes roll heavenward in silent amusement at the old lady's gluttony.

A teenaged daughter, upon being told by her parents that she may not attend a party where her parents know that the parents of the party giver will not be home will wail, "You never let me do anything . . . you hate me!" The parents will exchange the "look," and it's an expression of shared . . . endurance.

Since the "look" is not meant to be seen by its subject, it is an expression of solidarity against some aspect of the subject. It's a polite way of agreeing to disagree, without verbalizing.

To tell Grandma she's already had three servings of dressing and will doubtless have at least two servings of pie—"Both kinds look sooooo good . . . give me just a smidgen of each"—would be futile. Grandma is in her very late 70s. She won't change her eating habits for her health's sake, and certainly not for the sake of her children's approval. So behind her back, the "look" is exchanged as a substitute for confronting Grandma.

The "look" is a substitute for verbal and direct confrontation. It acknowledges a shared opinion or feeling concerning another person, often when it would be unkind or futile to express it directly.

It also expresses a lack of power. When used in the presence of a superior or an authority figure, it defuses the frustration, and perhaps anger, of those who are powerless to effect change of the "official" attitude.

When I am with my daughters, I sometimes feel the silent "look" exchanged at some terribly wise pronouncement of mine, and I realize that my statement was doubtless inappropriate, or repetitive . . . and I sigh and give the "look" to my . . . self.

Ritual

This assignment is bigger than any of the previous three and should incorporate what you learned from each. You are to record a ritual event, preferably freshly, but if not, then from memory.

From the map assignment: Observe accurately and minutely, including costuming and decorations.

From the private language assignment: Note the *exact words* used in the event. Thomas Mann said of language, "Language itself is a criticism of life; it calls by name, hits things off, characterizes, and passes judgements . . ." (in Angell, 1950:409). Every person who describes a given event defines it differently, and what you are seeking in this assignment, as well as in the big ethnography, is your informants' definitions, not your own. You will find this point reemphasized in the next chapter in the quotes by Sir Richard Burton and Samuel Johnson.

From the nonverbal communication assignment: Record the body language of participants. Does it reinforce or contradict what is said? Keep in mind that while telling lies is one of the survival techniques which language facilitates, it is harder (but not impossible) to lie with the body.

What is a ritual? You will find a detailed definition later. Consult it carefully and use it explicitly. The essence of this definition is the symbol. A ritual is almost always a collection of symbols, which a good analysis separates out and considers one by one. You may find an event that is entirely ritual, for instance, initiations, weddings, funerals, and other rites of passage, and rites of intensification like Christmas, Hanukkah, Thanksgiving, and the pledge of allegiance to the flag. The Roman Catholic mass, described by Dana Curtis in this section, is entirely ritual. You may, on the contrary, describe the ritual aspect of an event that is basically nonritual—for instance Joshua Keilty's analysis of the ritual imbedded in saying goodbye to a close friend or Renato Rosaldo's parody of a family breakfast. Meals, business meetings, sessions of college classes, and countless other cultural events and situations have ritual aspects even though they cannot be labeled primarily as rituals. Although most of the events described in the illustrations in this section are informal and private, you can learn a great deal by choosing an obvious public event and analyzing it thoroughly.

PURPOSE

Cultural systems are not just rules for behavior, ways of surviving, or strait-jackets to constrict free expression, as we remarked in the section on private language. All cultures, no matter how simple or sophisticated, are also rhythms, music, architecture, the dances of living. To look at culture as style applies particularly to the patterning of each language, as linguist Kenneth Pike used to tell his students—more broadly to cultural patterns themselves as ways to sing and to dance one's life. To look at culture as style is to look at ritual. (For a few years students and I experimented with adding an an-tiritual, or "ex-stasis" assignment, by way of contrast. The exercise threw rituals into perspective and was exciting to write and to read. But we decided that ecstasy is private by nature and that to write about it as an assignment was an invasion. You may, after you have become accustomed to the idea of ritual, want to write an antiritual for your own interest.)

If you become genuinely involved with this assignment, you will learn, as Josh Keilty says in his ritual of goodbye, that "almost every act in life is ritualistic" and ritual can be an instrumental act "charged with a special energy." By doing a good job, you will learn much about the heart of culture.

PROCEDURE

Divide this paper, like exercises 2 and 3, into two clearly marked sections. The second section should receive more attention then the first, and is often longer.

Section 1: Ethnography. Describe the setting and tell the events in their proper order. Describe the church and the weather and the stadium, the size and mood of the crowd. Don't start with "Here Comes the Bride" or with the opening kickoff.

As well as you are able, avoid interpretation. Instead of "the bride was nervous," go to the trouble of saying, "She twisted the bouquet as she stood at the altar; the veins in her hands stood out." *In short, do not label the emotions, but communicate them through your descriptive statements.* This is a difficult part of the assignment, designed to reduce the bias of ethnocentrism insofar as possible.

Section 2: Ethnographic Analysis. Your first task in this section is to defend the proposition that the events you have just described are in fact ritual and not merely habit. Once you have satisfied the definition, analyze your ethnographic data in terms of the typology offered later. What kinds of functions were performed? If the bride was nervous, why? Why did her mother cry? What may have made the groom drop the ring? If it is the wake after a funeral of an elderly person who died "in the fullness of time," how come sober faces gave way to good spirits and camaraderie? Aside from sadism, what made some fraternity boys wield the paddles and others meekly present their bare backsides? How come Casper Milquetoast became the life of the party? This part of the paper is the more important part, as it will demonstrate your subtlety, your ability to probe into the data you have collected, and your ability to stand back from your own culture and understand it as if it were foreign and you the visiting ethnographer. You will probably find that while your ritual fits best under one label, other labels fit subordinate aspects of the event (e.g., deference to the most important individual at a rite of intensification, or the intensification of a social group at the gathering following a rite of passage).

Limitations. You must have been either a participant or eyewitness to the event. If you are describing the ritual of a foreign culture, be prepared to supplement your own analysis by reading or asking questions of those who know the ritual better than you.

Range. Good papers have been submitted on topics ranging in size from a couple having a cup of coffee and a cigarette to a presidential inauguration. It matters relatively little what ritual you describe, and relatively much how sensitively you observe what transpired and analyze what needs were served. A sense of perspective (i.e., a sense of humor) is not essential, but it may help you do a good job if you use it with restraint. Papers for this assignment run about ten pages.

When casting about for a ritual to analyze, keep in mind that rituals can be both formal and informal, conservative and innovative. The examples here start with two descriptions of one of the most formal and conservative of Euro-American rituals—the Roman Catholic mass. The first description, by Dana Curtis, straightforwardly explains what is symbolized by various parts of a standard mass. Conservative rituals help to maintain the integrity of cultures. The second description of the mass is by Alan Stewart, a non-Catholic who brushes lightly over that part of the ceremony to focus on the military forms that honor a comrade fallen in the line of duty. The moral of the contrast between the two papers is that the study of ritual depends both on the ritual itself and on what the observer brings to it.

Alice Reich comments, in the context of women's spirituality, that rituals "create connections with larger communities of belief," and then she opens the door to individual creativity: "While many institutionalized rituals require hierarchy and authority for their performance, women's spirituality emphasizes the ability of each person to create and participate in ritual" (1993b:435). Men can be equally creative: Tony Muñoz's football ritual contains little hierarchy and perhaps no authority; Bill Dunbar's ritual of drinking simply invents itself as it goes along. Each student's part in creating and interpreting meaning is central to the sort of education that this field manual aims to promote.

DEFINITION AND ANALYSIS

There are many definitions of ritual. Some limit ritual to public ceremony. Several limit ritual to religion. The definition used here sets no limits on context, but insists instead on the functions performed by the event.

Our definition comes from several sources, the most important of which is John J. Honigmann, *The World of Man* (1959), Chapter 31, "Ritual," pp. 509–29, as reinterpreted by three decades of my students.

Definition

"Confucian philosophers of the second and third pre-Christian centuries spoke of ritual as the orderly expression of feelings appropriate to a social situation. . . . To rephrase this, ritual refers to the *symbolic expression of the sentiments which are attached to a given situation.* The term 'situation' should be taken to include person, place, time, conception, thing, or occasion. Marriage, death, Christmas, and Easter are prominent ceremonial occasions in Europe and America" (Honigmann, 1959:509; emphasis added). You will have no trouble distinguishing between symbolic and literal actions if you keep in mind that, by definition, symbols stand for other concepts, events, or emotions.

By stressing appropriate sentiments, Honigmann means to imply that ritual is form. You may find it helpful to think of ritual as a vessel (form) holding wine (the appropriate sentiments). If the ritual is vital to its culture, then it is a beautifully formed vessel full of good wine. If it is no longer functional, it is a dry vessel, empty. If the emotion is so great that the ritual structure cannot contain it, then it is a cup running over and the situation gets messy. A similar observation is made in an unexpected source—*Miss Manners' Guide to Excruciatingly Correct Behavior* (Martin, 1982:694): "The great art of etiquette was invented to translate the incoherent jumble of human feelings to which we are all subject into something more presentable. When we cast it aside and let our emotions run around naked and exposed to public comment . . . everybody suffers."

Whether the emotion is sincerely felt is an interesting question to be considered in the analysis, but not part of the definition; standardization of behavior is part of "orderly expression." Use the terms *sentiment* and *emotion* in their broadest sense.

The Aim of Analysis

The first three assignments were like finger exercises on the piano, designed to acquire (or to remind you that you already possessed) skills needed in the description of culture. With this assignment, you begin to play the music itself. You have by this point carefully and thoroughly described an event or series of events, and you have *explicitly* defended that event as ritual (your first analytic task). Now the real fun begins. Use the following classification of types systematically to exhaust the analytic possibilities. But don't stop there.

What is wanted is a probing analysis of the nuances of the ritual you have described. It is worth repeating that what you choose to describe is a comparatively trivial decision, but how well and delicately you tease apart the elements of the event and their implications is the critical part of the assignment and will help you to learn what ethnography can accomplish at its best.

There is also a dimension to analyzing a ritual that is *not* illustrated in the papers which follow, although the ambivalence Renato Rosaldo reports brings us close: Rituals are supposed to give symbolic expression to appropriate emotions, but the emotions people actually feel may be inappropriate and may actually be disruptive to the event. In short, the ritual (or any part of it) may not work. Despite the tendency of ethnographic writing of the past to depict all cultural systems as functional, sometimes they are dysfunctional. So in this assignment, look for the greed or glee that may accompany grief at a funeral, the jealousy at a wedding, the personal rivalries at a drinking bout (see Bill Dunbar's paper). One student paper, which cannot be published because there would be no way to mask identities, described how a broken and taped-back-together family constructed the funeral of its patriarch by inventing new rules for seating individuals who hated each other, for allowing alcoholic members to drink without destroying the proceedings, and small ways to symbolize the disapproval of the more moral participants against the choice of clothing of those who lived by looser codes. People do not have to be respectable in order to act ritually. How does the ritual you describe paper over, or accommodate, or fail in the face of "wrong" emotions? These tensions are the stuff of novels of manners like Jane Austen's *Pride and Prejudice*, William Makepeace Thackeray's *Vanity Fair*, or Edith Wharton's *Age of Innocence*. Amy Lowell in her poem "Patterns" (1916:3–9) jogs along for several pages with the underplayed tragedy of a noblewoman in her whaleboned and brocaded gown whose lover has just been killed "in a pattern called a war," and then shrieks out "Christ! What are patterns for?" These tensions are also the stuff of good analyses of ritual. (We return to the theme of dysfunction later, number 4 under "Pitfalls to Avoid.")

Classification of Types (Not Mutually Exclusive)

1. *Rites of Deference:* rituals that show difference in status, ranging from tipping a hat to a lady to prostrating oneself before a throne. These can be indirect, such as the right to interrupt another in conversation or to arrive late for an appointment.

2. *Rites of Passage:* rituals associated with the change of status of an individual or group of individuals—for example, christening, marriage, funeral, initiation. Functions of such rituals are as follows:

a. *Closure.* Rites of passage mark the end of stages of life or of situations. The more public and conscious the ritual, the more those involved are enabled to proceed to the next stage.

b. *Stressing Responsibility.* The new responsibilities taken on by those changing status are stressed—usually by stern injunctions, often by formal speeches. The more elaborate the ritual, the easier it is (ideally) for the individual to forget old habits and learn new ones appropriate to the new role.

c. *Promotion of Familiarity.* "The initiation ceremony . . . promotes stepped up social interaction between the new member and others in the association" (Honigmann, 1959:513). The wedding reception is sometimes the initial meeting and interaction between the family of the bride and the family of the groom, and (perhaps with the relaxation induced by alcohol) promotes their socializing.

d. *Aid in Readjustment.* Rites of passage almost always disrupt previously existing relations. The ceremony assists those concerned to restore equilibrium in the new arrangement. This function is particularly characteristic of the wake following the death and burial of a prominent and powerful individual. For example, after John F. Kennedy's funeral in 1963, the new president, Lyndon Johnson, held a reception for heads of state of all of the world's principal nations to reassure them that the U.S. government was stable and unshaken.

e. *Solidarity Is Enhanced.* The disrupted portion of society pulls together again and asserts that it is still viable and intact. Most poignant after funerals, but also characteristic of weddings, commencement parties, and so on.

3. *Rites of Intensification:* rituals, for which the main purpose is to reassert social relations, to intensify social bonds. Functions of such rituals are as follows:

a. *Solidarity Is Enhanced.* Most rites of passage are also rites of intensification. See 2e. Hannukah, Thanksgiving, Memorial Day, and weekly religious services are prominent examples of rites of intensification that are not rites of passage.

b. *Activation of Status Relationships.* Helps maintain status systems by giving them the excuse to operate (e.g., Rex and Comus at New Orleans Mardi Gras; inauguration of a president, coronation of a monarch). See also "Deference" (number 1). The four-day purification of Cherokee hunters or warriors as they return to the village marks their change of status, providing the decompression chamber during which men switch from red (war) to white (peace) organization of the village. See also 3d.

c. *Value Reiteration.* Patriotic (including academic) ceremony promotes loyalty and also the particular values for which the institution prides itself. Reaffirmations like the pledge of allegiance to the flag and the repetition of wedding vows by everyone in the congregation at a wedding are clear-cut examples. Similar but not identical to 3b.

d. *Achievement of New Adjustments.* See 3b. and 2d. In relation to a seasonal cycle, for instance, ritual helps a community switch from the activities appropriate to the growing portion of the year to those appropriate to the saving portion. Among the Chukchee, when the young men and women return seasonally with their reindeer herds to base camp, ritual helps them adjust back to stricter parental control.

4. *Rites of Reversal:* prohibitions normally enforced are lifted according to rules of their own—what we have called rules for breaking rules. The grand occasion is the Latin *carnaval,* as celebrated in New Orleans and Rio de Janeiro on the eve of Lent. Smaller occasions are found in smaller circumstances, for example, when the counselors wait on the campers or when (as in the 1950s and 1960s at Colorado College) the graduating seniors kidnap the faculty shortly before commencement, take them to a secluded campground, and get them drunk. One important function is catharsis.

5. *Instrumental Rites:* include magical incantations. Such rites are tricky because actions that to an outsider appear as ritual are likely to be seen by the actors as simply instrumental steps without symbolism (i.e., nonritual). Horace Miner's famous "Body Ritual Among the Nacirema" (1956) uses such contrary interpretations of what people do in the privacy of their bathrooms as material for cultural satire.

MISCELLANEOUS FUNCTIONS SERVED BY RITUAL

1. *Enhancement of Patriotism:* similar to 3c., but going further. For example, " . . . [in] segmentary tribes of Africa (for example, the Tallensi) each [clan] segment possesses crucial roles in a cycle of rituals that must be completed if *all* the segments are to prosper" (Honigmann, 1959:516). In Hopi, each clan is responsible for the dance rituals that it performs on behalf of the whole village—rain, good crops, and so on.

2. *Avoidance of Conflict:* often associated with kin (e.g., avoidance of mother-in-law among the Navajo to keep relations smooth). These are "zero rituals" because they symbolically express appropriate sentiments by *in*actions.

3. *Symbolic Suppression of Evil:* "Step on a crack, break you mother's back." Rites of purification, exorcism, expiation after crisis. "The gods are offended, we must propitiate them." In Western culture, the Lord's Prayer, the jail sentence, the fine, and the religious penance are important examples.

4. *Allaying Anxiety:* the psychosomatic aspect of ritual. The Hopi village feels better after the rain dance, whether rain comes or not. The athlete is not so disheartened after losing a game if he has done his psyching-up ritual correctly. "We have done all we mortals could do."

PITFALLS TO AVOID

1. Ritual and habit are conceptually different, although the performance of a familiar ritual can become habitual. One ties shoelaces the same way each time, cooks, perhaps even gets up and goes to work in the same sequence every morning, simply because repetition saves time and saves the energy of rethink-

ing familiar tasks. No particular sentiments, no symbolic expression. If you are in doubt whether the event you want to describe is ritual or mere habit, return to the definition and ask whether sentiments are being symbolically expressed.

2. The more emotional the situation, the more wine and the less vessel. For example, two students in three decades of ritual papers described coitus as a ritual. Both papers were failures because although the sentiments were abundant, their symbolic, orderly, publicly expected expression was absent. All wine, no vessel. (Sexual congress can be ritualized, but the sexual culture of young Americans is usually private and experimental, hence unlikely to convey the symbols of expected sentiment.)

The opposite, however (all vessel, no wine), is an opportunity and not a pitfall. If you find that the performers of the event you witness are only going through the motions without believing in the emotion or thing symbolized, the openings for analysis are rich. Why do people no longer believe? What cultural change has occurred to crack the vessel and/or evaporate the wine of emotion? We can generalize that cultural form lags somewhat behind changes in sentiment, whether we are talking ritual or some other aspect of culture. Two examples close to home will illustrate: Fathers traditionally escort brides down the wedding aisle, and the bride wears white. The historical significance of the first is that daughters must be protected by their fathers, who hand over that responsibility to husbands at the moment of marriage. As daughter and also as wife, a woman's chastity reflects on the good repute of her family. The historical significance of wearing white is virginity. Why do these customs persist in an age of gender equality, when a woman's marriageability is more likely to depend on her earning power than on her sexual decorum, and when if she is still a virgin by her mid-20s she is suspected of frigidity rather than virtue? The answers at this moment must be tentative: The first custom seems to be slipping away, in favor of rituals that better express not only the independence of young women but the equality of her parents (and of them with the parents of the groom); couples more frequently write their own rituals than they used to. The second custom is, I believe, more resistant to change: The form tends to remain the same, but wearing white is coming to symbolize not sexual purity but purity of soul or something else as nebulous. (But note that brides are still criticized if they wear white at subsequent weddings.) The moral for the student of ritual is that the interplay between form and function is as slippery as the interpretation of poetry.

3. Following logically on number 2, watch out lest the emotions that you as participant experienced during, leading up to, or as a result of, the ritual overwhelm your analysis. Discussion of your own emotions is permissible and may help clarify the analysis, but it is not the core of the task. That core is to discover the symbols used in the ritual to express expected emotions. Use your own emotions as the key to discovering what emotions are expected. But this is anthropology, not autobiography; reflexivity, not navel gazing. Your idiosyncratic life history is not the same thing as cultural interpretation.

4. Because anthropologists usually study what works rather than what doesn't—functions rather than dysfunctions—it would be natural to assume that every ritual works well and that if the analysis doesn't demonstrate how well it works, the student is doing a bad job. Not necessarily. To explain this problem, we shift our metaphor from a wine vessel to theater. I believe the desire to see human life as an art form is programmed in our genes (although I don't think I could prove the point to a sceptic). Certainly every language has its own music. Consistently, we should like all rituals to be harmonious and beautiful and to make their dramatic points with Shakespearean eloquence. But sadly, many dramatists have a poor sense of theater, and many rituals are just badly done. Here are two simple examples: College commencements are supposed to symbolize the best and the highest achievements of academic labor, and academic costuming harks back to our monastic beginnings. Yet many professors wear their regalia sloppily, with jeans and scruffy shoes protruding below their gowns, and some deans stumble over the names of the graduating seniors and can't even pronounce "summa cum laude" with the round sonority which highest honor deserves. (I decline the next obvious step, of complaining about graduating seniors who wear shorts under their gowns and pop champagne bottles as they walk across the podium, because they are often doing good theater of a different kind.) A second example is a court trial in Santa Fe which I both observed and participated in, late in 1967 while doing ethnography on a Spanish village in the Rio Arriba (Kutsche and Van Ness, 1981:166–83). We in the village were the defendants, and I wanted the enemy (the district attorney) to make his case with melodramatic flourishes. He disappointed us by bumbling and mumbling and showing so little preparation that the judge had to provide the case citations of precedents for him. The defense attorney wasn't much better. I felt cheated out of one of the great moments of theater of my professional life.

How are you to handle your ritual if you decide it makes bad theater? (None of the students whose papers are in this volume had to confront this problem.) First, state why you chose it despite its flaws. Second, explain how it lacks the appropriate expression of sentiments. And third, write the scenario it should have followed to express the appropriate sentiments well and memorably. To paraphrase what I have said in other contexts, one can learn as much from cultural forms that don't work as from those that do.

5. The most frequent error students make in this assignment is to get so caught up in telling a tale that they forget to analyze. Long rituals take many pages to describe adequately, and when one has written these pages it is easy to think that the job is done. The best strategy if you are describing, for instance, a wedding with all of its preparatory ceremonies, or the series of events that make a memorable childhood holiday, is to write a fast draft of the whole event, then pick the one portion of it which you want to focus on, writing up in detail only that portion and analyzing it exhaustively, using

the foregoing classification as your framework. Description without analysis is not ethnology at all, but an exercise in creative writing.

FURTHER IN THE SAME DIRECTION

In the long sweep of anthropology's short history, few questions have gripped more of us more deeply than the nature of ritual and its connections with religion, magic, myths, and symbols. In case this assignment whets your appetite, you may pursue the topic in an enormous literature. Useful starting places are two books: Arnold van Gennep, *The Rites of Passage* (1909), and Barbara Myerhoff, *Number Our Days* (1978); and two articles in the *International Encyclopaedia of the Social Sciences* (1968): "Ritual" by Edmund Leach and "Myth and Symbol" by Victor Turner.

Turner's article is curious in that it labels myth a "liminal phenomenon" which marks permanent cultural changes, each with its sequence of status, loss of status, assumption of new status (death/rebirth, infancy/adulthood, etc.), and then depends heavily on van Gennep and Mircea Eliade concerning rites of passage. Leach considers ritual almost exclusively as an aspect of religion. His approach to culture focuses on its public areas and its stability, in contrast to Honigmann's more flexible definition, applicable equally to public and private behavior. Unlike such feminists as Alice Reich, Leach says nothing about each individual's ability to create. For Leach, the sacred seems to occupy much the same place in the dynamics of ritual that the emotions do for Honigmann.

If your interest in ritual turns toward the reversals contained in Mardi Gras and other carnivals, then your best starting point is Mikhail Bakhtin, *Rabelais and His World* (1968). Rituals themselves, as well as the analysis of ritual, sometimes criticize social structures in poignant ways.

Finally, going "further in the same direction" may lead you to do original research on a topic which, as far as I know, has not been touched by scholars: changes in ritual style during a normal life cycle. People in their late teens and early twenties are usually more interested in rituals that they invent, while older people find that traditional ceremonies fit them better. An alumnus of my introductory course, now in his mid-forties, brought this dichotomy to my attention in 1997. He had been inventive and creative as an undergraduate. Now a business executive with a wife and two children, he travels frequently over much of the globe and must adapt himself to a variety of cultures, one after another—a classically postmodern situation. He told me that he began to experience difficulty finding his way back to domestic life in the suburbs of a big American city. He turned to his ancestral religion and found structure and predictability in its traditional rituals. As he understated it, "Now I know where my family and I will be at the end of every week."

Roman Catholic Mass

by Dana Curtis

*The first two student illustrations of ritual show what can be done with set-piece cer-
emonies—undeniable rituals. Both describe and analyze the Roman Catholic mass.
All of the rest of the papers describe newly created rituals that the author had a large
hand in designing.*

    *But note how different are the perspectives of the two authors: Although both
Curtis and Stewart (author of the second paper) had careers before college, and both
were students in the same class at Pikes Peak Community College in Colorado Springs,
Curtis is a practicing Roman Catholic who understands each part of the mass as a
believer. (If she had come from a non-Western culture, she would probably have described and analyzed the clothing of the congregation as a mark of deference to di-
vinity, but she is so familiar with Sunday clothes that they did not seem noteworthy.)
Stewart is a former sheriff's deputy who describes the mass with a few spare strokes
and then concentrates on the military ritual, which made an overwhelming impression on him.*

DATA

As we enter the church to begin the Sunday's celebration, we dip our fin-
gers into the Holy Water bowls, cross ourselves, genuflect facing the cross
hanging above the altar, kneel, say a brief private prayer, and take our seats
until the Mass begins.

INTRODUCTORY RITES

With the beginnings of the opening song, we stand for the first part of Mass.
The priest, altar servers, and proclaimers process from the back of the
church, up the main aisle, to the altar. This procession is led by the boy altar
server carrying a brass cross on a pole. The girl server follows directly behind him. Next, walking side by side, are the two proclaimers, or lectors, one
holding above his head the large, elaborately decorated, gold Bible. Finally
comes the priest, wearing a simple cream-colored vestment, singing from a
hymnal as he makes his way forward.

    As they arrive at the front of the church, the altar server places the
cross in its stand to the right of the altar, then servers and proclaimers take
their places behind the center of the altar as the priest begins the Mass.

Penitential Rite

All: "I confess to almighty God and to you, my brothers and sisters, that I have sinned through my own fault in my thoughts and in my words, in what I have done, and in what I have failed to do; and I ask blessed Mary, ever virgin, all the angels and saints, and you my brothers and sisters, to pray for me to the Lord Our God."

All: "Glory to God in the highest, and peace to his people on earth. Lord God, heavenly King, almighty God and Father, we worship you, we give you thanks, we praise you for your glory. Lord Jesus Christ, only Son of the Father, Lord God, Lamb of God, you take away the sins of the world: have mercy on us; you are seated at the right hand of the Father: receive our prayer. For you alone are the Holy One, you alone are the Lord, you alone are the Most High, Jesus Christ, with the Holy Spirit, in the Glory of God the Father. Amen."

LITURGY OF THE WORD

Responsorial Psalm

Song Leader: "The Lord is kind and merciful."

All: "The Lord is kind and merciful."

The song leader sings three or four different choruses and our response to each is the same.

Alleluia

All: (singing) "Al-le-lu-ia! Al-le-lu-ia! Al-le-lu-ia!"

The song leader sings the first refrain, and the people repeat him or her. This refrain/repeat lasts for three to four choruses. Then the congregation stands again for the gospel read by the priest.

Gospel Reading

Priest: "The Lord be with you."

All: "And also with you."

Priest: "A reading from the holy gospel to Matthew" (5:138–45). Everyone makes small crosses with their thumbs on their foreheads, mouths, and hearts.

Homily

During this time we take our seats as the celebrant or priest delivers the homily. It is a sunny but cold spring morning. The sun shines through the mosaic stained-glass windows, giving the sanctuary a calming glow. The altar is adorned in simple garments also: Its cloth is plain white with two cream-colored runners on either end. These runners have no ornamentation save a gold fringe along the bottom. There are several dozen Easter lilies on the floor directly in front of the altar as well as on numerous shelves around the front of the church. This gives a clear indication of the season we have just celebrated. The candelabras on and around the altar add to the glow and warmth of the building.

Profession of Faith

Nicene Creed (said as we once again stand)

> All: "We believe in one God, the Father, the Almighty, maker of heaven and earth, of all that is seen and unseen. We believe in one Lord, Jesus Christ, the only Son of God, eternally begotten of the Father, God from God, Light from Light, true God from true God, begotten, not made. For us men and for our salvation he came down from heaven: by the power of the Holy Spirit he was born of the Virgin Mary, and became man. For our sake he was crucified under Pontius Pilate; he suffered, died, and was buried. On the third day he rose again in fulfillment of the Scriptures; he ascended into heaven and is seated at the right hand of the Father. He will come again in glory to judge the living and the dead, and his kingdom will have no end. We believe in the Holy Spirit, the Lord, the giver of life, who proceeds from the Father and the Son. With the Father and the Son he is worshipped and glorified. He has spoken through the Prophets. We believe in one holy catholic and apostolic Church. We acknowledge one baptism for the forgiveness of sins. We look for the resurrection of the dead, and the life of the world to come. Amen.

LITURGY OF THE EUCHARIST

The girl server, with her dark hair tied neatly up in a bun, helps the priest to rinse his hands by holding a bowl underneath them and pouring water from a small glass pitcher onto them.

The congregation kneels on the "kneelers" in front of them.

Priest: "Let us offer a prayer . . ."
   All: "Amen."

Preface

Holy (sung by everyone present).

Memorial Acclamation

Priest: "Let us proclaim the mystery of faith."

All: (sung) "Dying you destroyed our death, rising you restored our life. Lord Jesus, come in glory."

Final Doxology

Priest: "Through Him, within Him, in Him, in the unity of the Holy Spirit, all glory and honor is yours, almighty Father, for ever and ever."

All: (sung) "A-men, a-men, a-men, a-men, a-men."

Communion Rite (The Lord's Prayer)

All: (holding hands after rising to our feet) "Our Father, who art in heaven . . . but deliver us from evil."

Priest: "Deliver us, Lord, from every evil, and grant us peace in our day. In your mercy keep us free from sin and protect us from all anxiety as we wait in joyful hope for the coming of our Savior, Jesus Christ."

All: (raising still-joined hands to the sky) "For the kingdom, the power and the glory are yours, now and forever."

Sign of Peace

Priest: "Lord Jesus Christ . . ."

All: "And also with you."

Priest: "The peace of the Lord be with you always."

All: "And also with you."

Priest: "Let us offer each other the sign of peace."

Parishioners greet other with handshakes and the words "Peace be with you."

Communion

From this point until the end of Communion we kneel.

Priest: "This is the Lamb of God who takes away the sins of the world. Happy are those who are called to his supper."

All: "Lord, I am not worthy to receive you, but only say the word and I shall be healed."

At Divine Redeemer, another hymn is sung as each of us, row by row, walk to the front of the church to receive communion.

All: "Amen."

CONCLUDING RITES

As the priest, proclaimers, and altar servers leave the altar, the priest once again bows; then the group turns and exits from the same central aisle they entered. The Mass has ended and the congregation genuflects one last time before they too leave the church.

ANALYSIS

One cannot help but wonder why church membership over the past century has sunk to an all-time low. One explanation could be the dominance of science. People are not conditioned to believe in the unseen and the unproven. Another possibility is that church membership requires a time commitment that busy people are unable or unwilling to give.

Some people attend church services merely out of habit: They feel that, for whatever reason (fear of what might happen if they don't attend, or because they were "brought up that way"), attending Mass is something they are just supposed to do. But despite this, thousands of Catholics still attend Mass regularly. For most, Mass is a deeply felt occasion that offers them something they could not fulfill elsewhere. It can offer personal peace, words of inspiration, or a chance to feel Christ's presence. What each person seeks is as unique and varied as the worshippers themselves.

The Catholic Mass celebrated daily in churches around the world is an age-old ritual. Like most religious ceremonies, it is a rite of intensification. But within this rite are other ritual categories as well, such as deference, suppression of evil, allaying anxiety, occasionally the enhancement of patriotism, and instrumental ritual elements. In addition to these specific functions, Mass is full of symbolism.

By definition, the main purpose of rites of intensification is to reassert social relations and intensify social bonds. Offering the sign of peace to one another is an obvious example of social bonding. Touching hands and greetings, offered with warm smiles, reaffirm that individuals form one community through God. Before approaching the altar to receive Jesus in Holy Communion, it is important to be at peace with one's family and neighbors. Following the church's custom of extending some sign of peace to those nearby ensures this sense of peacefulness and symbolizes peace with all people. Joining hands during the Lord's Supper also reaffirms the idea of community.

To further examine the intensification functtion we can look at several subcategories: First is the activation of status relationships, which is implied although never stated directly. People begin Mass burdened with sins and weaknesses from the outside world. The penitential rite is a confession of this sinfulness as well as a request that these sins and burdens be forgiven and lifted. During the course of the Mass petitioners are in a sense "renewed," and leave the church once again pure.

The Nicene Creed very effectively reaffirms the values of the Catholic Church. Every word, from "We believe in one God" to "Amen," redefines the foundation of the religion. The Catholic faith teaches that Jesus is true God and true Man—not "really" one or "really" the other. This doctrine of the Incarnation also says that Jesus is not some mixture of part divine and part human. This expression of the mystery of the incarnation is declared through the Nicene Creed, which was written in the third century A.D. and is still recited at Mass.

Rites of deference abound throughout the Mass. As worshippers arrive in the church, they genuflect to the crucifix hanging high on the wall behind the altar as a sign of their deference. This simple gesture is repeated as they prepare to leave the church. The congregation also kneels during the most significant part of the ritual, the preparation of the eucharist. This is again a deep sign of respect and acknowledgment of the importance of the act. The priest or celebrant also shows deference to God through his gestures. At the end of the procession, the priest stops to bow and kiss the altar. Since the altar is the central fixture of the eucharist preparation and the focal point of all during Mass, the priest's act confirms that it is holy and worthy of respect. The washing of the priest's hands is symbolic of the purification of the soul, so that he may approach the great sacrifice without blemish. As Christ enters the bread and wine and it becomes the body and blood, the priest genuflects as yet another act of deference and acknowledgment of Christ's presence. The priest bows to the altar again as he leaves the church.

There are at least three instrumental rites in the typical Mass: these are parts of the Mass that are sung instead of said—the Lord's Prayer, the Great Amen, and the Alleluia—because these words are directly spoken to God. Singing these parts gives the words a feeling of holiness as well as helping the people to pray and meditate.

The Lord's Prayer is also a suppression of evil. In this one brief prayer, God is asked to suppress evil of one sort or another several times. "Forgive us our debts as we forgive our debtors" is asking that wrongdoers of the earthly kind be held at bay. "Lead us not into temptation but deliver us from evil" requests that help be given with a supernatural foe. The priest's comments between the two parts of the prayer ask for the bread which is the Lord, and that others will be forgiven in the same way that each person wishes God to forgive them.

A general theme of the readings, songs, prayers, and homily is to allay anxiety. By Christ's teaching of "Be not afraid" and "Trust in the Lord," anxiety is reduced. These simple lines can do a great deal to help comfort worshippers and make it easier for them to face the challenges of the world.

Although not a part of the regular daily mass, during special occasions the altar is blessed and dedicated by the crossing of incense all around it. This again validates the altar as holy and an important element of the other rituals of the church.

As mentioned earlier, the washing of hands by the priest and the sign of peace are symbolic acts. But the most important symbolic aspect of the Mass is the eucharist and its preparation. At the Last Supper, the Lord surrounded the moment of sacrifice with ceremonies: The supper itself, the washing of feet, a sermon and a hymn. The Church does likewise: the Mass is filled with prayers, symbols and actions that help to recreate the Last Supper.

Most Catholics who attend Mass do so with little attention to the richness of ritual and symbolism. Through dissecting these rituals, one is truly able to understand the glory and wonder that is the Mass.

In the Line of Duty

by Alan N. Stewart

This paper is a success despite violating the guideline that descriptions should be exhaustively complete and analyses finely detailed. For Stewart, the core of this ritual is not the mass but the presence of the police and sheriff and the rituals that for them might be regarded as sacred. The event is stark and the author's prose style matches it.

Names of people are changed. The name of the city (Stockton, California) is not.

DATA

This is my recollection of a dark time several years ago when a fellow sheriff's officer lost his life in the line of duty; his name was Preston. I thought of him as a friend, though I was not really close to him. He was the type of person who always gave 110 percent. If one needed a favor or help with a case, he would come through if it was humanly possible. Some regarded him as a hot shot, since he always wore expensive suits when working in the investigations division. I saw him simply as a sharp professional.

Preston lost his life during a SWAT raid on the residence of a drug dealer. After clearing his assigned area, he moved to assist in the apprehension of the suspect in a trailer. When he came near a window, the suspect shot him in the head with a rifle. He was dead by the time he fell to the ground. The other officers then opened fire into the trailer, where the suspect was found to have bled to death from multiple gunshot wounds.

The funeral, in Stockton, California, was the first time that I had been exposed to any type of Catholic service. It was also the first funeral for an officer killed in the line of duty that I had witnessed or been a part of. Every deputy I knew of who was not on duty at the time was there. Everyone in uniform from our agency gathered in one area, to enter the church together in formation. We all wore our class A dress uniforms, including coat, hat, and tie. Several hundred officers, representing agencies all over California, attended in their dress uniforms as well, driving the newest polished patrol cars their agencies had available.

As we gathered in a staging area, I noticed that nearly everyone I saw had solemn expressions or frowns. Most had a look of pain in their eyes, even if the rest of their faces did not show emotion. A few of the newer officers in a group appeared to be uncomfortable. They were there, I assume, out of duty or respect, but they were probably thinking of their own mortality, as I was, since they could face life-ending dangers working in the jail or on patrol. They stood quietly talking among themselves and watching as officers from other agencies arrived. Most others stood silently looking at the ground.

We entered the church in a double marching line after family and other civilians were inside and seated. At the time, this seemed like just an orderly and respectful way of being seated, though now I see that it was part of the ceremony.

The church was a grand and beautiful building. The ceilings were high and very decorated with gold and paintings; there was an abundance of stained glass and burning candles.

Most of the service was performed by a man I knew as Ted. He was a deacon in the Catholic Church, and a lieutenant, but had also been my father's partner in a sheriff's office years ago. He seemed like a different person that day, quite a bit softer, wearing a decorated robe. I had always seen him wearing his uniform at work.

I had heard that Catholic services are very structured and ritualistic. I found this to be true today. Most of what was said seemed to be a matter of procedure: praying standardized prayers, quoting "generic" funeral scripture and other prose. Sure, there was emotion in Ted's voice, but his words could accomplish nothing for Preston. I had the feeling that for some this had meaning, but for me it was just going through the motions. I grew up in a Protestant church and believe that praying to statues of dead humans is idolatry and that you cannot pray a dead person into heaven. I recall images of the event more than the words that were said.

The exit procession was a reversal of the entrance procession. The double file line exited the building and then formed two ranks along either side of the walkway where the casket would be carried to the hearse by the color guard officers. We stood at attention as the congregation passed by and saluted as the casket was carried out. Though we stood motionless, many officers wiped their eyes after breaking ranks. A few of the female officers began to cry after the formation broke. Not many of the men did, at least not openly or loud enough to be heard by others.

There was a great deal of stress during the service, since we were expected to behave in a formal fashion, withholding emotion. During the time that the procession to the cemetery was forming, the air was a bit lighter. People were talking to each other. Some cried quietly while others hugged each other to give comfort. There were even some smiles, but only on the outskirts of the crowd, away from the family.

The procession to the cemetery I thought would never end. First the motorcade of police motorcycles in a v-shaped formation, then the mounted posse with the lead rider alone in front walking his horse. The hearse came next, followed by the family cars. Then what could only be described as a spectacle passed by. A line of probably two hundred law enforcement vehicles, brightly polished, with all their lights on and flashing, each filled with officers. It was said that the beginning of the procession arrived at the cemetery before the last cars left the church. I traveled to the cemetery with other officers in a personal car; we might as well have walked, since parking was so bad.

At the cemetery all the uniformed officers stood in formation while the graveside service lasted. There were probably between two and three hundred present. This was a very powerful sight. This show of numbers was not visible at the church due to its confined space. I was not close enough to the grave to see or hear the words, but could hear the great wailing from family and civilian friends. All the officers in formation stood at attention during the entire service. When a color guard played taps, all in formation stood at salute position until the bugler was silent. This was when I was moved to tears. There was something so moving at the sight of this great number of peace officers gathered, and the finality of taps. I was not alone, to judge from the red and wet eyes of the people around me.

When the graveside service was over, the ranks were dismissed. This was the end; there was no more formality or procession, just walking away from our fallen friend.

ANALYSIS

The dress uniform reserved for such occasions as this, the standing at attention, the saluting, are all marks of the special nature of this ritual. It conveyed the emotions expectable at the loss of a friend or coworker, the pain and emptiness that go with it, the comforting words that encourage closure and healing.

A funeral is a rite of passage. This one aided in the readjustment of those who lost the deceased. The church service contained many reassurances that Preston was in heaven with God, or at least on the way there. It comforted the people attending. There were also words of healing. There were attempts to uplift the mourners with recollections of positive things done by Preston in the line of duty and in his personal life.

The things that I considered empty in the church service were probably so only to me and to others who are not Catholic. To a Catholic, the reading of what I call standardized scripture would have more meaning, comfort, and encouragement. The intent of the reading, presumably, was to help fill the void in the minds of those who miss Preston.

There were also words intended to enhance the solidarity or unity that was disrupted. Being a "peacekeeper" was described as a blessed and honorable profession, a pillar of society, a noble career. These words were intended to reaffirm that being a police officer is truly a calling—to be proud and stand firm in one's choice to be an officer. It was also encouraging to those who were affected by the death of a fellow officer. This had impact, because Preston's death represented a chink in the armor of law enforcement. This was proof that we are not invincible and that life is precious and fragile. Nevertheless, the calling to be a peacekeeper is a strong one, worth the exposure to personal peril that comes with the duty of upholding the law.

This event also possessed an element of intensification and value reiteration. The motivating of the listeners to continue with their careers in law enforcement helped reaffirm individual desires to hold fast to deeply embedded ideals which drive officers to get up and do a job that few in our society would do—to be willing to lay down one's life for the noble cause of upholding the law.

The Formal Farewell

by Joshua Keilty

This paper is original in several respects. First, Keilty discovers that ritual is not so much a single action as it is an aspect of human actions in general. Second, he discovers something new (as far as I know) in the study of ritual: Special events are charged with energy, and, we might say, are ritualized in order to mark their specialness. Third, he is conscious that closeness between males in North American culture is regarded as dangerous, and he expresses that consciousness subtly. The ritual of goodbye which Josh and Bryan invent provides them with a means to open themselves emotionally to each other in a way that preserves their American masculinity. Finally, the author is the first student in my acquaintance to recognize gift exchange as a frequent aspect of rituals. Comparative ethnology contains countless illustrations of the exchange of objects as central to many ritual and nonritual categories of culture, but in one's own culture it is easy to overlook how important the transfer of goods is to personal relations.

Note how Keilty picks out the ritual significance of small items of behavior, like the choice of good rather than ordinary beer, avoiding the usual college dining hall, and playing a favorite game one last time. Note also that although the paper conflates data and analysis, it is thorough in both respects.

Keilty's enthusiasm for the experiential method in this and other courses led him, after graduating in comparative literature, to devise experiential programs for bright kids in New York City.

Goodbyes are rituals each person in our culture performs innumerable times in his or her life. They serve primarily as rites of passage, stabilizing a transformed relationship. But they may also be a rite of reversal where previously avoided acts are allowed to manifest themselves. I have experienced many goodbyes in my time but only my latest, that of my roommate, spurred the realization how ritualistic goodbyes really are.

Bryan and I didn't hit it off right away. Soon after we arrived, we each went his separate way and interacted very little. There was no avoidance and we spoke often, but a real friendship didn't develop until the end of fifth block. Bryan is a very intelligent guy and the more we talked the more I came to realize it. During the last couple of blocks he spent very little time in classes, slept away the days, and read and thought all night. He asked many questions of himself and the world around him and soon he drew me into conversations that lasted into the morning hours. We both benefited greatly from our talks and grew to love talking all night, interrupted only by a late meal or a racquetball game. Our friendship grew quite strong and we came to be able to talk about anything, no matter how personal. I guess we became as close as I've ever been with another person, so I was surprised when he said he was leaving. I came back to the room one day and he was packing.

Tuesday afternoon after lunch, I came back and made a reservation for the first symbolic act of Bryan's goodbye—a racquetball game. The entire time from that racquetball game to Wednesday morning, when he left, was charged with a special energy. It is this energy that made the acts ritualistic; it is the energy of private meaning, the nonverbal energy of the last time. It may be that energy of symbolic acts, but I'm hard pressed for words to carry the appropriate meaning. I only know that it is always present, underlying acts that are thought of as special.

Bryan and I have a peculiar way of playing racquetball, totally non-competitive. After our 2½-hour game, including lectures and lying silently on the floor exploring the roots of human competition, we adjourned to Benji's to spend the rest of his flex points on a late dinner. We do this because we detest being forced to eat the last meal of the day nine hours before we go to bed. Both the game and the late dinner were charged ritualistic acts. These were things that we always did together and even though we didn't need a workout and weren't hungry, we did them anyway. Both acts became rites of intensification that served to enhance our solidarity one last time.

Before returning to the room we stopped by the liquor store for one of the most important aspects of the ritual of goodbyes, a twelve-pack of good beer. The quality of the beer often indicates the value of the relationship. We bought good beer out of respect for each other. If the beer is good, one sips and the evening is long. Cheap beer goes down quickly, and the evening is short. Our long evening was a mutual salute to our friendship.

Beer also facilitates a rite of reversal within a goodbye. In order to have a proper goodbye, the relationship must be laid out completely. Thoughts previously left unsaid for various reasons must be brought out into the open. Our relationship needed to be stabilized before it could be successfully transformed; loose ends must be tied off. After the third beer or so the conversation changed and became more emotional. We spoke of worry for the future, love, parents, decisions, confusion, and missing each other. Bryan and I are equally subject to the fear of emotional relations with other men, like many in our rather homophobic culture. Although this pressure doesn't have to limit a man's social interactions, it is sometimes useful to have a little social lubricant to pull up the blinds that conceal open fraternity. These blinds are usually manifested in nonverbal communication and private language where the socially unspeakable can be brought out in a more comfortable manner. The more beer flowed the easier it was for feelings to be spoken of; many were released in the form of jokes. We joked about becoming fellow bums in New York, teenage fathers, wandering gurus—all products of the private language developed in our endless evening talks. As the beer ran out, so did the conversation, and we sacked out. Bryan and I had said everything left to be said and there was nothing more to hamper the transformation. We had come to terms with our relationship and it was now ready for change.

Wednesday morning following breakfast, the goodbye ritual continued. It was now time for the gift exchange. During the goodbye it is many times helpful to exchange a reminder of the past relationship to aid in readjustment. Memory serves as a buffer to abrupt change such as loss of a friend. It may be as formal as an initialed keepsake or maybe just some unpacked junk. I gave Bryan a pot I had thrown and my copy of Ayn Rand's *Fountainhead*. He gave me a pair of pants someone had left in his car. Both gifts were emotionally charged; I had always coveted the pants and he loved the *Fountainhead*. He also constantly complained of my pottery cluttering the room, so I gave him a piece just in case he would miss it. The object exchanged is secondary to the meaning behind the gift. It is a symbolic act that helps stabilize the relationship in preparation for readjustment. With all that out of the way it was time to perform the final acts of the ritualistic goodbye.

After the fourth or fifth scour of the room, we went down to his waiting car. At this point there was much stalling. We checked and rechecked the room, and reorganized the car. Conversation was disjointed and sporadic, often punctuated with private jokes. This was the last few minutes, and each of us wanted to touch all the bases before it was too late. We made promises to write, to take care, and to see each other again. We checked the car for the third unnecessary time and did a lot of idle pacing back and forth looking in the car windows. Finally, as words ran out, he opened the driver's door signaling the time to depart. This was the last time to say what we wanted so we tried to keep our cool and speak the right words. All that was said was gibberish. A hug signaled the closing and he started up the car and drove off with a honk, leaving me waving on the curb. The ritual of goodbye was complete.

This was a paper of discovery for me. The more I looked the more I found that almost every act in life is ritualistic. The more emotionally important an act is, the more ritualistic it becomes. In an activity as difficult as goodbye can be, it is not surprising how complicated the ritual is. Goodbyes are rites of passage to aid in readjustment, but they contain many other rites to help in the process. There are rites of intensification and reversal. After we had further cemented our friendship and then cleared up the loose ends between us, our friendship was ready for change. The stalling by the car and the obligatory farewell words were part of the final rite where respect was shown. After that, there was nothing left but to leave. We had prepared, so each could walk away feeling good, and so the relationship could be renewed another time. As in any ritual, many things are done the same every time, but also there is a special energy that fills the form and gives it meaning, and that is new every time. Our goodbye had that energy and was very successful because of it. I'll miss Bryan.

Leaving the House

by Carla Miller

"We decided to have a ritual, " says Miller, a social worker in Grand Rapids, Michigan, who as a newly divorced mother recognized that she and her children needed to come to closure with the house where they had lived for a long time. In a geographically and socially mobile society, every life is periodically uprooted and set down in new channels. Unless the uprooted individuals make a conscious effort, they will carry too much psychological baggage from one phase to the next and eventually may find themselves sorting it all out on the therapist's couch.

Ritual helps people to declare one portion of existence ended, to close it out, and to facilitate getting on with the next. All rites of passage are closures, and graduation ceremonies are probably the most successful of them. Joshua Keilty's ritual of saying goodbye was also a closure ritual, but I had not yet recognized and listed the category when he took the course.

Miller's reminiscence is reprinted with her permission from Seeds: A Family Resource for Liberal Religion *(Grand Rapids: Fountain Street Church, 1992).*

When it was time to sell and leave the family home in which all of the children had spent most of their childhood, I wondered how we could say goodbye to this wonderful house that had been our home for so many years. There had been many happy years, but we were also in the process of divorce, so the memories were important to hang on to and also let go. The children were by this time all living somewhere else but often "in and out." It was still home to us all. As we planned to gather at Christmastime, knowing it would be our last time together in that home, we decided to have a ritual to remember our times there and also say goodbye. We agreed to gather on an appointed evening and go from room to room, weaving a tale of history and memories as we told stories about what we remembered about each space.

I lit a large candle and we gathered, feeling a bit silly and nervous. A little afraid that we just couldn't do this, we were also eager to share some of the things we remembered. We started in the kitchen, remembering all the remodeling changes and how we all really lived in that room most of the time. The children recalled how it felt coming home from school, where the jackets were hung, and where I would stand while they told me about what had happened that day at school. We moved from room to room, remembering details, fears, things that had happened, friends who had been present with us. The dark scary basement hosted images of playing and hiding and huge piles of laundry that were never sorted. Bedroom tales were interesting (to me). Slamming doors, tales of sneaking out at night were confessed—I'm glad I didn't know everything at the time it happened! The wallpaper, where the dog used to sleep, the kitten that got stuck in the laundry chute, the "noises" in the ceiling that turned out to be honeybees' nests—we laughed and fondly remembered our life together. Then we ended in the living room, in front of the fireplace. One daughter brought a record that she'd recently heard on the radio. Deeply touched by the lyrics, she drove all the way to Kentucky to find the record after weeping through it in five o'clock freeway traffic. The country western tune was about an old family home being left and what it might say if it could talk. We played the song and listened. Then we cried.

Finally we stood together in a circle and expressed our wishes and hopes for that great house. We wondered aloud who would live here. We imagined a new family. Hope was expressed, hope that others would experience some of what we had in that dwelling. Each person spoke softly, tearfully, about the emotions and activities that had been most important to her or him in this house. It had hosted babies, animals, children, friends, music, dance, fears, happiness, sorrow, joy, coming together, and now going apart.

We honored the house as the great container it had been for us. And then we blew out the candle.

It is interesting that we have been able to let go of that house so well. We often drive by and look, feeling good. It is not where we are anymore. In a way, our ritual allowed us to both honor that period of our lives together and grieve the loss of it as well.

If Miller's paper had been written for the course, it would have contained an "Analysis" section emphasizing 2a, "Closure," with mention of "Aid in Readjustment" and "Enhancement of Solidarity," and would have commented on the use of candles as a way of heightening the impact of the ceremony—"Charging with special energy" as Keilty would have said—and pointed to the daughter's trip to Kentucky to find a particular record as a mark of the importance of the event to its participants.

Psyching Up

by Tony Muñoz

Almost everybody is familiar with the ritual of psyching oneself up before an intercollegiate or interscholastic athletic event. This paper is unusual for its elaborateness and for the author's ability to see the variety of functions that it performs. Although the section labeled "Analysis" is far too brief, the data section contains a lot of implied analysis.

"Psyche-ups" are a ritual each athlete in our culture performs innumerable times in his or her life. They serve a primary service as a rite of intensification and a secondary service as an activation of status relationships and a third miscellaneous function, allaying anxiety. I have experienced many psyche-ups and will continue to do so during my next three years of collegiate athletics. The following ritual was performed every year before the Delta (Colorado) High School homecoming football game. It was such a part of the mental process of preparation that I never thought to label it, until now.

DATA

All of the homecoming activities have ended and the decorations, speeches, and hype are all put aside; it's showtime. It began every year on the Friday of homecoming at 1:32 P.M. My best friend, Tim, and I would leave school and go to our separate homes to shower and cleanse ourselves. At about 2 o'clock I would go over to Tim's house for a 32-ounce glass of water and to watch an NFL Greatest Hits video. We would sit there for the next hour and a half and comment, respect, and admire the vicious patterns of hits, collisions, and helmet decapitations. All the while, we were wearing our chosen war garb. Mine were a pair of padded linebacker gloves and Tim's was a single headband that he wore around his neck, to "keep the helmet rash off."

After the film, it was time to secure ourselves the next vital liquid: Jolt, a double caffeinated carbonated soda. With a six-pack each, we would then drive down to the playing field and examine it. One soda would be finished by the time we got there; another two would be taken with us to examine the field. When we go to Panther Stadium, we would get out and enjoy the serenity of the scene: The stands would be empty, the grass neatly trimmed, the decorations swaying in the gentle breeze, and calm silence would encase it all. We'd casually stroll to the field, carefully looking at the grass down the center strip and the other two strips along the left and right hash marks. This was done because here the game would be played and the condition of the field determined the size of the cleat that we would wear and our ability to push off from the grass.

By the time we got back to the car, our bottles were empty and ready to be deposited. We would then sit on the hood of the car and drink our fourth Jolt. We would remark on the validity of the phrase, "the calm before the storm." In just a few hours the stands would be filled with spectators teeming with the anticipation of a win, the yell team would begin to psyche up the crowd and anticipate the crunch of helmets, the fieldlights would split the approaching darkness. Then we would dismiss our conversation with a surly, "Yeah, whatever!" and start up the engine and travel to the "Den of Skulls."

The music from the car radio blared as we ascended the hills near our high school and lyrics of destruction and pillage filled our minds. The Den of Skull was a valley about a half mile from our high school where we, the Delta High football team, had dug thirteen graves. Each grave was for one of the thirteen teams that we would have to defeat on our way to the state championships. The graves were 3 feet wide and 6 feet long. Our way of burying the enemy after defeat was similar to the ritual performed by the Cheyenne Dog Soldier.

According to legend, the Dog Soldier would take an item, such as a spear or an arrow, from an enemy he had killed and bury it so that the spirit of the deceased could not seek revenge in the next life. This was done as a gesture of respect for his enemy as well as for his own social honor. Similarly we, after a victorious game, would return immediately and bring with us scouting reports, a piece of the opposing team's jersey or cleat, anything that was symbolic of the other team, and bury it. It was to remind us of what we have done and of other goals that need to be fulfilled.

We finally arrived at the makeshift parking area and got out of the car with our two remaining Jolts. We trod up the hill thankful that no one else was paying their respects, for if someone had been there we would have had to come back at another time. We finally reached the Den and quickly made our way to the fourth grave, passing the three filled graves. We saw that others had been before us and left their offerings.

Tim was the team's center and defensive lineman; he "believed" in a lineman god known as The Viking God. The Viking God was a mythic figure on the field that determined whether you, as a lineman, had worked hard enough to become a "hog," the self-given name of the linemen. An offering was expected in order to have a good game. Since I was a linebacker, no offering was expected, but since I was a starter it was frowned upon if I didn't contribute to the hogs' effort to appease their god.

No words were spoken, just a lowering of two full bottles of Jolt into the grave and a throwing of a handful of dirt to begin the job that we were soon to finish. We opened our last Jolt, silently toasted the Viking God, and began to walk back to the car.

During the drive back we reminded each other of the other team's favorite plays and formations. We went over motion and coverage assignments as well as blocking assignments. By the time we got to the locker rooms we were beginning to feel the effect of the caffeine. We locker right next to each other and begin the next stage of the psyche-up, the individual stage.

I dig into my locker and retrieve my contact pads, my helmet, my shoulder pads, and most importantly a portable stereo. Soon the air surrounding my locker is filled with songs that both Tim and I chose. The lyrics are filled with words of motivation, such as "Seek and . . . Seek and Destroy." I begin to put my pads in their corresponding pockets and cinch up the strings on my shoulder pads. Next I get air for the air bladders in my helmet. After that is done I consult Tim on the size of cleat that I should install in my shoes. We agree on a size 3 cleat, which is about medium. The lawns had just been cut so there was no need for any larger cleat.

It is now about 4:10 and I get dressed. I begin with an athletic supporter and protective cup followed by a support girdle. I then put on a half shirt and training shorts. I proceed to the training room for tape support on my ankles and wrists. My right wrist then my right ankle followed by my left wrist and then my left ankle. Afterward I begin the individual wrapping of my knuckles, starting with my left hand from pinkie to thumb and then my right hand following the same pattern. All of this is done by 4:30 and then I finish getting dressed. My game pants with pads are put on followed by socks and cleats: right sock and cleat, then left sock and cleat. I wait until we get to the field to put on my helmet and shoulder pads. I now sit down and review my scouting reports and refresh myself on their plays and tendencies.

The coach calls everyone into meeting about 5 o'clock and the rest of the coaches take their places. First we meet with the defensive position coach and then with the offensive position coach. The coach has his usual game face on along with his customary lip full of chew. All the coaches have emerald green coaching shirts with gray pants, black shoes, and matching green caps. The players are equipped with green jerseys, black game pants with a green stripe down them, black cleats, and green helmets with white decals. We load up on a bus and take a trip to the Den of Skulls to pay respects as a team and then are taken to Panther Stadium.

The bus is as quiet as a funeral parlor. Everyone is thinking about what is going to happen during the next three hours. The week's training and preparations are going to pay their dividends or losses in less than an hour and a half. There is no laughing, no giggling, no smiles—only solemn faces, scowls, and silence.

The bus unloads and we stalk to our locker room and the final stage begins, the team psyche. The shoulder pads are donned and the sleeves rolled and taped. The helmets are at the ready. There is a lot of whooping, helmet bashing, shoulder popping, and locker slamming. Team captains pose challenges to everyone to "Kick ass and take names." The word "house" is frequently used to describe our stadium and hometown; when you have unwanted guests in your house then the socially acceptable reaction is to put them in a sling and show them the door.

About 5:45 Coach takes the "specialists," field goal kickers and their holders, long snappers, punters, and kick returners, onto the field to warm up. Quarterbacks and receivers begin to warm up indoors and positions groups huddle to put the finishing touches on the preparations.

Now the Jolt is beginning to take effect. The bands strike up the fight song and the adrenaline begins to flow. That ice water in your veins causes you to pump up the somewhat warmed-up "specialists" as they come in around 6:15. Coach senses the anxiety and gives his last pep talk followed by giving us our "present," a T-shirt that is the same color as the opposite team's jersey with their mascot's name printed on it. The jersey is thrown into the mass of waiting battle-starved warriors and it is promptly shredded and distributed to put in our left shoes—another offering to the Viking God, for after the game.

The captains lead the team to the field at 6:25 for a fifteen-minute warm-up, and at 6:50 the national anthem is played and the crowd approvingly responds. At 6:55 the captains march to the center of the field to take part in the coin toss while the rest of the team watches and eyes the opposition. The referee indicates the winner of the toss and who will defend which goal. The team huddles for their last bonding moment and lets loose a war cry for the other team and the stands to hear and revere. The kick-off team takes the field, the referee blows his whistle, the kick-off team points to the stands and yells, "Delta," the sidelines point to the opposite stands and yell, "Panthers." The ritual is complete. Now it's showtime!

ANALYSIS

Indeed, the ritual is complete. But to stand back and begin to understand its undertakings is another matter. In order for this ritual to be easily studied, it is necessary to divide it into three sections: rites of intensification, activation of status relationships, and allaying anxiety.

The broadest spectrum is that of a rite of intensification. This ritual's purpose was to intensify social bonds. It was necessary for the graves to be dug by everyone so that all would feel the burning sensations of blisters after their turn with the pick or feel that sense of accomplishment after the coaches approved the graves' craftsmanship. The Den of Skulls was a place that was common to all the players, starters and nonstarters alike. Likewise, in relation to the leaving of offerings, it was a bonding unit between the starters. When the final huddle was gathered no one was left out. And finally, as those who were on the field yelled their final challenge and those on the sideline gave theirs, it was a cooperative action that signaled the beginning of another ritual—the game—and the end of the psyche-up.

The next largest category is the activation of status relationships. By definition this is necessary to maintain status systems by giving them the excuse to operate. Under no other circumstances would I subject my body to the ingestion of enough caffeine to run a power plant. It was a socially acceptable reason to drink the caffeine in such abundant amounts. Why else would a football team imitate a semiwarrior society that has gone the way of the dodo bird? And at the very least, why would one submit oneself to the tedious processes of dressing in the exact same way every time a fall Friday evening came around? The reason is the ritual.

Last but not least we come to the psychosomatic aspect of our ritual, the allaying of anxiety. An athlete does not feel so disheartened after a failing effort if he has slammed enough lockers, butted enough heads, or popped enough shoulders. If he has fulfilled the tedious dressing techniques and drunk enough caffeine then surely it will be enough for The Viking God to grant them victory.

To sum up, it is difficult for someone to read this and actually believe that this happens, but as the saying goes, "you'd have to have been there." Otherwise you can simply read and disbelieve. The ritual provides one with an aura of invincibility that can be relived by the witnessing of it, over and over again. My rituals will always be powerful and if The Viking God sees fit then I will remain successful.

By the way, we won that game.

Friday Night

by Bill Dunbar

Drinking is ritualized in a great many cultures, perhaps because to eat and drink are so close to physical survival and are usually social activities. All drinking rituals are rites of intensification, as this one so conspicuously is. Dunbar's analysis is impressive in seeing also the rite of passage (the initiation) and the rite of reversal, which this event shares with Mardi Gras and similar ceremonies of license.

Note that the author first teases out the significance of details within the Friday nights and then attacks the ritual as a whole. This procedure is almost always productive. Note also that the ritual is held at The Tavern because that is where it is held: Most rituals are partly arbitrary, and arbitrariness often plays a part in ritualizing an act.

Many people have rituals that involve drinking alcohol. Mine comes from Australia where I spent a few months of 1992, working as a volunteer in conservation in Melbourne. The ritual I describe took place every Friday night at a place called The London Tavern, which will be called simply "The Tavern" here because that was what we called it. The work was done weekdays, whether in Melbourne or in some other base camp, with weekends free in Melbourne. Friday night became the official pub night and the official unwinding time for us workers.

DATA

The pub was smoky and warmed up by the point in the evening when we would arrive, as many locals frequent the place on weekends. Toward the end of my stay in Australia, I could recognize a good number of the locals who hung around the bar, although I can't claim to have spoken to any of them, except for a brief exchange while urinating. Usually such exchanges would consist of the local asking if we were some kind of school group or something, and I would respond that we were actually doing some sort of construction or other labor in the field, which was only slightly true. These locals were never invited to join us, nor would the ritual have been complete if outsiders had been present.

The bartenders, sharp in white shirts with black ties and pants, were an integral part of the ritual, because we ordered drinks from them and because they learned our names, our orders, and would often rib us about stupid things we had done or outlandish things we had drunk the week before.

Most of us would never have gone to this clean, well-cared-for pub had it not been the only one within walking distance of our house. Sometimes on other nights we went to dirtier, cheaper pubs where more people who were closer to our age would be found, but it was absolutely imperative to go to The Tavern on Friday night for the simple reason that it was the ritual and the ritual would have been incorrect if we had gone anywhere else.

We would arrive between 8 and 8 P.M., after having made and eaten dinner amid a jungle of good-natured arguing, yelling, blaring music, and flying objects at the house. The Tavern was only about five minutes walk from the house if one knew all of the shortcuts and back alleys to get there. The first order of business was to find two or three tables to pull together and many stools so that our large group could be accommodated as a unit. Our group numbered between ten and twenty people on any given Friday. Next, half or slightly less than half of us would proceed to the bar and each order a jug of Carlton Draught for A$6.75. Those of us who knew the bartender would usually spend a minute or two chatting with him before returning to the table. Those who did not buy at first would be expected to buy next.

So the drinking would begin. Sitting at this table with a beer in one hand and a cigarette in the other was the perfect opportunity to survey and reflect on the friends who were around you. These particular friends were a mix of American and English volunteer conservation workers, that is, students taking time off from school and traveling to exotic places. These were the sort of friends with whom one has a very short intense relationship because one spent twenty-four hours a day with them for a few weeks, and was unlikely ever to see them again. That aspect of the relationship was important in that almost every week we were saying goodbye to someone close to us. As was to be expected, the mix of Americans and Englishmen led to a great deal of lighthearted patriotic rivalry and argument. A good deal of the conversation at the table was geared toward how stupid the other culture's customs were. I'm sure that the Queen of England took more abuse from Americans in The Tavern than any person deserves. The two major rivals at all times were John, a large, boisterous lacrosse player from Princeton, and Adrian, a blond Englishman. While John and Adrian would argue incessantly about big bombs and whether there is a "u" in "color," the rest of us would throw in side comments and generally make noise.

There were several other ritual procedures. The first was the drinking game, "Chug." It started only after we were in the pub for half an hour to an hour, because it required at least mild intoxication, as well as a working knowledge of one's opponents. The rules of the game are simple: One drinker challenges another to take the remainder of his glass of beer at one gulp. The challenged will then consider whether it is in fact a good idea for him to do so. If not, he will then refuse and challenge his opponent to do the same. Hence a debate will ensue until one or the other is fully convinced that he in fact must chug and does so. "Do it for the Queen" or "do it for Norman Schwartzkopf" were foolproof challenges to use on Adrian or John, respectively. Anyone may challenge any other to chug at any time, but must be willing to pay the consequences.

Another major event was shot time. Shot time could officially happen at any time a drinker would feel moved, but it almost invariably occurred late in the evening in an advanced state of intoxication. Shot time was called when two drinkers, usually but not always very close friends, would make eye contact and one of them called "shot time!" Both would proceed to the bar, where the one who shouted would buy himself and his partner a shot of either Southern Comfort or Jack Daniels, to be consumed immediately, before returning to the table. Reciprocation was not expected.

At 12 o'clock, last call was made at the pub, and what money we had left was pooled to buy last-minute jugs, to be consumed before 1 o'clock closing time. Then came the stumble through the back alleys and side streets that led to our house. The evening wound down with large quantities of water, and usually some macaroni and cheese. Finally we would all fall asleep, content that the evening had been a success. All of these events were secondary to the true drinking ritual, which was often the highlight of the whole week. Despite all of the conservation work we did, some of my most dear and most vivid memories of Australia come from those four hours a week spent in The Tavern.

ANALYSIS

These Friday nights were a ritual as opposed to a habit. A habit is like a ritual in that it is performed regularly and always in the same manner. How-

ever, a habit does not contain any deeper emotions than are necessary to fulfill its purpose. If our Friday evenings had been merely an attempt to get
drunk, then they probably would have happened differently. For example, it
would have been cheaper and easier to go to another pub, but for some reason we always went to The Tavern. The reason for this was simply that Friday
night was the time when we went to The Tavern. Also, there was no utilitar-
ian reasoning behind shot time or any of the other aspects of the ritual besides the emotions involved, which I discuss later. The point is that, although
much of the purpose of Friday night was to get drunk, the particular manner in which it was carried out was not just habitual but truly ritual.

Now I would like to examine the various aspects of the ritual individually, as well as the ritual as a whole, classify the types, and analyze the emotional content of each. I will start with the first part of the ritual, which was
the buying and, more importantly, sharing of the jugs of beer. This was primarily a rite of intensification, by which I mean that its main purpose was
to intensify social bonds between the members of our group. By both buying beer and sharing it with others, one is extending his generosity to his
fellows and showing them that he considers them to be true friends. He is
saying to them that they are a part of his life. The primary function of this
ritual is the promotion of solidarity, that is, the strengthening of friendship
bonds between various members of the group. This served as an excellent
opportunity to strengthen a relationship with someone whom you had not
had the opportunity to approach before. Sharing beer was a symbolic gesture in that it showed people you felt an emotional bond with them in an
accepted, embarrassment-free context with no difficult words necessary. Even
John and Adrian shared great amounts of beer as they viciously attacked
each other's homeland. Any other display of their true feelings would have
meant a loss of face and was therefore impossible.

The conversation, which was certainly a part of the ritual, goes hand
in hand with the sharing of beer because it was also a rite of intensification.
In this case, it created solidarity among the members of each nationality
group, and enhanced their patriotism.

"Chug" began as merely a drinking game that was good for a few
laughs, but it became an initiation rite as well, because everyone had to take
part in the game in order to be a full-fledged member of the group. If you
were challenged to chug your beer, and you simply refused despite all of the
pressure applied by your peers, you would not be openly rejected, but everyone would conclude that you were not willing to observe the rules of the ritual, and you would have slightly alienated yourself. Likewise, if you always
convinced your opponent to chug, you would also alienate yourself because
it was an unspoken rule of the game that everyone involved actually wanted
to chug, and the argument was just a façade put up to save face. Those who
participated most actively and correctly in the game were assuring themselves

passage to the center of the group. The primary function of the game was to promote familiarity because although I have been calling the players "opponents," your opponent was, in fact, your closest social contact for the brief minutes that the game involved. It was a symbolic manifestation of your affection for your opponent, as well as a chance to assert your prowess both in argument and in drinking.

Shot time was the purest and most gratifying of the events involved in the drinking ritual. It was a display of pure generosity. Shot time only happened between two of the closest friends. It was both a rite of deference and a rite of intensification. I call it deference because when you offered a shot to someone you were putting yourself in a position below them by admitting that you were willing to spend your own money to make yourself closer to them. It was a rite of intensification within the larger rite of intensification because two members would separate themselves from the rest of the group to share a moment to themselves. Shot time was the true test of friendship, that is, one could treat another any way during the week, but if he bought that person a shot, that was enough to express real friendship. Again the emotions behind the ritual were affection and a desire to elevate the relationship, and these unspoken emotions could be relayed simply by yelling "shot time!" I think it is worth noting that Jack Daniels and Southern Comfort were among the most expensive shots available at The Tavern.

The ritual as a whole is difficult to analyze because it has so many different facets. First and foremost, it was a rite of intensification for the obvious reason that every aspect of it was to some extent geared toward strengthening the social framework of the group. Even the more individual of the rites were instrumental in strengthening the group as a whole because every individual relationship was vital to the overall strength of the group, just as every link in a chain must be strong for the chain as a whole to be strong. Secondly, Friday drinking was a rite of reversal in that, while we were not exactly tame throughout the week, the ritual and the alcohol allowed us to say and do things we would not say or do throughout the week. Thus, our behavior was to an extent reversed for a few hours each week, and we were able to purge ourselves of any tendencies that had been dormant during the week. Thirdly, the ritual often served as a rite of passage in a more general sense than the chugging game did. Almost every week would see a new member just arrived or an old one leaving. On these occasions part of the evening would be dedicated to toasting those people or reminiscing with them or welcoming them. Thus the Friday evening ritual became the medium for those people to either pass into the group or to pass back into the rest of the world.

The primary function of the ritual was to promote solidarity among the group. Had we all gone to different pubs around the city, a bunch of separate smaller groups would probably have formed, who would not have spent much time together. But due to the Friday night ritual, each of us became good friends with everybody. The ritual also had the function of helping us to readjust to a more relaxed atmosphere after a hard week of work, and to allay anxiety about a number of things, such as the week ahead, or the loss of friends, or even our own leaving. I remember my last Friday evening well, and I know that leaving would have been much more difficult without that final farewell and reassertion that the people I was leaving were truly my friends. My last shot time, called by my friend Spencer, was a very important step toward being able to leave the group happy.

When I think back on Australia, I can easily pull up memories of any given Friday evening, although I would be hard pressed to remember a good part of the work. I consider this sufficient evidence of the importance of this weekly ritual in my life. An interesting feature of this particular ritual is the fact that it cannot be repeated, as those people will never be together in the same place again. Even by the time I left, the ritual was somewhat different than it was when I arrived. It makes me wonder what the workers will be doing there this Friday night.

The Family Breakfast

by Renato Rosaldo

The following ritual event was recorded/invented by Renato Rosaldo, professor of anthropology at Stanford University, and is reprinted by permission of the publisher from Culture and Truth *(Boston: Beacon Press, 1989). It does not quite follow the format prescribed for you, but it makes explicit some points that student rituals often unconsciously expose: Finding ritual in one's own culture may have a humorous element, describing a ceremonial event in one's own culture may have elements of parody, and it objectifies what may have been as invisible as the air one breathes. (Rosaldo then proceeds to a discussion of validity in ethnography, which goes beyond our concern here.)*

Your description and analysis of a ritual may or may not find itself parodying or satirizing your own culture; most likely it will not. But if it does, you are in good company. You are probably already discovering that doing ethnography makes one more conscious of culture and one's dual relations to it—carrier and creator.

After falling head over heels in love, I paid a ceremonial visit, during the summer of 1983, to the "family cottage" on the shores of Lake Huron in western Ontario. Much as one would expect (unless one was, as I was, too much in the thick of things), my prospective parents-in-law treated me, their prospective son-in-law, with reserve and suspicion. Such occasions are rarely easy, and this one was no exception. Not unlike other rites of passage, my mid-life courtship was a blend of conventional form and unique personal experience.

My peculiar position, literally surrounded by potential in-laws, nourished a project that unfolded over a two-week-period in barely conscious daydreams. The daily family breakfast started turning in my mind into a ritual described in the distanced normalizing mode of a classic ethnography. On the morning of my departure, while we were eating breakfast, I revealed my feelings of tender malice by telling my potential in-laws the "true" ethnography of their family breakfast: "Every morning the reigning patriarch, as if just in from the hunt, shouts from the kitchen, 'How many people would like a poached egg?' Women and children take turns saying yes or no.

"In the meantime, the women talk among themselves and designate one among them the toast maker. As the eggs near readiness, the reigning patriarch calls out to the designated toast maker, 'The eggs are about ready. Is there enough toast?'

"'Yes,' comes the deferential reply. 'The last two pieces are about to pop up.' The reigning patriarch then proudly enters bearing a plate of poached eggs before him.

"Throughout the course of the meal, the women and children, including the designated toast maker, perform the obligatory ritual praise song, saying, 'These sure are great eggs, Dad.'"

My rendition of a family breakfast in the ethnographic present transformed a relatively spontaneous event into a generic cultural form. It became a caricatured analysis of rituals of dominance and deference organized along lines of gender and generation.

This microethnography shifted jaggedly between words ordinarily used by the family (mainly in such direct quotes as "These sure are great eggs, Dad") and those never used by them (such as "reigning patriarch," "designated toast maker," and "obligatory ritual praise song"). The jargon displayed a degree of hostility toward my potential father-in-law (the reigning patriarch) and hesitant sympathy with my potential sisters-in-law (the designated toast maker and the singers of the praise song). Far from being a definitive objective statement, my microethnography turned out to be a timely intervention that altered mealtime practices without destroying them. The father approaching retirement and his daughters already established in their careers were in the process of remolding their relations with one another. For all its deliberate caricature, my description contained an analysis that of-

fered my potential in-laws a measure of insight into how their family breakfast routines, by then approaching empty ritual, embodied increasingly ar-
chaic familial relations of gender and hierarchy. Indeed, subsequent
observations have confirmed that the ritual praise songs honoring the
poached eggs and their maker have continued to be sung, but with tongue
in cheek. To defamiliarize the family breakfast was to transform its taken-for-
granted routines.

THE BIG
ETHNOGRAPHY

Doing serious ethnographic work was traditionally the preserve of professional anthropologists possessing, or working toward, their doctorates. Fieldwork took anywhere from nine months to several years, plus time to write up the data, and was conducted in exotic climes. In 1972 James Spradley and David McCurdy stood that conventional wisdom on its head in *The Cultural Experience*, a how-to for introductory students, which empowered all who came after to become ethnographers, not merely to read the ethnographies of others. Spradley and McCurdy's technique is to abandon the idea of a whole study of a whole society in favor of finding a "cultural scene," which they define somewhat inadequately as "the information shared by two or more people that defines some aspect of their experience" (1972:24). More completely, a cultural scene may be defined as *a geographic or symbolic place where two or more people repeatedly share activities that lead to shared understandings.* Within the cities and towns where most institutions of higher education are located, examples of cultural scenes range from a mom-and-pop store to a street gang to a classroom or playground to a drug ring to a convent to a house of prostitution to a hospital ward to a junkyard. They are large and small, legal and illegal, related to making money and spending it, open and secret. There are no limits to what may constitute cultural scenes except that they must be social, the scenes of repeated activities by the same people, and serve as incubators which generate cultural (i.e., language) understanding. The classroom in which you take this course is a cultural scene.

Although Spradley and McCurdy showed us all how to do what we could not do before, their method has two important limitations: It fails to allow for different constructions of reality between the individuals who share the scene, and it is exclusively intellective (i.e., related to processes of the intellect), not at all affective (related to the emotions, or even to motivation). The first time that a Colorado College (CC) student found a cultural scene which the people concerned defined differently (Jeff White on the Broadmoor police force, reproduced later), we began to realize that we had to move past the confines of cognitive analysis. Anthony F.C. Wallace made our job easier by replacing the "replication of uniformity" assumption made by Spradley and McCurdy and most of their predecessors about cultural behavior, with what Wallace called "the organization of diversity" (1970). Making sense out of the oxymoron that people can interact successfully while failing to share culture perfectly has proven to make our task more lively and to produce cultural analyses that are closer to commonsense reality.

Putting affect, both ours and our informants', to work for us in ethnographic reconstruction and analysis was a slower process. It received a boost when Renato Rosaldo (1989) insisted on looking emotions in the face in his statement on rage among headhunters and rage in himself when his wife Michelle Zimbalist Rosaldo (whom he was courting in the last chapter's breakfast scene) died unexpectedly and violently on a trail in the Philippines. Among the smaller papers in this book, Tony Muñoz handles his own emotions very productively; among the big ethnographies, Jennifer Sands is conspicuous. Andy Lewis uses his emotions to get him going.

Finally, here is a thought to keep before you as you work with your informants and as you analyze your field notes: David Warren, an historian of Brazil who is a native of Santa Clara Pueblo in New Mexico and works with Indian, Hispanic, and Anglo cultures in the United States, advises those who would advance multicultural understanding, "Once you get to know their realities, you can communicate with anyone." You will know that you are close to finishing your ethnography when you begin to understand the realities of the people whose cultural scene you are studying.

PROCEDURE

Before you do anything else, reread the section on ethics at the beginning of the book. If you pay close attention to it, you and your informants will have a positive and memorable experience.

We shall proceed now in stately but not very ritual fashion with this biggest field assignment and break it down into a summary of four stages. Following the summary, the stages are spelled out in greater detail.

1. Find yourself a cultural scene off campus. Possible scenes may include the following: an occupation you are considering entering, but do not already know (see White's and Goodwin's papers in this volume); a way to get out of your present cultural confines (see Andy Lewis's paper); or an alternative lifestyle you may have been curious about' but lacked the courage/excuse to investigate (see the Cunningham-Hayes paper). At the same time, use prosaic criteria such as accessibility of the site vis-à-vis your means of transportation, resistance of informants to be studied, and complexity of the scene in relation to the time at your disposal. Introduce yourself to informants and get their permission for you to do the work. In the case of some bureaucracies, this step may require a letter from the instructor. You will be expected to report that you have made a start to the instructor or the student assistants on or before a date to be announced.

2. Spend time with your informants on a regular schedule, preferably over a month's time, preferably at different times of the day, to understand variations in the routine. Ask what Spradley calls "grand tour questions" early on—that is, "Describe a typical day," or "How does this store/office/school run, week by week?" Such questions will give you a framework within which to pursue more detailed questions as your knowledge opens them up to you.

Get as close as you honorably can to your informants. This is called establishing rapport, and means presenting yourself to the people who are teaching you in such a way that they will welcome you on subsequent visits. Be as open with them about yourself as you hope they will be with you; successful cultural communication is a two-way street.

Check your information with your best informants as it takes shape. They will often be able to correct your interpretations. They may be pleased to see themselves through your eyes, or they may not. You will be expected to report to the assistants that you are well along with collecting information and to discuss with them questions of analysis on or before a date to be announced. "I've done what you told me to, I've asked all the questions. It just doesn't add up to anything," is a frequent complaint at this stage. Take heart. Many people experience this dilemma, and almost everyone, with help, pushes beyond.

3. The last period of the field assignment is devoted to analyzing your material and making sense of it. Diagramming the intellective understanding is useful (see Christopher Goodwin's paper).

During this period of fieldwork, concentrate on pulling together the threads and fragments of your understanding into a single well-organized whole. But do not impose organization on a scene that is disorganized, and do not assume perfectly shared understanding if in fact people share only partially. Two distinguished anthropologists offered helpful advice concerning the analysis of imperfect systems. David Aberle used to tell his students, "All systems have bugs in them." And A.F.C. Wallace believes that understanding is never shared entirely. He contrasts the "replication of uniformity" approach to culture, which is implicit in old-fashioned ethnography, with an "organization of diversity" approach, which assumes that cultural understanding is always partial and results from the intersection of different understandings of the same data (Wallace, 1970:123–29). You will be expected to report to the student assistants your progress with analysis and any analytic problems on or before a date to be announced.

4. Hand in a beautifully thought out and written paper on the due date and enjoy the praise that comes from creative work well executed. These papers tend to run about twenty pages.

You or your instructor may wonder why "construct a hypothesis" or at least "set yourself a research problem" is not among the procedures I recommend. After more than forty years in cultural anthropology, I am a little cynical about hypotheses that are more often constructed after than before the fact. For beginning students I am convinced that theory before practice is cart before horse. Ethnography is almost always opportunistic in any event. Stephanie Smith's experience in finding what to emphasize when studying a racetrack is typical of the bright and flexible student.

I. CHOOSING A SCENE

What will be the topic of your big ethnography? Consider the following questions among others as you make up your mind:

1. What profession(s) am I interested in but know too little about to decide if I want to enter?

2. What are my nonprofessional interests that I never had time or opportunity to inquire into?

3. What sorts of experience has my upbringing not opened me to? What fantasies have I about "life on the other side" that I might explore? *Stretch yourself.*

4. How mobile am I? What means of transportation are available to me?

5. Given the severe time pressure, how big an ethnographic bite can I chew?

6. What linguistic or other interpersonal skills do I possess that I can put to use in gathering information?

Note that the first three questions ask you to expand yourself, the last three to bring yourself back down to earth.

Discuss the possibilities with the staff—the instructor and the assistants. Put out feelers, using whatever contacts you may have, plus any that the staff may add. Do this early in the course, anticipating that several requests may be turned down by potential informants. Some organizations (e.g., city government) may require letters of introduction from the instructor, and a few will require you to sign waivers of liability. These steps take time.

Parameters

The parameters of the possible are wide, but not infinite. First, the various scenes of your own college or university are off limits. Here you are a player, and gaining perspective on your own scene would be a formidable task for any ethnographer; it is too daunting for the first attempt. Avoid noncampus scenes you already know. On the one hand, they are so easy that they are a copout. But at the same time they will betray you into neglecting to ask pertinent questions because you know, or think you know, the answers. If you want to learn the properties of water, don't ask a fish.

What about sex? Stephen O. Murray published an amusing paper on sleeping with the natives as a source of data (1996), which makes some serious points, including the caution that informants often react sexually to the ethnographer as foreigner differently from the way they would with people in their own society and that consequently this kind of participant observation is going to skew the data more than most. Your informants are not likely to be very foreign from yourself and yet, as more than a few ethnographers have found, perspective is hard to gain or maintain while in bed with the scene. All things considered, it is better to limit your contact with informants to the particular scene you are studying during your maiden effort at ethnography. Save the arpeggios of more difficult field techniques for later in your career.

Exchange

Always remember that informants have no obligation to you or to your institution, and consequently you have no rights to their time or their cooperation. I remember that when the Eastern Cherokee of North Carolina failed to provide information as enthusiastically as I would have liked, or failed to keep their appointments to look at the Rorschach cards during my doctoral fieldwork, my first reaction was, "I came all the way down here from Philadelphia to work with you guys. Now cooperate, damn it!" That irrational reaction was ridiculous, of course, and it helped me realize how necessary it was to present myself to the Cherokee in such a way that they would rather provide information about their culture than not. Otherwise, as one saucy young girl of Big Cove remarked, "Why should we answer your silly questions? Just so that you can go back North and teach other people to sit around all day and do nothing, like you?"

What can you offer informants, then, in exchange for their information? The most important answer is the flattery of your interest in their lives, and the fact that you regard their culture as worth the effort of learning, with themselves as teachers. Sometimes you can perform specific tasks they want done; this is an important part of participant observation, the method that is the hallmark of ethnography as opposed to other means of eliciting information. You will also find that information sharing is a two-way street, and your informants may be as interested in learning about your life as you are about theirs. Be prepared to give as much as you get. Finally, you have amusement value; you are a diversion in what may (or may not) be dull routine lives.

Pitfalls to Avoid in Choosing a Scene

1. If your informants are people much like yourself (e.g., young adults working in a record store), you will be hard put to stand at what is called ethnographic distance so as to see them with some perspective. Your rapport may be great, but your gaze myopic. Try for a scene as different from your own as you dare. See "Parameters." (Not all of my colleagues would agree with me. Some ethnographic research is done by "native informants," i.e., by those already part of the scene. What seems obvious and easy is, however, so difficult that I cannot recommend it for beginners.)

2. Religious institutions are tricky. The foregoing procedural guides might seem to imply that they would be ideal, for you are asked to collaborate with your informants in a student-teacher relation and to report what your informants want known about them. Religious institutions, especially those that are evangelical, are happy to regard you as a neophyte who can be taught/converted. And they have their versions of the truth that they disseminate. The problem is that you may find it difficult to obtain anything from them *but* their truth, which is probably already published. A theological statement is not, after all, the same as the model of how a sociocultural system in fact works. This caution is not intended to put all religious scenes off limits. An excellent study was done by a shy Jewish male student of a Roman Catholic convent; somehow, the personal chemistry clicked, and the nuns did not try to convert the Jew.

3. The one-person scene. A single informant does, of course, derive cultural understanding from many others, so one could argue that such a scene is composed of "two or more people." The ethnographer exercises fewer skills, however, in interviewing and interacting with one person than with several, whose varying accounts of reality he or she must accommodate in the report.

4. Breaking the law. Illegal activities are as cultural as any other, often as rule bound, and at least as interesting to study. But you must be crystal clear whether studying such activity requires you to break the law yourself. Most colleges and universities, because of fear of lawsuits, will not permit students to break laws in the pursuit of course credit. Check carefully and concretely with your instructor (not, in this one case, with the student assistants) to find out what rules govern your own situation. This caution is not meant to discourage you from studying illegal cultural understandings, but to help you and your institution avoid trouble. Even if you manage to

study lawless behavior while staying clear of it yourself, be forewarned that you have no immunity from testifying if called on by legal authorities to do so. If you nobly refuse, the American Anthropological Association may praise you, but the judge is likely to find you in contempt of court.

WHAT MAKES A GOOD INFORMANT?

Once you have chosen a scene, you may hope to have some choice among informants. The criteria that follow will help you choose among several places where similar scenes are played or to select among the people on the particular stage you have chosen.

Don't expect that just because you are the ethnographer and they are the informants, all relationships will work. You don't like all your fellow students or your teachers either, and personality clashes will make some informants good and others bad, quite apart from whether they are knowledgeable about the scene. Beat your head against no brick walls. Here are some criteria for good informants, adapted from James Spradley's *Ethnographic Interview* (1979:45–54):

1. Thorough enculturation. It takes a while for anyone to know the scene. Make sure he or she has been in it long enough to know it inside and out.

2. Current involvement. We all grow rusty quickly. You would no longer be adequate informants for high school culture or for the daily life of the family in which you grew up. Likewise, someone who has left the scene you want to understand won't do. Ethnography went through a long period of collecting "memory culture." In the case of Native American societies which had ceased to exist when the information was collected from the mythic "last survivor," it was either use that technique or lose the whole record. (Theodora Kroeber's *Ishi in Two Worlds* [1961] is a touching comment on this technique.) Ruth Benedict (1946) constructed an ethnography of Japan from interviewing Japanese people in the United States when Japan was unreachable because of World War II. You yourself have just described several small ethnographic scenes from memory. But we know such records to be faulty, and we don't collect them when we have alternatives.

3. Adequate time. Even if they are willing, some potential informants don't have time to cooperate with you in the patient probing, questioning, and requestioning that make a thorough ethnography. Physicians, surgeons, and attorneys are notoriously busy. They may give you a friendly initial interview, then turn you over to their receptionists, which is fine if the focus of your study is the culture of the office, but fatal if you want to learn the culture of the profession.

4. Analytic ability. You want intelligent reflective informants, who are willing to talk about their activity in the scene, hopefully willing to say when appropriate, "How interesting. I never thought about how the parts of the scene go together until I began to explain it to you." The clearest argument that I have seen for encouraging informants to help shape the analysis was made by Roger Lancaster in the introduction to his study of religion among poor people in Sandinista Nicaragua (1988:4):

> I see anthropology [read "ethnography"] ... as an "intersubjective" practice, wherein the subjectivity of the people under study is understood by honest but no less subjective observers. . . . [M]y informants were always reminding me that they, too, were watching me, learning about my beliefs, and assuming a give-and-take in our relations. Commonly, my informants would ask me: "And what are you writing in your notes about us today?" and then proceed to offer suggestions on the interpretation of their own culture and practices. . . . Far from being inhibited by this type of interest, I was often able to refine and sometimes completely revise my models.

II. WORKING WITH INFORMANTS

Recording Data

The most important part of your ethnographic record will consist of field notes. You may also collect tape recordings, photographs, and other material.

You will find it useful to play an intellectual game as you compile your field notes: Assume, even though it may seem on the face of it absurd, that you speak one language (we could call it the ethnographer's language) and that your informants speak another. You will find the germ of truth in this fantasy if you write down the words of your informants exactly as they are spoken. Exert a lot of effort to catch their turns of phrase. It is entirely possible that different informants will speak different languages within the same scene. The very keen ear will hear women's versus men's language, boss's versus employee's language, the language of the old versus the language of the young. In the terminology of literary criticism, these differences in language and points of view are referred to as different voices. This is what David Warren tried to tell us a few pages back.

It is impossible to exaggerate the importance of learning the language because at the same time you will be doing a task that sounds identical but is not: understanding the scene. Learning something new means translating the unfamiliar into terms one already understands. In a foreign language class one translates literally, but in every other discipline one translates from the new to the old, from the unknown to the known, or one cannot reach understanding. Your final product, your ethnographic report, will be written in your language. But it will be a far better report if it is richly illustrated by the language of the informants. It will take you a while to tune your ear to catch the difference between your language and that of informants. This is yet another reason not to seek informants of your own sort, who speak your own language in every sense of the term. A number of the papers that follow here are conspicuously successful in recording the speech of informants.

Taking notes: You will quickly discover whether your informants are most comfortable if you tape-record, take copious notes in their presence, or note nothing until you leave. Perhaps you will find that in more formal interaction on the ethnographic stage you can record in detail, but that while informally participating you cannot. Among the tricks of the trade for the latter occasions are to keep pencil and bits of paper in your pocket, so that the moment you leave your informants you can record key words and phrases as aids to your memory when later you write up your notes. A trip to the lavatory just after memorable statements or action may provide the few moments of privacy needed to save important nuggets.

Write out those fragmentary notes in full as soon as you possibly can— at least once a day. However good your memory may be for the gist of what has been said, you are not likely to remember the exact words, or even the exact sequence of events, for more than a few hours. A biographer of Sir Richard Burton, the famous nineteenth-century explorer, says that "Burton owed his success as a narrator in great measure to his habit of transferring impressions to paper the moment he received them," and credits the idea to Dr. Samuel Johnson, an equally famous eighteenth-century traveler and lexicographer: "An observer deeply impressed by any remarkable spectacle . . . does not suppose that the traces will soon vanish from his mind. . . . [T]he succession of objects will be broken . . . separate parts will be confused . . . and many practical features and discriminations will be found compressed and conglobated [conflated] into one gross and general idea" (Johnson's *Journey to the Western Islands*, and comments on Burton, in Wright, 1906:149).

Your success as a narrator is even more important, in a discipline that reveres the specific voices which utter culture. In this volume, Elizabeth Cunningham and Kathryn Hayes's paper captures those voices especially well.

Every day, read over all of your notes. For this small assignment, they will not be so long that this task will become a great burden. Ask yourself as you read what patterns emerge that had not occurred to you. Ask also what gaps appear, so that you can return to the scene and fill them. Make hypotheses as you go along, to test by tomorrow's fieldwork.

Asking Questions

First, you and your informants must become familiar enough with each other so that information flows freely. Expect apprehension from both of you at first and be patient with it. At the extreme, informants sometimes suspect that ethnographers are undercover agents. Each of us has favorite stories about such misapprehensions. When I appeared among highlanders in Eastern Kentucky in 1956, where coal mine owners and United Mine Workers had gone through bloody confrontations during the preceding decades, some of the inhabitants of "Henry's Branch" thought I was a secret land buyer for the Ford Motor Company because I wore clumsy army surplus ski boots of a design they had never seen before. If your scene involves activities of questionable legality or respectability, you can be sure that it will cost you time and effort to reassure your informants that you are what you say you are and can be trusted.

Once you begin to overcome your and your informants' apprehensions (i.e., once you have established rapport), you can begin in earnest the stages of exploration, cooperation, and participation. If you want to become an expert interviewer, a goal usually beyond the aim of an introductory course, you will profit by using Spradley's *The Ethnographic Interview* (1979), which has detailed guides for asking questions in a way that will elicit the data you need in the informants' own voices.

At the same time you are practicing how to capture other people's voices, record your own reactions and your own actions. This process is a necessary part of ethnography in the postmodern era. It is called reflexivity, and we say more about it later. Ethnography is, as noted earlier, a two-way exchange of information. It is also, as Clifford Geertz declared, "an interpretive [discipline] in search of meaning" (1973:5). That meaning, so most of us now believe, is constructed, not discovered, by ethnographers as they put their own culture into contact with the culture of the informant. During this stage of your ethnographic work it is sufficient to take note of yourself-with-your-informants, as well as to note what your informants say and do.

Saying Goodbye

By the time you read this section you have ideally established friendly relations with your informants, have quite possibly got to know them, and they you, better than you know many people with whom you have had long-term casual acquaintance. The relations between informant and ethnographer are very often among the more intimate in European and American life.

How do you take leave? The answer is not so self-evident as you may think. Your fieldwork, if you established good rapport and if you and your teachers/informants made discoveries about their culture, themselves, and yourself, was one of the closest relationships you have ever established. One student of field methods, in fact, jokingly says that making and breaking field ties is like making and breaking a love affair: "It has been pointed out that with sexual liaisons, getting *out* of bed gracefully requires more art than getting in it" (Wolcott, 1995:125).

So take leave formally, even ritually (reread Josh Keilty's ritual paper). Recognize that the familiar "Bye. See you around," won't do. Prepare your speech. Drop hints during the few visits before the very last one about how much you will miss them. Then shake all the hands that need to be shaken, hug all the people who need to be hugged. Thank all of the people you have worked with, taking care to give each one the specific thanks appropriate to the specific help he or she has given and/or specific incidents you have shared. If you agreed to give one or all of them a copy of your paper, keep that promise. Assure them you will continue to think of them.

Your aim is to leave them feeling enriched by your presence as you are by theirs, glad they took the time and energy to share their lives with you, and receptive to the next anthropology student who may knock at their door. The casualness that marks most American personal encounters is totally inappropriate and would leave your informants feeling exploited. If you think you might visit them at some time in the future, it is better not to promise but do it than it is to promise and not do it.

III. ANALYSIS AND INTERPRETATION

By this stage you are well along in data collection or feel you are almost finished. You have asked the grand tour and the mini-tour questions. Your informants have opened up the connections between their participation in the scene and at least some aspects of their lives away from the scene. You have offered a good deal of information about yourself. Perhaps you are beginning to question some of your own long-held values and beliefs as you are challenged by the different beliefs of informants you are learning to respect. This is a normal process in good ethnographic fieldwork. You may have consulted the student assistants and/or the instructor about these doubts. If you have done all or most of these things, you are ready to turn the bulk of your attention to the second large procedural task—analyzing and interpreting your field data. Some students approach this point desperately, asking us, "I have done everything I was supposed to and I have all this information [here they may spread out reams of paper on the table] and it doesn't add up to anything. What do I do now?"

There are many approaches to that question, and we do not have dogmatic answers, because ethnography in the late twentieth century is not one technique or a single methodology, but a variety of approaches to understanding culture. We do have a number of suggestions—ways of looking at your data.

Wendy Davis's experience was one that beginning ethnographers frequently run up against. She assigned herself the task of discovering the structure of employee authority and relations in a motel. Like Goodwin, Davis was handed a table of organization. She talked to most of the employees, decided she liked them (some more than others, and the bartender who hit on her not very much at all), that they were interesting people. "But what does it add up to as far as the motel is concerned?"

It added up, as she learned by a systematic comparison of her data with the official statement, to a complex operation that succeeded very well by short circuiting. The manager managed, but below him people took informal charge of various relations with clients (especially reservations and rapport) according to their talents instead of according to their assigned duties. As Davis began to find her way through the masses of interview notes she had collected, she discovered also that employees covered for each other, both in the limited sense of doing each other's jobs when necessary and in the broader sense of helping each other cope with their personal and emotional problems and keeping up each other's morale. The motel was successful, but it succeeded because of informal ties that corporate headquarters would never have recognized and might have disapproved of. The theme of Davis's paper became the informal mutual support structure of work in this small bureaucracy.

What you are after is a model that will make sense of what your informants do. Ruth Benedict, in *Patterns of Culture* (1934), constructs her models around themes, for example, the Zuñi of western New Mexico are Apollonian, the Kwakiutl of the Northwest Coast are Dionysian, the Dobu of Melanesia are prudish, cutthroat, magic-ridden. You may find that some attitudes and opinions recur like leitmotifs in the talk and behavior of your informants, and these motifs can be used as an armature (to borrow a term from sculpture) on which to place the field data in your notes and in your head. Remember that you are constructing a model of a culture, not telling *the* truth about your data; there are numerous truths.

Whether you find themes or not, set out an outline of the information you have. You may be able to do this by yourself; if not, do so in consultation with the instructor and/or the staff, who can help you talk your outline onto paper. Then organize your information according to the outline. Keep in mind that the outline itself is a tool and is likely to change as you work on it. Once you have key points written in outline form, then you can move the points around as the argument of your paper dictates.

A second suggestion is that you organize your data around a narrative sequence. You may tell the story of a day or a week in the lives of your informants; indeed, they may have given you information in these terms in response to grand tour questions. This device can lead to an interesting paper, if it is preceded, followed, and perhaps interspersed with more purely explanatory and interpretive sections. In fact, once you have organized your data in such a fashion, a number of interpretive sections will probably appear to you as necessary in order to make the cultural scene clear to your readers. Ask a friend or one of the course assistants to read this draft, to see what aspects of the scene are unclear to someone who has not been there as you have been, and let these recommendations guide you concerning the additional passages.

A third suggestion is that you ask your informants to help you structure your report. They can sometimes help you with the outline, which means they have their own ideas what order information best goes in, what follows what, and so on. Even if they cannot do this, they are likely to be able to edit your report for accuracy. "You almost understood what we're about, but you didn't quite get it right at this point" is one of the more helpful responses an informant can offer. And this stage of consultation may lead to further information on key matters that the informant neglected to describe and you didn't know to ask about before you started analyzing and writing. Not all informants can or are willing to read your report, and you may have good reasons for not wanting them to see it before you have finished. But if your aims and needs come together with their desires and abilities, few techniques are more effective for representing other people's culture through their own eyes than to let informants literally help you write about them. (No, this is not a violation of your school's honor code because the informant is helping you revise your draft, not originating it, and because you and not he or she is responsible for the coherence of the model you construct. What it is, or can be, is your own work raised to a higher level of sophistication.)

Whatever technique you employ to analyze your field information, read over your notes several times, making notes on the notes, both concerning outline and further information you need to fill in gaps. And whatever technique you employ, keep in mind that one of the unique properties of *Homo sapiens* is to impose meaning on what we do. Your informants find meaning in their scene; they probably won't agree perfectly on what the meaning is, but they will all be able to interpret it for you. Your task as a student of culture is to construct a model of the scene that shows its meaning. Your model may agree with informants' models; more likely, it will partly agree, partly disagree.

Model and "Truth"

It is time for me to say explicitly what I mean by the term *model*, and to describe the relation between models and facts, and between both and the "truth." Not many decades ago, ethnographers aimed to discover scientific truth and record it in their reports. We have abandoned the search for that kind of truth, in favor of recognizing the multiplicity of truth and of interpreting the interaction between ethnographer and informants. This approach is sometimes called reflexive ethnography. Consider your report as one among a number of possible models.

The aim of a contemporary cultural model is to construct a conceptual picture of a culture or cultural scene that accounts for all of the data you collected. The ethnologist Ward H. Goodenough (personal communication) described ethnographic information as a hierarchy: The primary level consists of what happens; the secondary is what the ethnographer observes, recognizing that he or she is incapable of observing everything; the third is what the ethnographer records in field notes; the fourth is the model of the culture, derived from those notes. You are working toward level 4 (A fifth level, says Goodenough, is ethnological theory, which is built from separate models of separate cultures. Theory is studied in more advanced courses.)

A model can be defined as a theoretical system, or more poetically as a "scientific metaphor." It is an analogy to data. (These terms are from Pelto, 1970:13.)

Models have certain properties if they are to be useful in science. Claude Lévi-Strauss (1953:525) lists four, of which two are pertinent to our discussion: First, "the structure exhibits the characteristics of a system," a statement which Pelto echoes; and fourth, "the model should be constituted so as to make immediately intelligible all the observed facts."

Your model of your cultural scene will be a system; That is, it should be internally consistent, except where inconsistencies in the behavior and statements of your informants require you, in effect, to make plural models. And your model should take account of all the data available to you. If you find you can reduce some of the relationships of system to charts and diagrams, then you will be quite literally modeling (see Goodwin's charts of an intensive care unit and White's model of the world of a police officer). Sophisticated models often use sophisticated mathematics, but in your first serious approach to ethnography it will be enough to be aware that you are constructing a verbal, and perhaps a pictorial, model.

Of course, there is no such thing as *the* adequate model for a given set of "observed facts." But not all models are equally valid, either. Lévi-Strauss again: "the best model will always be . . . the simplest possible model which, while being extracted exclusively from the facts under consideration, also makes it possible to account for all of them" (1953:526). In all scholarly work, as in art, simplicity is elegance, and it is worth striving toward. Robbins Burling (1964), in a humorous critique of the pretensions of componential analysis to show us how informants really think, says that for any set of facts there are plural adequate models, equally valid, sometimes equally simple. But there is not an infinite number of adequate models. Reach for simplicity. Reach also for your informants' models, for they may have speculated as much about what their activities mean as you have. Compare your model to theirs. If the two models are radically different, discuss the differences between them—with the staff in the course if you have time, and with yourself in any event. The disparity will be profitable to explore, as we implied earlier.

You may think that the material with which you construct your model consists only of the tapes, notes, pictures, and whatever else you have recorded, and of nothing else. Not so. The heart of your field knowledge is in your memory, while the material record you have compiled is best thought of as a mnemonic device to call it up. This may sound unreasonable. Ethnologists classically thought that we wrote down (or otherwise recorded) everything we knew, until Frederik Barth inherited the field notes on the Marri Baluch of Pakistan left behind by his colleague Robert Pehrson on the latter's death. Since Pehrson was a thorough and careful scholar, Barth assumed he could write up the notes for publication without complication. He could not. The notes (by extension, all field notes) were tantalizingly fragmentary. Barth found that he had to go to Pakistan himself and spend five weeks doing participant observation with Pehrson's informants, building on the field records Pehrson had compiled (Pehrson, 1966:vii–xii).

Barth apologetically called the Pehrson-Barth sequence of learning about a culture "a makeshift procedure" and "a serious methodological weakness" in the discipline (Pehrson, 1966:xi), but few ethnologists of the 1990s would agree. We now regard the subjectivity of models as intrinsic to all ethnographic work. Most of us, I think, concur with Goodenough (1991), who declares, "I take the position, widely held among modern scientists, that the world out there 'as it really is' and the truth with a capital 'T' are beyond the human capacity to know. We can only have propositions about our world. . . ."

George Mills, an ethnologist decades ahead of his time and a student of the relation of art styles to culture (Mills, 1959), told his students back in the 1960s that if a red ethnographer studied a blue culture, the resulting ethnography would be purple, whereas if the ethnographer were yellow, the result would be green. You must do your best to understand how your self and your culture interact with your informants and their cultures and write honestly about the juxtaposition, at the same time working hard to avoid distortion or inaccuracy. (Reread the quote from Roger Lancaster in the section "Choosing a Scene." Take another look also at Adán Trujillo's desert-born eye on a tree-lined street, and at the contrast between what Dana Curtis and Alan Stewart found worth recording about a mass.)

Your field notes, tapes, photographs, and introspections are therefore necessary but not sufficient materials with which you construct your ethnographic model. They will assist you in making that model (note that the verb is "making," not "discovering" the model). The structure you create is in your mind.

Your final product, then, will be you as well as they or, to use the jargon of the trade, will be Self as well as Other. It will be, whether you intend it to be or not, a dialogue between yourself and your informants. Since it *will* be so, you may as well do it consciously. Most of the student papers that follow contain Self/Other dialogues, each expressed in a voice which fits the writer's own experience.

Once you have decided your focus and the aspects of the culture you wish to stress in your ethnography, look yet again at your own likes and dislikes, your relations with your informants, your motives for choosing the particular scene, your reactions to it, and put them consciously into the paper.

This procedure has more than one advantage. In no particular order, they include the following (and perhaps others of which I am not conscious).

First, in good Freudian style, you can handle your bias better if you deal with it over rather than under the table of your consciousness. You may discover aspects of your bias of which you had been unaware, and counter them in the analysis.

Second, you acknowledge by putting yourself on your own stage that the human psyche is an imprecise recording instrument, and you are likely to describe the culture more modestly, more tentatively, with more humanity—all desirable qualities in scholarship as well as in other pursuits.

Third, you give your readers information they can use to discount your bias and also credit your special access to information. To manufacture a few simple examples, if you are premed and do your fieldwork in a hospital, the reader can simultaneously watch out for your medical prejudices and be more likely to accept your interpretation of some aspects of hospital work. If you are gay and writing about a gay scene, the reader can simultaneously discount your bias and assume that you are likely to have an ear well tuned to the kind of information your informants can tell you. The permutations of interest, bias, and special access are infinite.

Fourth, you can enter one of the most interesting discussions now going on in ethnology—reflexivity, and the assumption that all ethnography is a dialogue between Self and Other, which both parties to the dialogue help to shape, the assumption that if there is any such abstract and fixed entity as "the culture of X," it cannot be apprehended by ethnography or any other means we can now conceive (see Goodenough on page 99), and that the best and most honest we can do is to publish our Self-Other dialogues, always remembering what other Selves we write for. (In academic assignments, one unavoidable other Self is the instructor, and all students know how much instructors' expectations influence the way they write.)

What happens to "truth?" Does it disappear in a semantic shuffle? If you define truth as single and absolute, forget it. But if you define it as accuracy, then its importance cannot be overemphasized. Reread the admonitions to set down your informants' ideas in their own words, exactly as they say them, complete with gesture and inflection. Make sure your own observations about the setting are as accurate as you can make them. *Never cook the data* (that is, don't distort the facts). And, although in your paper you cannot include every statement from every page of your field notes, be self-critical so your selection leaves "the system" intact insofar as it is within your power to do so. "Truth" is like absolute zero—impossible to attain, but a useful concept and worth all the effort it takes to approach it.

In sum, honor the facts, set them forth as fully and accurately as you can. Seek the truth. But be always aware that you are constructing your model of the scene, which is not likely to be identical to the informants' model, and which will depend, among other things, on the personal experience and the theoretical (or, more generally, intellectual) set you bring to the fieldwork.

IV. WRITING THE PAPER

What will your paper look like? Ethnographic reports vary enormously; the student authors of the papers in this volume use widely disparate strategies to organize their field experiences. But all ethnographies should be organized according to the topics you decide characterize your particular cultural scene. Your paper should present a vivid enough picture so that readers can say, as Clifford Geertz (1988) said in a slightly different context, "I am there because you were there." It will be well if your report has a central theme, but do not strain for one.

Wendy Davis, one of the best former student assistants in my course, suggests that it may be useful to "attack writing as if you are trying to prove that the scene is 'cultural.' Go back to earlier assignments and break down this big one in terms of the smaller ones: categorize the information into a physical map, language, ritual, and your reactions as ethnographer" (personal communication).

To recapitulate, put yourself deliberately into the scene, and describe your interactions with the actors on that stage and your reactions to them and to the scene. Neither hog the stage nor pretend you are absent. Although ethnographic reports describe interaction between Self and Other, nevertheless they are not psychological navel gazing; spend more energy trying to understand the Other (using their words to do so) than you do indulging the Self, and keep a balance between the two.

Quite a number of authors, both student and professional, suffer from writer's block. It is not the end of the world, although it may seem like it. If the advice here doesn't work, just start writing—anywhere. You will almost certainly throw away the first few pages of desperation writing, but the dam will have broken and the flow started.

FURTHER IN VARIOUS DIRECTIONS

Beyond the present assignment you should choose among the alternative methods that ethnologists use in doing field ethnography, of course mixing them according to your taste, but recognizing their differences. The Spradleyan method is widely esteemed and goes by the name of ethnoscience, sometimes (because it focuses so strongly on what people say and how they say it) ethnolinguistics. Sociologists using such an approach tend to label it ethnomethodology (e.g., Van Maanen, 1988). The simplest guide to doing ethnography written from that point of view is Spradley and

McCurdy's *The Cultural Experience* (1972), already mentioned. Virtually any other book or article that Spradley wrote before his untimely death is also useful. I recommend especially *The Ethnographic Interview* (1979), which will lead you step by step through a productive way to interview informants. Other guides in the ethnoscience tradition are Harry Wolcott's somewhat chatty *The Art of Fieldwork* (1995), an accessible discussion of many of the personal and professional problems the ethnoscientist is likely to run into, and Oswald Werner and Mark Schoepfle's exhaustive two-volume *Systematic Fieldwork* (1987), a treatise more useful to graduate students and professionals than to undergraduates. Both contain long bibliographies on the topic. Russell Bernard's *Research Methods in Cultural Anthropology* (2nd ed., 1994) has often been used by undergraduates, although it is not for beginners. It is positivist, stresses scientific method, the use of electronic technology, and sophisticated data management.

To the best of my knowledge, no field manual stresses the cultural ecological method. That is unfortunate, because it is conceptually simpler than ethnoscience and can be used by advanced undergraduates (although the most sophisticated ecological work tries to understand such intricate pressures and counterpressures between environment and culture that they tax the minds even of professionals). Nor, so far as I am aware, has any postmodernist entered the lists.

Beyond such field guides for graduate and advanced undergraduate students as those mentioned here, you must swim with the rest of us in the endless sea of literature on ethnological theory, much of which carries implications for field methods although not written primarily with the field in mind. I confess a bias toward postmodern questions such as the interpenetration of cultures and identities and the uses of reflexivity. Paul Rabinow's *Reflections on Fieldwork in Morocco* (1977) is regarded as a founding document on reflexivity. Rosaldo's *Culture and Truth* (1989), which I have referred to several times already, is a favorite of mine on several postmodern topics and has deeply influenced my own work. Even reflexivity, as a subcategory of postmodern theory, has an enormous and constantly expanding literature.

Student Illustrative Ethnographies

Ethnography of Police Work in an Affluent Community

by Otis Jeffrey White

Spradley and McCurdy's guide to doing field ethnography was published in 1972, and I used it immediately in the Introduction to Cultural Anthropology class. Their assumption that culture consists of shared cognition showed strain early on, but students and the instructor pulled and tugged to fit data onto the Procrustean bed. Jeff White's research in 1975 broke the bed because his two principal informants flatly disagreed on an essential part of their scene—how to respond to lawbreakers. From that point, the guidelines for analyzing field data steadily changed in the course as they were changing in the profession, where they come temporarily to rest in a postmodern, polyvocal, reflexive frame.

White's paper is interesting as a transition piece in that he shows concretely where cognition is shared, where the map is the same for both informants and where it diverges (Appendix 1). Appendix 2, the classification of residents of the area, is the same for both informants. Note that he asked his informants to check the adequacy of his model of their culture. White also offers useful biographical background on his informants, which rigidly cognitive ethnographers do not seek.

White intended a career in criminology, but he became a banker.

INTRODUCTION

With few exceptions, I think it can be asserted that almost every city, town, and community in the United States, regardless of size, has some form of law enforcement. I maintain with equal conviction that those portions of society with greater monetary influence than the masses have usually demanded, and more often than not received, better quality in the goods and services rendered. The community of Broadmoor and the service of law enforcement in Broadmoor are no exceptions to these assertions.

Broadmoor is outside of the Colorado Springs city limits, therefore is the responsibility of the El Paso County Sheriff's Office. *[Since White graduated, Colorado Springs expanded to include Broadmoor, and provides its police protection. So White's ethnography is now part of the historical record.]* Several years ago, certain residents of Broadmoor expressed concern about the lack of adequate protection for their community, and the alleged inefficiency with which the Sheriff's Office handled law enforcement problems occurring in the community. The fact that Broadmoor was (and still is) a wealthy area combined with little police protection seemed an invitation to crime. The Broadmoor Improvement Society (hereafter BIS) was formed, whose main function is the collection of membership dues to pay the wages and operational expenses of the newly formed Broadmoor Police Department. Anyone living in Broadmoor can join the BIS, and upon payment of yearly dues is issued a "glow-in-the-dark" decal to proudly display on their mailbox. Of course this assures the best protection possible. The paradox is that the Broadmoor police do not deny protection to nonmembers: They patrol their assigned district just as other police would patrol their entire districts. As one of my informants told me, "The smart ones know damn well that we watch their houses and respond to their calls too, whether they're members or not. The others just have to keep up with the Joneses." Alas, it seems as though a decal on one's mailbox is yet another way to enhance one's status. Another plausible explanation is simply that most residents enjoy the increased protection, and realize that someone must "fork over" to ensure its continuance.

Even though the Broadmoor police are called "rent-a-cops" by many youth of the community, they are all trained law enforcement officers commissioned by the El Paso County Sheriff's Office, hence are legitimate police officers for all of El Paso County. Because they are deputy sheriffs, they are often called to assist other sheriffs outside of the Broadmoor district on what is referred to as a "cover-call."

Important to the framework of this ethnography are my concepts of culture and cultural scene as they apply to this paper. One can find thousands of definitions for culture, but I think the most concise and tangible is, "The knowledge people use to generate and interpret social behavior. This knowledge is learned, and to a degree shared" (Spradley & McCurdy, 1972:8). This definition is also useful in describing a cultural scene: "the knowledge actors employ in a social situation; the latter is the observable place, events, objects, and persons seen by an investigator" (Spradley & McCurdy, 1972:27).

The culture of the Broadmoor police is the knowledge they possess which influences their behavior and their interpretations of the behavior of others in a given situation of interaction. For instance, the event of an officer stopping a traffic violator can be thought of as a social situation. The officer enters the interaction influenced by his enculturation as a policeman, with expectations of what is to happen and knowledge of what he must do. Utilizing this set of cognitive skills now creates a cultural scene.

Quite obviously law enforcement could embody several cultural scenes depending on the varied social situations an officer encounters. To simplify terminology and alleviate confusion (if not for the reader, then for myself) I will allude to only one broad generalized cultural scene—both the everyday activities and peculiar interactions. I think all these can be lumped together and considered a single cultural scene because the culture of the officer, the knowledge he uses to generate his own behavior and interpret that of others, is still the same from one social situation and interaction to another. Whether stopping a suspicious car or responding to an armed robbery, the officer employs the same cognitions of his enculturation as a policeman.

I respond differently to a professor in class than I do to my employer at work, because I am a member of both the cultures of student and employee. I have different cognitions influencing my behavior in the different interactions. Yet in a given day of police work, knowledge from the police culture must be employed in every interaction although those interactions may be different.

In this paper I describe the daily routine of the Broadmoor police and their responses to both ordinary and infrequent calls. The main emphasis is the plural cognitive mapping of my two informants, and how this free variation within their culture affects their self-images and the execution of duties.

Fieldwork Methods

When this ethnography was assigned, my first idea was to study some aspect of police work, preferably a squad car. This seemed a reasonable choice because I hope to enter some aspect of criminology, and thought squad car patrol would present most clearly the culture of a police officer.

I encountered several problems at the outset of my research. Chief Oren Boling of the Colorado Springs Police Department denied a request to allow students from CC [Colorado College] to ride in squad cars. Alternative suggestions were made, few of which appealed to me. I then contacted a lieutenant in the city police SACS (Special Anti-Crime Squad) unit, and received the "pass-the-buck" routine which I was quite used to by that time. Disgusted, I met with Marion Shipley, sheriff of El Paso County, fully expecting similar treatment. It would be an understatement to say that I was astonished when granted permission to ride in any squad car of my choice. They practically gave me a badge and a car of my own.

I chose the Broadmoor police to ride with because of their small size (three officers), hoping I could better understand the cultural scene of law enforcement of an affluent community.

Once I was granted permission to ride in a squad car, I signed a release freeing the Sheriff's Office from any liability, and had it notarized. I next went to the Broadmoor police office and requested their permission to ride, which was granted with enthusiasm. I explained the purpose of my project, what it would entail, how long it would require, and what I hoped to achieve.

My two informants are named Earl and George; Earl is approximately 50 and George is 40. Both are veterans of the Vietnam War and served several years in the military prior to their tours in Southeast Asia. Earl has been a Broadmoor policeman for the past three years; George has been there about nine months. George was a helicopter pilot in the army, and he piloted a helicopter as a Missouri State Trooper prior to his employment as a Broadmoor policeman.

Earl was rather quiet but always very willing to answer my questions. George was quite garrulous, seemed to enjoy my company, and was equally willing to answer questions.

My fieldwork methods were simple enough: I observed, then recorded what I saw as objectively as possible. I continually reminded myself to be objective and attempt to record data without bias, suppressing any preconceptions I might have had about police, the law, or violators.

For the first few days I concentrated mainly on collecting data about the daily routine. I provided my informants with a model of what I thought to be normal daily procedure, based on my notes, and asked for their responses. With their comments and corrections, I determined a chronological pattern of what they considered to be their daily routine duties. I then was able to concentrate on collecting data about how my informants responded to calls, viewed themselves, and organized their universes.

I scribbled my notes (often in the dark) in a method I'm sure appears organized only to myself. The next day I transcribed my notes onto 3x5 cards, condensing and categorizing them according to the informant involved, event that occurred, and method employed to cope with the problem.

SETTING

The physical setting that encompasses my cultural scene cannot be described in explicit detail as might the setting of an elementary school classroom or jewelry store. Broadmoor is an expansive community situated on a small table-mesa southwest of Colorado Springs. The district of the Broadmoor police is bounded on the west by the Old Stage Road, on the north by Cheyenne Road, on the east by State Highway 115, and extends southward to the NORAD (North American Air Defense) complex.

Obviously, when my informants respond to a cover call outside of their district, the cultural scene also extends beyond its normal boundaries. These cover-calls are seldom farther away than Skyway to the north or Interstate 25 to the east.

I stated earlier that my two informants have different cognitive maps and that these in turn affect the organization of their universes, self-images, and methods of operation as police officers. Therefore the domains stressed in this paper are those that illustrate the free variation possible when executing duties in the culture of a Broadmoor policeman. Also included are those domains shared by my informants included in the realm of police procedure and daily routine.

CULTURAL DESCRIPTION

The plural cognitive mapping of my informants that I referred to seems to operate when they are responding to calls and not during the performance of routine duties.

The Broadmoor police work in three shifts, two of which overlap somewhat. The chief (not an informant because his duties are mainly public relations work rather than patrol) arrives at the office at 8 A.M. and departs at 8 P.M. Earl comes on duty at 8 P.M. and stays until usually 5 A.M. the following morning. Each man has two consecutive days off during the week, and is covered by the other officers at that time, who then work about twelve hours each of the two days. These schedules are highly flexible; often Earl and George both work twelve hours or more and will trade off shifts to alleviate too much of the graveyard shift for one individual.

One of my first insights was that both informants are exceedingly dedicated to their jobs. They are paid a yearly salary based upon an eight-hour day and a five-day week, but while I was riding with them neither worked less than ten hours and often would work on their days off when needed. When questioned about this, my informants responded with answers that confirmed my insight. Earl stated, "If I leave before 3 A.M., all hell is sure to break loose, so I usually stay late." George's response was similar: "I hate to leave early even if everything is quiet; I just feel as though I'm deserting the community and leaving it unprotected."

The Chief's main duties appear to be making the pot of coffee when he arrives, and answering minor complaints. At 9 A.M. he stations himself at the elementary school crosswalk to escort the children across the street.

George assumes the duty of patrol when he arrives in the morning and answers calls in his district aired over the radio by the Sheriff's Office dispatcher. The Broadmoor police radios are equipped with three channels: (1) the El Paso County Sheriff, (2) the local volunteer fire departments, but the third channel is not operational. They have no direct contact with either the city police or the state patrol, only with other deputy sheriffs.

At 3 P.M. the elementary school is dismissed and the officers station themselves at two different crosswalks. Routine patrol and public relations work continues until Earl comes on duty in the evening. This P.R. work entails responding to complaints and reports of menacing, vandalism, and other ex post facto incidents. Paperwork is also done during the day (i.e. accident & burglary reports, etc.). Any court appearances that may be necessary are of course made during the day.

The night shift begins by playing back the telephone recorder and responding to any calls that were made via telephone in the absence of the officers. Emergency calls are never made in this manner, and they usually amount to only doing a little P.R. work—consoling people about possible prowlers the previous evening, assuring neighbors that loud parties next door will not continue to occur, or listening to family quarrels.

After this task is completed, both of my informants always stop at the World Arena (an ice rink owned by the Broadmoor Hotel) to drink a cup of coffee and chat with the ladies who work at the concessions counter. After about fifteen minutes, routine patrol resumes with emphasis on checking vacant houses. Residents phone the office to report when they will be vacationing, and this is recorded in a notebook. At night when an officer arrives at one of these homes during his routine patrol, he will get out of the car and thoroughly check the premises. This is usually done only once or twice per evening because overconcentration on the vacationing residents' homes would limit overall efficiency. At half past ten, the officer on duty must go to the World Arena to escort the money courier to the Broadmoor Hotel for deposit.

The officer then returns to the office and again checks the recorder for phone calls and responds accordingly. After this is accomplished, routine patrol is again resumed until about midnight. At this time the officer goes temporarily "out of service" to eat. The places they eat are the I-HOP in Southgate Shopping Center, the kitchen of the Broadmoor Hotel, and the Hatchcover restaurant in the Country Club Corners complex west of highway 115.

Food is free at the Hatchcover and the hotel kitchen, and 50 percent off at the I-HOP. When questioned why this was, both informants were reluctant to state that it was a type of bribe, but both agreed that it sealed a type of understanding; "If anything happens at one of these places, you're supposed to bust your ass to get there since they've been nice to you" (George).

Once the meal is finished, patrol resumes. The difference, though, is that after midnight any cars or persons not known by the officer are immediately stopped and investigated. A registration check is radioed to the Sheriff's Office and run through the computer. In this way the officer can find out in thirty seconds or less if the vehicle is stolen, whom the plates are registered to, and the registrant's address. If the person or persons stopped do not have a valid reason for their presence in the area, they are strongly advised to depart and are usually tailed until they do so.

Patrol is continued in this fashion until about 5 A.M., at which time the officer radios in that he is off duty. On his way home, he takes all documents and reports accumulated during the previous day and night to the Sheriff's Office in downtown Colorado Springs. This daily routine is strictly followed by both informants, the execution of the duties involved being the same.

Of course, the major part of the officer's job is responding to calls from the dispatcher pertaining to incidents occurring in the Broadmoor district, or covering calls in nearby districts. The only call that occurs in Broadmoor so often that it can be considered almost routine is potential prowlers. This occurs several times during a given evening, and both informants respond by thoroughly searching the area, then consoling the reporting residents. Should a prowler be caught, identity is established and investigation into the alleged "prowl" is conducted. A prowler cannot be held on any charges and is released with the advice to depart from the area.

The plural cognitive mapping I have alluded to occurs when they respond to a call and are coping with the problem encountered. In each of the incidents I cite that illustrate the plural cognitive mapping of my informants, they are attempting to achieve the same goals through different means. Although their means of coping with the actual problem differ, both share the same procedure prior to their distinct methodologies. I am referring to police procedure and it is shared by all trained law enforcement officials in the country (see Appendix 1). The main purposes of adhering to basic police procedure are to protect the welfare of the officer involved and any innocent bystanders, and to gather and establish evidence that will hold up in court. In short, both informants would approach a suspicious vehicle in the same way, cover an armed robbery or conduct a search the same.

At different times, both of my informants stopped young drivers who lived in Broadmoor and who did not possess drivers' licenses because they had been revoked due to past driving records. Earl lectured his violator, called the parents, but did not write a ticket. George, on the other hand, did issue a ticket to his violator.

While I rode with Earl he stopped several traffic violators, yet issued only warnings. If the violation was serious and involved a teenager of the community, he usually lectured briefly and talked with the parents. George is fairly lenient with traffic violators, but serious infractions are met with tickets. If he deems the violation serious enough to warrant a ticket, he will issue one without hesitation whether the violator is a resident of Broadmoor or not.

Public disturbance calls are received relatively often, and my informants handle these quite differently. One night Earl responded to a disturbance call that turned out to be a fight involving about ten youths, most of whom lived in Broadmoor. He broke the fight up, took the boys who live in Broadmoor to his office, and phoned the parents to come pick up their sons at which time Earl spoke with them about the incident. George responded to a similar disturbance involving some rather inebriated youths who were causing a great deal of commotion in a public place. Without hesitation, he took them to the county jail on charges of drunk and disorderly conduct. They too were residents of Broadmoor.

Another example of the free variation of operation of my informants is a pair of "hit and run" traffic accidents involving teenagers of Broadmoor. Late one evening, a Jeep (whose driver was drunk) hit another auto head on, and simply drove away despite injuries and heavy damage to both vehicles. Earl responded to the call and later picked up the responsible youth at his home. He convinced the victims to refrain from pressing charges, both parties met with each other, including the parents of the boy and Earl, and reached a settlement out of court. The parents also applied some punitive measures to their son. In the contrasting case, George responded to another "hit and run" call at a later date: A Mountain Bell phone truck had been hit and extensively damaged as it was parked next to a phone pole. George found the responsible vehicle about a mile up the road, trying to escape despite heavy damage and two flat tires. All occupants of the vehicle had been drinking heavily and were arrested at the scene and taken to the county jail. (Some were underage, and this is why the passengers were also arrested even though they were later released without charges; the driver was charged for drunk driving and hit and run.)

Minor drug and alcohol violations are also handled differently by my two informants. Whenever Earl caught youngsters in possession of marijuana, no matter what quantity, he followed the same procedure. He immediately confiscated it, took the former possessor to his office for a lecture, then contacted the parents of the youth. Once this was accomplished, he would sit down with the parents and youth and discuss the incident. Whenever George encountered the same problem, he adhered strictly to the law. If it was a first offense for the individual or the amount confiscated was less than half an ounce, he would release the violator with a strong warning and sometimes contact the parents, depending on the age of the individual. He stated, "If they have less than half an ounce on them, it is left to the arresting officer's discretion whether to press charges or not, but I usually let 'em go after I give 'em hell." If the amount of possession was more than half an ounce, George arrested the violator and filed charges. (This occurred only twice while I rode with him, but George told me he "stuck strictly to the law set down" and would treat all violators the same.)

Perhaps the best example I recorded involved burglary. Both instances involved burglaries of Broadmoor homes, and both burglars were young men who resided in the community with their parents. Earl responded to a burglary call one evening, and found that a stereo system had been stolen. A few days later he stopped a youth for a minor traffic violation, and discovered a stereo in the rear seat that matched the description of the one reported stolen in the earlier burglary. The youth finally confessed to having broken into the home and taking the unit. Instead of filing charges, Earl contacted the owners of the stereo and pleaded with them not to press charges against the youth because it was a first offense. They finally agreed, and the youth was released with the stern warning that another such incident would require prosecution. The entire ordeal lasted several days, during which time Earl met often with the boy involved, his parents, and the victims of the burglary. He also indicated to the youth that he was placed on an implicit probation with the Broadmoor police and that he had "better not screw up again or we'll nail him to the wall."

George caught a youth in a similar incident with goods that had been stolen in a burglary two months prior. He was able to prove beyond doubt that the youth was indeed guilty, and urged the victims to press charges, which they did.

In all of these examples, both informants are trying to achieve the same end result—stopping a youth from stealing again, getting drivers to adhere to traffic laws, and so on. The difference is in the way they believe they can accomplish the desired result, and consequently the action they take.

I maintain that these contrasts in coping with the same problems exist because of the officers' self-images, and the people whom they feel they are responsible to. When questioned about this, George said he saw himself as a law enforcement officer, and that he would "uphold the law whether I personally believe it is right or not." He also stated that since he was an El Paso County deputy sheriff, "I'm responsible to all the people of the county at all times, and not just those in my district."

Earl views himself as a security guard whose responsibilities are mainly to the BIS members. "I'm just a 'doorshaker'; I'll never be a cop and I don't want to be." I assert that with this view, he feels he is directly responsible to the residents of Broadmoor and in particular the members of BIS. He feels that he can better handle internal problems by keeping them that way, as opposed to turning the problem over to the judicial system. (I found that although lenient, Earl tended to adhere more to the law if an incident occurred outside of his district or if it involved individuals who were not Broadmoor residents. He answered cover calls as George did, but considered coping with problems outside of Broadmoor to be "a pain in the ass," a duty outside of the realm of his real duties.)

SPECIAL LANGUAGE AND CATEGORIZATION

The Broadmoor police don't really have an elaborate special language. At least if they do, I didn't notice it and they wouldn't reveal it when questioned.

They do, of course, use the 10-call system, as do all police departments. Other than this, their only language that is shared is their categorization of people who reside in Broadmoor. Their district, although large, is highly personal and they know the majority of residents by name and usually their addresses also. The purpose of the categorization of residents is, as Earl states, "To keep a tab on everyone, know where you stand with someone, and what you can expect of them; it's especially helpful and wise to know as much as you can about kids" (see Appendix 2).

Youth belong to four divisions according to their position in school, each of which is further subdivided. Elementary school children can either be "brats" or "good kids" depending on whether they're courteous or rude when escorted across the crosswalk.

The major subcategory of junior high youths are the long-haired boys. Kids who have been known to steal are referred to as "future crooks" and must be watched very closely. Girls who may act "sleazy" or who wear too much makeup are "Jr. whores." There is no name for other girls.

Senior high youths comprise the largest category. There are "druggies" and they are subdivided into "hards," who take a variety of drugs, "dopers" who only smoke marijuana, and "pushers," which is self-explanatory. Rumor usually establishes the identity of individuals placed in this category.

"Cowboys" are the next category, and these can be "drugstore" or "real cowboys" depending on whether they just wear Western-style clothes or really have ranch experience.

"Troublemakers" establish their reputation through actual past experience, and "death seekers" are those who "drive like hell" in George's terms. "Smart-asses" is a self-explanatory term, and "dumb broads" are those females who cannot carry on an intelligent conversation. "Potential housekeepers" are good-looking girls whom the officers enjoy looking at and flirting with. When asked about the term *housekeeper*, Earl said, "'Cause if my wife weren't home, I'd take her home and let her clean my room, if you know what I mean." (The adjective "potential" means that the girl is really a little too young for this, but that she will certainly do in a couple of years.)

Those youth in the community that aren't in school but living with their parents are either "workers" or "f——offs," both self-explanatory.

The category of adults in Broadmoor is also fairly large. "Richeys" (wealthy) and "partyers" are obvious. "Nomads" are those people who are always vacationing, "flirts" are the women of Broadmoor that the officers think flirt with them, and "housekeepers" are good-looking women that they likewise admire and would like to take home in the absence of their wives.

About a dozen people in Broadmoor own radio scanners, and often listen in on the radio frequency of the Sheriff's Office to the Broadmoor police. These people are termed "big brothers," and therefore one must be cautious about language and be sure to respond immediately to all calls or the "big brothers" will report the incident the following day to the chief.

"Friendly neighborhood contributors" are those people who always leave their garage doors open at night, inviting burglars.

"Whiners" are those who always "cry wolf," as George says.

People who aren't classified in any of the mentioned categories, and who are unfriendly or disliked by the officers, are called "s——heads," a term which my informants use quite often when referring to individuals.

GAMES

There are a few things to do or "games" to be played during spare time that are shared by my informants. They only participate in these games when the district has been patrolled several times and the area is calm and the radio quiet.

The game most often played is "tinkering with the traffic," the officer who plays it being termed at the time "traffic happy." This is when an officer hides on a side street next to a larger street known to have a heavy flow of traffic. The purpose is to stop as many cars as possible, or to stop them for trivial violations. Only warning tickets are issued for these offenses.

Another game both informants seemed to enjoy was to find another sheriff, and either follow him or drive ahead of him with lights blacked out. The purpose was to elicit an investigation by the other sheriff into the mysterious automobile. They seemed to delight in the embarrassment the other sheriff displayed when he pulled him over only to discover that he had stopped another sheriff.

The last game played is to roust people parking on side streets, at the World Arena parking lot, or North and South Cheyenne Canyons. When both Earl and George are on duty in different cars, the game is even more fun. One officer will seek parkers and tell them that a good place to go where no one will object is the Cheyenne Mountain Zoo parking lot. He will even given them directions how to get there. Once they depart, he radios the other officer and tells him to "go get 'em." This mild harassment seems to be their favorite game, but lately they have had a difficult time locating parkers. Earl's hypothesis of this situation is that, "with the economy and all, everyone is so hard up they can't afford to make babies anymore." I think perhaps that people have just figured out the game and would prefer not to be victimized participants.

CONCLUSION

I'm reluctant to admit that a large proportion of the data I collected is not included in this paper primarily because much of it didn't pertain to the main theme. *[All good ethnographers collect far more data than they can use.]*

My conclusion about the Broadmoor police took me by surprise. I had preconceptions that they were merely a guard service and envisioned their duties to be very passive and relatively simple. I realize now that their operation is not at all like this, and that they really are what I consider to be law enforcement officials.

The plural cognitive mapping of my informants does not seem to hinder performance or effectiveness of coping with the law enforcement problems of Broadmoor and nearby districts. It appears as though the great contrasts in methodology might upset some of the residents of an affluent community, but I certainly did not witness any evidence that might suggest so. This may be due in part to the fact that George has worked there for only nine months, and perhaps the residents expect him to mellow with time, or even may demand his firing in the future. Quite obviously, only future research could confirm or deny this, the results of which certainly can't be included in this paper due to my "publisher's" deadline.

APPENDIX 1

Event is the same, and standard police procedure is shared by both individuals. When coping with the actual problem, their methodologies diverge, yet the purpose of each is to achieve the same end.

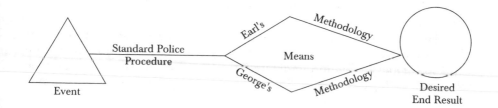

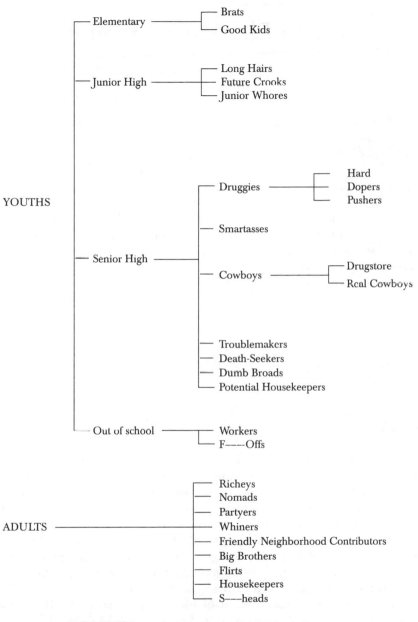

APPENDIX 2 Categorization of People Living in Broadmoor

North Elementary School

by Jenny Irving and Michael Allen

The reflexive and method portions of Irving and Allen's study of an elementary school are important to include in this volume, although the entire paper is too long to reproduce. The authors were first-year students when they wrote it. Their tentative, open, even naïve and feel-your-way style may give other students courage to strike out into their own uncharted territories. If you are debating whether to work alone or in a team, read their discussion of the pros and cons of teamwork with particular care.

Note that Irving and Allen were willing to shape their research question as they went along, after getting some idea of the school through talking with Allen's mother and with the principal. In many sciences good procedure requires the investigator to develop an hypothesis in considerable detail before proceeding to the laboratory. But ethnographic fieldwork is necessarily opportunistic because one must adapt one's purpose to the field situation. Note especially, "These ideas changed and metamorphosed into others." Don't be afraid to change your own ideas as you discover what you can and cannot do.

Both authors share their biases with the reader as much as they consciously can. Allen's decision to use his mother as an informant is highly unusual. It seems to have worked, but I don't recommend it.

PREFACE

When we began writing about the society of North Elementary, we had to ask ourselves the question, "How can we present our data in a way that most faithfully reflects the culture of the school?" Since the school's society was so diverse, we decided to observe a cross section of classrooms in order to narrow our study. In trying to delineate the culture of an elementary school, we saw the school's atmosphere best reflected in the individual classrooms, especially by the relationships between the instructors and their students. Therefore, in our ethnography we have chosen to present specific slices of the extremely diverse culture of the school to better represent the bigger picture. We feel close examination of individual classrooms will provide a picture that corresponds more readily to the manifold cultural influences enclosed by the school. We hope this eclectic approach presents a better metaphor for culture, one that expresses the culture of a society, while keeping in mind that the latter is composed of many smaller groups.

Before we began our ethnography, we were told not to try to decide on a specific focus before we had waited to see what ideas presented themselves. We went in with really no idea of what to expect. For this reason we arranged with Mr. Castle, the principal, to visit a variety of classrooms and thereby gain different insights to help us eventually decide on a focus. As the time we spent at the school increased we started coming up with ideas. These ideas changed and metamorphosed into others. At 'first we wanted to just focus on the kids. Later on we decided that the kids were not enough and that we needed to study the entire school environment, especially the teachers. So, we decided on a view of the whole school, then we talked of focusing on one specific classroom. Eventually as our ideas grew and changed we came back to the whole school idea. But this time we decided to focus on the school as one culture with many different and distinct micro-cultures within it. The particular micro-cultures we studied were Mrs. Rael's second grade class, Mr. Wallace's fifth/sixth split class, Mr. Burdekin's sixth grade class, and Mrs. Allen's special education classroom.

SUBJECTIVITY OF ETHNOGRAPHY

As discussed repeatedly both in our cultural anthropology class and between us, ethnographies are not absolute. Every ethnography, no matter how carefully conducted, contains subjectivity. Cultural and personal biases are impossible to do away with completely. This ethnography is no different. We have tried our hardest to exclude personal biases and judgments, but by no means is this ethnography completely objective. This paper inherently contains our opinions because it is a study based on personal observations leading to subjective analysis of the data. Hopefully though, all of our opinions and analyses are supported by the information we present.

Some problems that we encountered may affect the outcome of the ethnography. One specific problem is the relatively short amount of time we were able to spend gathering data. There were surely important interactions we missed because that there was not enough time to get to know our informers more intimately.

In order to aid readers in discerning for themselves the most true model of North Elementary, we present our personal biases and motivations that we feel may have affected the objectivity of this ethnography.

PERSONAL BIASES AND MOTIVATIONS FOR DOING THIS ETHNOGRAPHY

Jenny

When I first heard of this assignment I started trying to think of ideas. Many went through my mind, but the one that stuck was that I really liked kids and would like to do something that dealt with them. Mike and I decided to work together and that we would like to focus on a grade school. That was about as far as our focus went at that point. We are both very interested in children and thought it would be entertaining and informative to watch them as our informants. Along with my interest in children there was an interest in the whole education system. For as long as I can remember I have loved teaching and the process of learning. I would spend hours teaching reading and math to my little brother or the little neighbor girl. This probably came about because my mother is a teacher and loves her job. I have had a very stable home life. I grew up in the same house in a nice neighborhood since I was 4 years old. I always attended mostly white middle-class schools and I thought it would be interesting and informative to study a school that was not the same sort that I attended. Another significant reason I wanted to study an elementary school was my desire to recapture the lost years of my childhood. I wanted to experience them again firsthand. Each time I saw the kids again I realized how much I was missing now from that time and how little I can actually recollect. From the time we spent in North Elementary watching the kids and the teachers, I have seriously questioned my decision not to become a teacher.

Michael

I was born into a military family that has traveled all around the globe, living in California, Texas, Stuttgart (Germany), Missouri, and Colorado Springs. I have lived in Colorado Springs for a total of eight years. I graduated from Cheyenne Mountain High School and entered Colorado College in 1992. Living in the Colorado Springs area for this length of time has given me intimate knowledge of most of the city. I feel this intimacy does not necessarily affect my ethnographic objectivity to any great degree. I had previously visited North Elementary for half an hour two years ago when my mother accepted a position as a special education teacher there. The connection of my mother to the school led only to that one brief visit to the school. The visit did not allow time to formulate ideas concerning the culture of the school, therefore I consider the time spent in North Elementary for this ethnography unbiased by prior contact. Conversations with my mother about her students and colleagues at the school before this writing are considered irrelevant and are not included in this study.

Having my mother as a primary connection to the school definitely influences my ethnographic viewpoint to some degree. The fact that my mother has been an elementary school teacher as long as I can remember is not necessarily a deterrent in understanding the workings of an elementary school. I have heard many dinnertime conversations from my mother relating countless stories about her students, her peers, and her administrators. In hearing these stories for much of my life, I feel that my ability to sift through the confusing array of influences on the society of an elementary school has been enhanced to some degree. When one's parent is a teacher, one gets a better feel for what it must be like when compared to someone whose parent is not a teacher.

I have an interest in children in general. I like to watch and interact with them. I am very interested in how they learn and how they are taught. What exactly schoolchildren learn is a question we hope to answer in this ethnography. It became immediately apparent that what students learn in school is not reflected only by tests and papers.

My interest in child development, especially linguistic development, drew me toward an ethnography of a school. Also, an elementary school provided a good situation to examine social organization and interaction, which also interests me greatly.

In recent months, I have speculated about the possibilities of becoming a teacher myself. I have always loved how a good teacher not only teaches facts and skills but also involves and entertains the students. I felt this ethnography might expose more of what teaching is about and in doing so help me to find out what career I might enjoy.

REASONS FOR TWO ETHNOGRAPHERS

Fairly early on, we decided to work together. With a grade school as our focus we combined our mutual interest in children, education, and the fact that we both have parents who were teachers. Working as a team rather than separately had many redeeming and important aspects that overshadowed the obstacles. Working together meant being able to split the work and so concentrate on what most interested us individually. A primary reason we had for working together at first was the fact that we would be able to divide observation time so Mike could use his mother less as an informant. In collaborating we were able to obtain different perspectives on the same observations. Our different backgrounds and genders contributed unique outlooks. In this way, we could reduce some of the personal biases that are inevitably a part of any ethnography. Our different perspectives provided us with alternative interpretations and led to discussion about differences we perceived. These discussions brought about new ideas. In the actual observations we each kept notes that we did not share until it came time to write. We shared observations and ideas and did a lot of talking, but not about specifics while in the classroom. This kept us from influencing each other's biases.

The involvement of two ethnographers offers many advantages and disadvantages in examining a culture. We felt that differing perspectives would enhance the overall picture as more reflective of the multifaceted attributes of the culture in a school. An extremely diverse collection of people are involved with North Elementary, and two people may offer a more adequate description of such an inherently diverse culture as a school.

Two ethnographers were also important because Michael's mother was to be a principal informant. Their connection impairs objective analysis of this informant from Michael's point of view but not from Jenny's. Two ethnographers aids in collecting objective data from this particular informant. The mother-son intimacy cannot be considered good or bad, but pains were taken to present an unbiased model of Mrs. Allen's classroom.

The common interest of the two ethnographers in children and the educational system they inhabit provides a melding of ethnographic views. Sincere interest of the two ethnographers on a common topic allows more in-depth examination of a culture because they can work together to formulate a more fair model of the culture.

METHODS

The time we spent at North Elementary School was organized many different ways. We spent five out of ten school days observing at the school. The first time we went was to speak with the principal, Mr. Castle. This meeting was arranged through Mike's mother, Mrs. Allen. We talked with Mr. Castle about who we were and what we wanted to do at his school. He was very careful to make sure we would not be interviewing or testing the children. After our good intentions were established we began talking in earnest about what we would like to do.

First we talked with Mr. Castle about what our focus would be. At this point we were unsure. The decision was made that we would spend time in three different classrooms (a second grade class, a fifth or sixth grade class, and a special education class) for an overview so we could decide on a focus. Mr. Castle made the arrangements with the teachers he thought would be most amenable to our presence.

The first morning before school began we spent time watching and talking to the kids out on the playground. Then we both sat in Mrs. Rael's second grade class where we observed and took notes. Next we moved on to Mr. Wallace's fifth/sixth split class where we did the same thing. The next day Jenny spent a longer period of time alone in Mrs. Rael's class while Mike observed Mr. Wallace's and Mrs. Allen's special ed. class. That afternoon we both sat in Mr. Wallace's class again and then Mrs. Allen's. The next day was spent in Mr. Burdekin's sixth grade class and the special ed. class. The last day was spent revisiting all of the classrooms and getting more information from the teachers. During these days we observed and took notes, talked to the kids, and interviewed the teachers and other staff. Everyone was very helpful and encouraging.

ANXIETIES

Going in to the school for the first time, we really had no idea of what to expect. We did not know how well we would be accepted or what quality of data we would get. We also had very little clue about the type of data we would discover. We were anxious to be accepted by the teachers and the kids. We feared the data would not furnish us with a reliable ethnography. We also wondered if our presence there would affect the normal behavior of the classroom. We were nervous we might not be able to collect enough data. From our first day there, and even our first meeting with Mr. Castle, we were very excited. The kids were great and very welcoming. They were entertaining to watch and full of great data. The teachers were also very agreeable to our being there and very helpful. Our concerns about not being accepted or not getting good data were allayed. Many of these fears disappeared in the very beginning, but some lasted even until the final draft was handed in. Some doubts about the faithful representation of the school we have presented are still there and probably always will be.

[Descriptions of each classroom follow.]

CONCLUSION

We went into North Elementary School with little idea of what to expect. Our conceptions that a school was a relatively uncomplicated society changed quickly. What we found was a lot more than we expected. The school environment is much more complex than a group of teachers instructing kids in math, reading, social studies, and science. It is a complex blend of student and teacher values and peer interactions. School has become not only a place of teaching reading and math, but an institution taking the place of parents, church, and society. It must provide these for kids who lack much of it in their home lives. In this ethnography, we have attempted to give a faithful representation of the culture in an elementary school. By presenting this culture in slices, represented by the different classrooms, we hope readers can combine the parts into their own model of this culture. We have examined the slices independently and although the differences between them are large, we have discovered some common attributes that we feel partially define the culture found at North Elementary.

All of the teachers we talked to expressed a love of teaching. Each one said that he or she kept teaching not for money or power but because the teacher enjoyed doing it. Teaching is a job that requires endless patience. Students come and go from a teacher's sphere of influence, yet all of the teachers we talked to had been teachers for years or, if they were just starting, expected to keep on teaching. If teachers did not love what they do, we don't think they could keep doing it for years and years.

All the teachers, in their actions if not vocally, expressed the satisfaction of knowing that they were making a difference in a child's life. For better or for worse, elementary school teachers spend many hours in contact with young kids. When the student makes progress, a teacher gains personal satisfaction in knowing they had a hand in that student's progress. Teachers provide their students with skills that allow them to become functional members of society.

But the skills taught by the teachers we spent time with did not stop with reading, writing, and arithmetic. The teachers also provided a sanctuary within which kids could learn social skills, character development, and self-esteem in a nonthreatening environment. Some of these kids could not get such a shelter at home because in many families both parents work. This leaves kids without structure. Teachers in the school environment provide a safe place for the kids to be in for six and a half hours a day. There they can learn the skills they need to be a fully adapted member of society. Teachers teach kids a lot about the world in general. Granted, not every teacher succeeds in teaching these skills to every student. But to make a difference in one student's life seemed enough for the teachers at North Elementary.

All the teachers we spoke to thought that reading and writing were very important in the education of young people today. The general sentiment was that math was less important than reading and writing because if children can't express themselves in writing or read the words of other people, then . . . .

Most importantly, we saw the teachers as the preservers of culture. A few saw themselves in this way. Teachers pass on the tradition of knowledge. At first, it seems very basic, but what is our culture without knowledge? If the connection were broken, American society would have a very difficult time adjusting to a nation without communication. Teachers preserve the American way of life, for if there were no teachers, technology and philosophy would not advance. We feel this is true because, as linguistic beings, ideas must be expressed through words. If a group of people cannot communicate ideas between themselves, then how can they adapt to a changing world?

The morning we arrived at the school for our last day of observations the sky was blue, without a cloud. We talked to three of the teachers for the last time at lunch. Each of them mentioned that their kids were especially jumpy that day. Mr. Burdekin joked that a storm must be moving in, considering how his kids were behaving. An hour later as we drove away, rain sprinkled the windshield of our car. On the drive home, we laughed at the mysterious correlation. Then we got to thinking about it. We decided that schoolchildren were excellent barometers but not just for weather predictions. The changes in the United States regarding the increase of women in the work force, single-parent homes, and questionable economic times may be directly reflected in the culture of schools. Teachers have always helped to develop social skills, character, and upright moral stature in their students, but many teachers believe they must emphasize these skills more than in the past. Some teachers feel that schools are taking the place of parents in some respects. At any rate, changes in education directly reflect other changes in society. In times of drastic national and worldwide change, perhaps the youngest people of the new generation are the most sensitive to drastic change because they are the first to experience its ramifications. Maybe schoolchildren are as effective barometers as they are indicators of cultural change. Perhaps the restlessness of the kids reflects the restlessness of the world.

Intensive Care: An Ethnography of a Critical Care Unit

by Christopher Goodwin

Goodwin combined enthusiasm and discipline to a rare degree. His paper, as a result, is both exuberant and thorough. He offers rich reflexive comments and he covers the bases of data, methodology, and implications. Note that he defines "culture" and "society" explicitly, and gives his sources. An advanced student would be asked to go to the original passage for the quotes from Clifford Geertz, but in an introductory course, with the emphasis on field data and not on the literature, it is acceptable for Goodwin to quote Geertz out of Keiser, whose case study of black gangs in Chicago was one of those assigned at the time. Note also that his description of culture is largely a description of the language his informants use. Here, as in most ethnographies, culture is the symbolic expression of shared understandings, and symbols are usually (although not necessarily) words.

Goodwin uses his concepts rigorously and spells out the terminology thoroughly. Yet he makes us realize the equal importance of recording his enthusiasm; that is, he is at once an ethnolinguist and a reflexive postmodernist.

The most original aspect of his ethnography is his challenge of the official vertical table of organization with his own construct: a patient-centered model which indicates what actually goes on within intensive care. This construct shows us not only a creative mind at work, but the practical counsel which ethnographic field workers in their role as applied anthropologists can sometimes offer to clients. In this case the hospital director and other staff members were intrigued to see their institution through an outsider's eyes.

The paper was written in 1984. Goodwin completed medical school at Dartmouth and as this book goes to press is a family practitioner, obstetrician, father of five children, and playwright.

PREFACE

> 4/12/84 Today was my second full day (7–3 shift) in the Intensive Care Unit. My experience truly has been one of culture shock . . . the language (the terminology), the equipment, the technology, is all so foreign to me. I've left both days awestruck, fascinated, a little intimidated, and more certain then ever before that I want to be in medicine [from my journal].

This journal entry reflects the sense of excitement that has filled my three weeks of fieldwork at the Intensive Care Unit of Penrose Hospital. I chose the ICU for my ethnography initially because of my interest in the health professions and desire to go to medical school. My interest as a premed student remained strong—and increased—over the three weeks. Nevertheless, I did obtain useful ethnographic data both by intentional and accidental means, perhaps more by the latter.

The product of these past three weeks I hope is well documented here, not only as cultural description of a particular critical care unit, but as an ethnographer's experience as well, observing and participating for the first time in just one of many cultural scenes of the health professions in which this ethnographer will one day be an actor.

Words marked with an asterisk in the text are defined in the glossary at the end of the paper.

INTRODUCTION

Because the major purpose of the fieldwork assignment is to produce an ethnography, it is important to make clear just how I define ethnography. Ethnography is cultural description, understanding that to describe a culture "is not to recount the events of a society but to specify what one must know to make those events maximally possible" (Charles O. Frake 1964, quoted in Spradley and McCurdy, 1972:59).

Let it be understood that the "events of a society" correspond to the social system and "what one must know . . ." corresponds to the cultural system. The definitions of social and cultural system provided by Clifford Geertz are followed in this study:

On the one level there is the framework of beliefs, expressive symbols, and values in terms of which individuals define their world, express their feelings, and make their judgements; on the other level there is the ongoing process of interactive behavior, whose persistent form we call social structure. Culture is the fabric of meaning in terms of which human beings interpret their experience and guide their action; social structure is the form that action takes, the actually existing network of social relations. (Geertz, 1957; quoted in Keiser, 1979: viii)

My ethnography consists of the applications of these concepts of social and cultural system as observed in the cultural scene of an intensive care unit.

GETTING ESTABLISHED

Once I had decided to choose an area for my fieldwork that related to my interest in medicine, several possibilities came to mind. I have always been drawn toward situations that seem adventurous or exciting in some way. A trauma unit, critical care unit, or emergency room environment, it seemed to me, would provide a perfect context to observe people acting and reacting in situations uncommon to myself yet very common to themselves.

I also wanted to see how I would react in a tense, potentially life-or-death situation. First attempts at the emergency room of St. Francis Hospital led to a sequence of "I'm not sure who you'd need to talk to about that. . . ." I then called Dr. Donald Dawson, a pathologist at Penrose Hospital and, more importantly from the perspective of an ethnographer, a family friend and thus a potential connection or liaison. A short phone call explaining that I wanted to observe a critical care unit gave me the response, "I'll find out who you need to talk to. Call me back tomorrow morning and I'll let you know." I called the next morning and sure enough, he told me to call the Clinical Director of Special Care Services at Penrose Hospital, Joanne Petrick.

By now I had had several practice runs at trying to explain specifically what I was honestly rather unsure about. In other words, I had now focused my aim on one particular unit—the Intensive Care Unit at Penrose Hospital—and my interest was primarily as a premed student curious about the nature of such a unit.

When I first met with Joanne to explain this to her, I watched her carefully and was doubtful what her response might be. Yet as I began to speak, Joanne sat back and smiled lightly and maintained eye contact throughout my first breath of who I am and why I'm here. The sense of relief and new optimism was wonderful.

The initial contact with what would have been the necessary administrative approval became an inspiring, relaxed conversation with an interested, considerate person. I then mentioned the cultural anthropology class, which led to a discussion of some recent work she had done in the department that she felt was relevant. She then asked why I chose Penrose. For some reason I said because I was born at Penrose and that I live just down the street and that it only made sense to choose Penrose. I hadn't even thought of that before. I'm not sure why not, but it did seem perfect now, in a poetic way.

I received approval and encouragement to begin as soon as I desired. Joanne said she would "pass the word" on to nurses that I would be coming in. She suggested I report the next day at 7 A.M.

My gaining entree was greatly facilitated by being a premed student. Establishing rapport with my informants followed equally well. My informants were principally the nursing staff of the Intensive Care Unit (also the Coronary Care nurses, since the ICU and CCU nurses are all one staff). I did meet, observe, and interview others as well, which I discuss later. What is significant here is that I felt generally accepted by all I met in the unit.

I attribute my acceptance to a relationship that I noticed developed quickly between myself and an informant, even if the informant was initially suspicious about my intentions. This relationship was one of student and teacher. My excitement and curiosity as a premed student raised countless questions. My interest was genuine, even if the interest was in something bound to be explained in terms completely incomprehensible to me.

At first I was hesitant to bother anyone in the unit, afraid to interfere with such serious responsibilities, but I found they didn't mind. In fact, nearly all my informants seemed to love to teach (often more than I could understand!) and they said if they were busy they would simply tell me so.

FIELDWORK METHODS

I took this student-teacher relationship and ran with it as my main method for collecting data. After several conversations about what was going on medically in the unit I could get to questions about social and cultural aspects of the unit.

Typically there are always certain aspects of a given culture of which the data are simply unavailable to the ethnographer. Whether it be a gender, racial (as in Keiser's experience: Keiser, 1979:89), or even as age limitation, an ethnographer is just not going to have access to all the potential data. My limitation was of a different nature. I found my informants very open and willing to discuss any aspect of what I observed. I was limited by not remembering to focus on just the cultural data when that was what I was after. So often I was fascinated by what was going on medically and I would spend all my time asking medically related questions. I had to constantly remind myself, even with a note to myself in large letters at the top of my notepad: DON'T FORGET ETHNOG!

As I wrote in my journal entry on the second day of my fieldwork, I experienced culture shock because so much was foreign to me. This was especially true of the language. When nurses and/or physicians would talk, much would go right by because of the technical language of medicine. Of course they don't always talk in complex terms, but I would miss even some of the casual conversation and idle humor. As I reflect on the past three weeks, I can now see how this became less of a limitation as I learned more of the vocabulary. In fact, I even found myself using some of it!

THE SETTING

Penrose Hospital is located in the North End of Colorado Springs, at 2215 N. Cascade. The Intensive Care and Coronary Care Units are located in the southwest corner on the second floor. Though separate units, they are quite similar. As stated in a brochure on coronary and intensive care, "The purpose of the Intensive Care and Coronary Care Units is to provide the best patient care through the use of specially trained personnel and monitoring devices." Thus the kind of patient who is admitted to the ICU is the "critically ill" patient who needs close monitoring and possible help with respiration. These patients are not typically people with one ailment, but those afflicted with several interrelated complications. The Intensive Care Unit is set up to best serve this sort of patient (see Figure 1).

The central islands serve primarily as the nurse's station. The phones, H.P. heart monitor,* lab computer and house* computer and patient's charts are all on the north island. The south island has phones and an H.P. monitor with printout.

Each of the twelve rooms has a glass wall and sliding glass facing the center islands. Rooms 1–6 have windows allowing ample natural light by day. Rooms 7–12 are completely enclosed except for the glass front. Because of this, nurses like to fill rooms 1–4 first when possible. Beds 10–12 tend to fill next because of the proximity to the computers and charts located on the north island. Rooms 5–7 were never occupied while I was there. Each room is equipped to power all sorts of gadgetry: monitors, respirators (or ventilators),* infusion pumps,* hypothermia units,* suction lines, and so on.

There are three points of access to the ICU plus a fire escape in the southwest corner. The east door is the main door used by visitors and staff alike as well as for transporting patients. The two northern doors are used solely by hospital staff and physicians. The northwest doorway is a short hall connecting the ICU and the CCU The northeast door leads to the linen room and the hallway by the main elevators.

This setting allows for efficient monitoring and observation of the patients. The unit's compact nature means that a nurse, doctor, or respiratory therapist can respond to any situation within the unit without having to travel more than 14 or 15 meters. It also means that those who work the same shift are in immediate proximity of one another all the time.

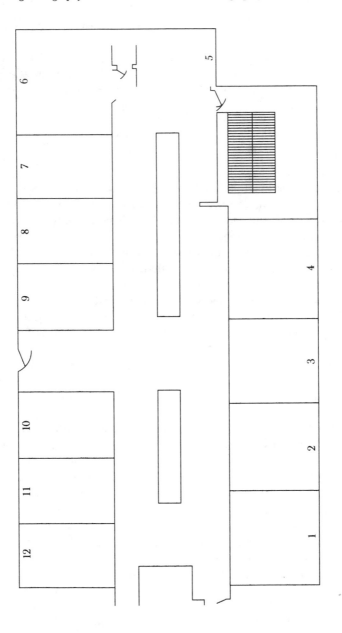

FIGURE 1

THE SOCIAL SYSTEM: ROLES

Geertz defines a social system as "the pattern of social interaction itself," as opposed to a cultural system which is "an ordered system of meaning and symbols in terms of which social interaction takes place" (in Keiser, 1979: viii). A hospital is one environment in which social interaction is given a very specific framework in which to take place.

The social roles of those working in a hospital are very stratified and task specific. Each status is well defined and can be found labeled on each person's lapel. That is, name tags include a title and/or school degree and the department for which the person works. Interestingly, none of the physicians I saw in the ICU wore name tags, although one always wore a white lab coat over his coat and tie that has his name and "MD" embroidered on it.

In the ICU I observed three positions: physician, nurse, and respiratory therapist. Of course, many people would be in and out of the unit all day: housekeeping, pastoral care, central services, and various technicians and administrators. I do not intend to ignore the diverse personalities of the individuals I worked with and observed, but I won't focus on them or use names for everyone. The three positions I chose to observe were those that were most often present and working in the unit. Because of this almost all my data center on the ICU nurses, with lesser amounts on physicians and respiratory therapists. Each of these positions has a varying degree of internal hierarchy. Where appropriate or relevant I discuss this hierarchy.

I was able to read several job descriptions, like that of a staff nurse and a head nurse. But here I give a description of the roles for each position as I observed it, as well as include descriptions and responsibilities as reported in interviews. Then I give several examples of kinds of social situations.

[Descriptions of the roles of physicians and respiratory therapists are omitted to save space.]

Nurses

Within the nursing staff I observed much more division or hierarchy as it related to the unit. The clinical director was the highest level administrator with whom I spent any time. She is a registered nurse and has worked in critical care units. At Penrose her function is the directing of special care services, which the ICU, CCU, and several other units fall under. This director is the one whom I obtained permission from to do my fieldwork. She was very helpful in providing all sorts of information.

Another administrator frequently seen in the unit was the administrative supervisor, whose territory is the whole house. This supervisor comes through to see how things are as part of monitoring all parts of the house and to make sure that areas are not under- or overstaffed on the particular shift. The administrative supervisor also directs the crisis nurse* to whatever area of the house as needed. The administrative supervisor is also an RN. Another responsibility of the admin. supervisor is to respond to all blues (also called "code blue" or "Dr. Blue")* and record all that takes place.

The actual nurses on duty in the unit consist of either a head nurse or assistant head nurse and several staff nurses. The number of them depends on the census* in the unit at the time. The pool of CCU-ICU nurses is 44 strong. The head nurse is the highest administrative liaison who actually works in the unit side by side with the other nurses.

On any given shift there is a charge nurse (either the head nurse, assistant head nurse, or a staff nurse on a rotating basis) who acts as a link with the previous shift by reporting* to the rest of the oncoming shift. The charge nurse must be familiar with each patient's chart* and condition and be ready to respond to help any staff nurse with a patient when the need is urgent.

The specific duties of an ICU nurse consist of highly skilled care to all types of severely ill patients. Here are a few of these duties:

* to provide emotional support to patients and family. I observed even when patients were unconscious or comatose the nurses talked to them, loudly if need be, to explain what they were doing and to reassure the patient.
* to take care of the patient's hygiene.
* to recognize immediately changes in the patient's condition and act accordingly.
* to use all sorts of highly specialized equipment.
* to start and administer intravenous medication and accurately monitor exact fluid intake and output when specified, to intubate and extubate.
* to know the protocol for responding to a life-threatening situation (as in code blues) without the actual direction of the physician.

Several factors seem to set the ICU nurses apart from other nurses. An interview one morning at 5:30 A.M. with the administrative supervisor, Betty Hagge, provided one perspective: "[The ICU nurses] are very skilled clinically, technically. Monitors, respirators, other machinery. . . . They keep their knowledge up and seem to thirst for new knowledge all the time. Colorado law requires that nurses have 30 hours each two years of inservice workshops. These [ICU] nurses probably have 60 hours a *year!*"

THE SOCIAL SYSTEM: SITUATIONS

The dominating factor in the Intensive Care Unit was the consistent low census. Out of a twelve-bed capacity, on the average four beds were occupied. For one twelve-hour period there was only one critically ill patient, so the unit was closed and the patient was moved into Coronary Care for the night.

The advantage of this was that it allowed me much more time to ask questions. Before my first day I had images of standing in a corner afraid to move while people raced back and forth not even noticing me. The nurses confirmed my beliefs by saying if the census were high, all I could do would be to stay out of the way because they'd be running.

The disadvantage of the low census is that I was rarely able to see the staff work in its most demanding and fast-paced situations. On two occasions I was able to get a glimpse of the staff when it was busy. Once was when the staff was short-handed and they had a code blue; the other time was when the census reached almost 75 percent capacity.

Although I observed the three positions described (physicians, nurses, respiratory therapists), almost all of the situations and interaction involved the nurses more than anyone else as they were always present and in the greatest numbers. Here are a few examples of typical situations:

Most of the casual talk among the nurses was focused in some way on the effects DRGs*—a prospective payment system—will have when they are implemented this July. In fact, nurses, doctors, and resp. therapists alike told me the main reason census was low was one result already of DRGs as the hospital prepares to switch over to the new system. This was all rather confusing at first. And it took a while to ask the right questions. On one of the first days while standing around the center island with several nurses I was told, "We're used to a fast pace. This [low census] is hard for us." The other nurses nodded in agreement. Initially I assumed it would be nice for a unit, which must normally be so stressed, to have some slow time to relax.

I still didn't know what was causing census to be low.

"Is census low through the hospital, or just in the ICU?" I asked one of the nurses.

"I think it is especially true in ICU with the DRGs coming in. Fewer people are coming in here," was the nurse's response. I was a little confused. Even if payment systems and the amount to be paid are changing, people still become critically ill, don't they? So why wouldn't the unit be just as busy as in the past? This confusion was straightened out in the following conversations:

1st Nurse:	The physicians decide if they want to admit their patient to the ICU. Soon it will be too expensive for many types of diagnoses and treatments to put a patient in here. Floor nurses are going to see sicker people . . . .
C.L.G.:	You said earlier that your role is changing. What has it been traditionally and what will it be?
1st Nurse:	For ICU nurses? We will be doing pretty much the same thing, treating very sick people, but so will other floors.
2nd Nurse:	I think the length of stay in ICU will shorten, census will rarely be high. And already we're decreasing our staff by attrition.
C.L.G.:	Do you feel that your job security is threatened?
2nd Nurse:	Well . . . some nurses think so, but I think we will just have to be more flexible and be prepared to float* more often.

A few days later, a conversation with another nurse finally helped me understand why low census was so frustrating to the staff:

C.L.G.: Things look pretty slow again today.

Nurse: I know. I don't want to talk about it, it's terrible!

C.L.G.: You know, a lot of people with service-oriented careers like it when they can say things are slow. They don't feel so stressed or pressured. Why is it that everyone here [the ICU staff] hates low census?

Nurse: We really like our work, Chris. We like working together. We don't like working on other floors [being floated] with nurses we don't know. And the type of care just isn't as challenging up there [on other floors]. And some days you don't even float, but are sent home to miss eight hours' pay.

C.L.G.: Then it isn't when you are here in the unit during low census that you don't like, it's the being floated or sent home that bothers you?

Nurse: Pretty much, yes. But like I said, when it's busy it's more challenging, and more of the people we like to work with are here working as well.

Another situation that is recurring in the unit is having to deal with a death and the constant possibility of a life-threatening (code blue) situation developing suddenly. During the three weeks I was doing my fieldwork 41 patients were admitted to the unit for an average stay of two days (at which point they are stabilized enough to move to another floor). Four of those patients expired* while in the unit.

The staff members I asked about how they dealt with death all gave responses similar in some way. Many joked about it. Once while I was there when they were telling death jokes one of the nurses turned and said to me rather self-consciously, "You probably think we have a pretty strange view of death . . . ." They all laughed. A resp. therapist walking by the island said to the nurse who just spoke to me, "You better be careful and watch him," she said smiling at me, "He's probably writing down everything you say!" and we all laughed.

Joking, or "cutting up," as one nurse calls it, is obviously a good pressure valve to relieve tension. But the joking doesn't seem to deal with the cases that really bother the staff. Some told me they get really involved in the follow-up. Others said they would become a little isolated and concentrate intensely on their other patients. Some said they thought the idea of an in-house support group was a good idea.

One answer I received from several nurses as well as one of the cardiologists was worded well by the cardiologist:

Psychologically? How do I deal with death? It depends how well I know the patient. When I'm on weekend call and it is someone who I didn't know at all it isn't very hard. But if it is an old friend as well as a patient it is real tough. Or if it is a young patient—a child—or a patient you've been treating for a long time. . . . But as long as you know you've done the correct thing, all that you're trained to do . . . all that is medically and humanly possible, it's in God's hands. . . . Can't get bogged down in self-blame.

The fact that doctors and nurses who work often in the ICU may have similar responses is best understood when they are seen working together in the social situation of a code blue. Here is one of my journal entries describing such a situation:

> 4/23/84 . . . I couldn't believe how quiet and calm everyone appeared as I entered the room. It was almost surreal. A frail, naked body was sprawled on an emergency backboard on the bed. There were 8 people in there excluding me. Two physicians, two resp. therapists, three nurses, and the Admin. Supervisor in the doorway scribbling down all that was happening. I looked at the monitor and recognized the "V-Tach" rhythm I had been taught the day before. That registered an alarm in my mind that said, my god this person is dying. But all those in the room were calm—too calm, I thought. One of the doctors looked over at me and said hello. I think I nodded. One of the nurses told him who I was and that I was here to observe. The doctor smiled at me, but immediately returned his focus to the monitor.
>
> Faces were calm, someone made a light joke, barely audible. Everyone chuckled. But by the way hands were moving swiftly and concisely, nurses setting up IV's,* one resp. therapist drawing blood gases, the other bagging* the patient with one hand while adjusting knobs and preparing a ventilator with the other hand . . . it was obvious they meant business. There was a quiet aggressiveness and determination in their actions which yanked at my heart and chilled me as I realized for the first time in my life I was standing in the same room where life and death were both so fantastically present.

I stood at the end of the bed next to one of the physicians. Pen and pad in hand, I was awestruck and unable to record anything. I tried to refocus and be an ethnographer, but that seemed so trivial compared with the struggle to save a patient's life. I didn't record any of the dialogue at the time, or anything else for that matter, but I do remember a good deal of it vividly.

This situation was intense, but obviously routine for the staff treating the patient. The doctor stood at the foot of the bed watching monitor and readings and then telling the others what to do. He was directing the activity, but wasn't actually doing any of the treatment. All his attention was on monitoring and quickly deciding what action to take. The doctor anticipated a change and ordered a nurse to get ready to shock him (i.e., defibrillate* him). Just then the patient's heart rhythm deteriorated from the V-Tach* to V-Fib.* A nurse calmly said "all clear" and pressed the defib. pads to the patient's chest. The still body jerked and stiffened and then went limp again. The shock restored a somewhat stable rhythm . . . at least for a while.

The team effort was the most striking element. The nurses were rushing to set up infusion pumps and IV lines; the resp. therapist who had drawn the blood gases ran back into the room with the lab results scribbled on a torn-off corner of scratch paper and read them off. A nurse predicted a treatment by asking if she should start a certain amount of one of the medicines in an IV line. The doctor nodded, but adjusted the amount a little. In the same breath he gave another nurse an order. In the twenty to thirty minutes I was there, more wires and tubes were hooked to the patient than I could count. Each member of the team was depending on every other member surrounding the bed. Time seemed to be the controlling factor.

The team was able to stabilize the patient and, slowly, as fewer people were needed, they went back to what they were doing before. The next day I heard that they had needed to shock the patient many times throughout the evening. After twenty-two defibrillations and seven hours later, the doctor and the patient's family decided to let him go. He expired sometime before midnight.

THE CULTURAL SYSTEM

Once again, the definition being used here for culture is "The framework of beliefs, expressive symbols, values by which they [a society] define their world, express feelings, make judgements." (Geertz, 1957; quoted in Keiser, 1979:viii).

Two aspects that strongly exemplify the cultural system of the Penrose Intensive Care Unit are the ways in which categories are organized and the main values, or ideologies as they will be called here, which the ICU staff hold in common.

The categories used by my informants are in two groups: the categories for patients and the categories for each other.

The categories for patients emphasize the task-oriented nature of the unit. While considerate, sensitive, and very human with the patients, among themselves the ICU staff acted more like mechanics. More often than referring to a patient by name, they would refer to the patient by the illness. Here are a few examples:

CATEGORY	DESCRIPTION
bleeder	a bleeding patient
GI bleeder	gastrointestinal bleeding
bypass	a heart operation, or an abdominal op. when called "gastric bypass"
heart	or sometimes "valve"; typically someone back from heart surgery other than a bypass
crani (pronounced cray-nee)	for head injuries and surgeries like a subdural hematoma, or bleeding under the skull

The list is nearly endless, as a patient can be categorized in terms of his or her ailment. The way the staff would talk about "the heart in 4" (i.e., room 4) or "the crani in 10" revealed that their primary motive was to get that "heart" and that "crani" stabilized and moved onto another floor and calmer environment.

Although there probably are nicknames and labels that the nurses use for certain doctors, and labels the doctors use for different nurses, I never heard any. Of course, the major categories used in the ICU correspond to the roles played by each individual. In an environment where each role is so well defined and task specific, and where each person depends so much on each other person to perform his or her duties competently, it only makes sense that the categories reflect each person's actual function.

This became clear to me one morning. I was standing in a patient's doorway watching a nurse and doctor treat the patient. When the doctor turned to leave and walked toward me we made eye contact and each of us silently recognized the other by a slight nod, but just then his eyes quickly diverted to my left breast pocket and then straight ahead, as he walked by me. I looked down at my white lab coat and realized that unlike almost everyone else I had no name tag! I imagined right then—and still think today—that the doctor was not completely aware that he looked to see who I was and what I was; there was such a reflex nature about his movements.

The way in which the categories are organized by the hospital, compared to the organization I observed in the unit, became a fascinating puzzle. The hospital organizes categories from an administrative perspective, typified by the organizational tree (see Figure 2) which I found pinned up in many of the administrators' offices.

This tree organizes the categories (or in actuality, the physical locations that correspond to the categories found there) both laterally and vertically. The vertical orientation shows where the power lies and suggests that the staff nurses are near the bottom of the tree and powerless. I'm sure this organizational tree was not in any way intended to show the relation of the patient to the rest of the hospital, but merely the internal structure of the hospital. Nevertheless, if a hospital's foremost concern is the patient, it would be useful to have a model of the organizational structure which incorporated the patient in some way. Without the patient included in the model there is no indication as to who has what amount of impact on the patient.

From my observations in the ICU, I found a quite different organization of the categories. I have attempted to represent pictorially the organizational structure I observed (see Figure 3).

This model is patient oriented, patient targeted. The model is designed to show both the relative amount of time spent with the patient by proximity to the patient and relative width of the ring. Who gives whom direction is shown by one ring encircling another. So even though the staff nurse is the lowest in terms of power to implement policy in both models, this model shows how it is the staff nurse who spends by far the greatest amount of time with the patient. Thus the staff nurse has the potential for

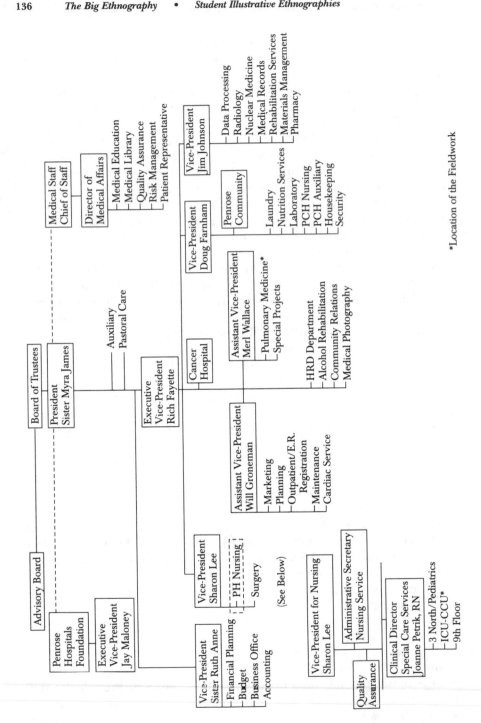

FIGURE 2

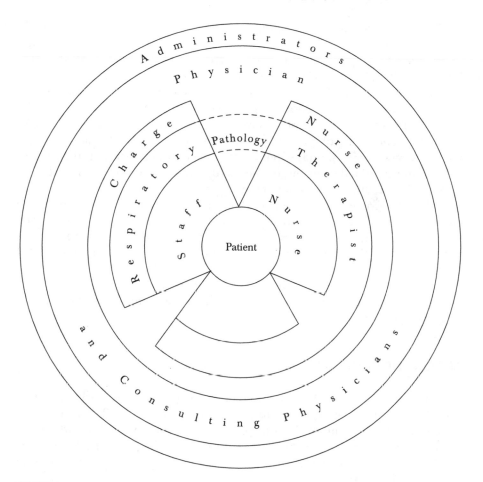

FIGURE 3

the greatest impact on the patient's recovery and attitude about the care he or she is receiving.

The respiratory therapist is not intended to appear to have more power or supervision over the staff nurse, but merely is the next ring away because of the amount of time spent with the patient. Here lies another difference between the two models. In the hospital's schema, the resp. therapists appear under "Pulmonary Medicine" which is quite removed from "ICU-CCU" (see Figure 2 where highlighted). The tree model provides no clue that resp. therapists and ICU nurses work together so closely.

I do not argue that the circular model ought to replace the tree model. For one, the organizational tree is for the whole hospital, whereas the patient-targeted model was designed only from observations in the ICU and is meant to show how different categories of individuals have shared values and common purpose. In fact, this model came to mind after I observed a code blue and the cohesive team effort became so apparent to me. Up to that point, almost all my data were exclusively from nurse informants. At the code blue I saw that all three of the categories I chose to concentrate on have not only a common goal (i.e., to do whatever possible to save a patient), but shared values and beliefs about how to best meet that goal.

To provide the best patient care is the lowest common denominator—a shared value or ideology—of not only the ICU but of the hospital as a whole. A moot point perhaps, but as it has been demonstrated, the patient can be unintentionally left out of the picture and temporarily lost in the administrative organizational complexity.

If the hospital were to be considered a complex society that holds one cultural value in common throughout the community, the ICU could be seen as a subculture; it has its own ideology which dictates how ICU staff pattern the way they pursue the common goal of providing the best patient care.

The unique ideology that the ICU team hold in common transcends the administrative organizational tree and operates more as the patient-targeted model demonstrates.

AGGRESSIVE IDEOLOGY

Several interviews brought out the idea of "aggressive care," which at first sounded horribly inappropriate to me. How, in such a fragile, critical environment, can a patient be treated aggressively? In one interview with an administrative supervisor who knows the nurses in all parts of the house (she has been a nurse at Penrose for fourteen years), I asked her to explain what she meant by aggressive.

"For one," she began, "there are more no-blues in Intensive now, especially cancer patients . . . even more young no-blues . . . so many new drugs, treatments and equipment, these [ICU] nurses will be aggressive all the way to the end; they won't quit. They've bought five to six months for people that way."

"So by aggressive, do you mean they don't quit?" I asked.

"Well, yes, but it's more than that. . . . They must be aggressive nurses: they'll bitch, complain, find things wrong. They'll stand up to a doctor—not afraid to call a doctor day or night. They're aggressive to each other. They will call another nurse on her methods if they don't think she is performing effectively. They want to get people well and get them off all that equipment as soon as they can. Most of them are perfectionists—they have to be, have to pay attention to detail."

I asked the same sort of questions of one of the doctors I saw often in the unit.

"They are very different than other nurses," he explained. "On wards there aren't even IVs. Here [ICU] there are tubes in and out of every orifice. ICU nurses have to know just what they are working with. . . . TLC isn't as important in here as it is on other wards. Traditionally ER and ICU appeals to younger nurses who like the intense atmosphere . . . it can be grueling. They have to be able to handle sudden changes and sudden death. It takes a certain nurse to do that."

The aggressive method became most clear to me when I observed the code blue. Despite the superficial calmness, everyone in the room was focused on that patient and doing everything they could to bring him back. Aggressive treatment does not mean the ICU staff is callous, but is the way they exhibit how much they care and want to move the patient on to better health. Aggressive also connotes confidence and decisiveness. In an environment where sudden changes occur, the staff must be able to act swiftly, confidently, decisively. The aggressive ideology is also reflected by the staff's thirst for new knowledge.

CONTINUAL LEARNING IDEOLOGY

Every day I observed the staff asking each other questions and exchanging knowledge about different methods and treatments. As the administrative supervisor I interviewed said, "So many of the nurses are timid. Not critical care nurses. If they don't understand something, they'll ask a doctor why. And the doctors like that because it isn't criticism but a true desire to learn. And doctors love to teach. That's how these kids learn."

They also share their knowledge and learn a good deal from each other. It is this ideology from which I learned so much as a premed student and gained so much as an ethnographer.

CONSTANT CHALLENGE IDEOLOGY

I finally established some of the reasons the ICU nurses dislike low census so much. One of these was the dread of being floated to another floor and having to give less challenging, less specialized care. As one nurse told me about floating, "I don't like running up and down the halls giving pain pills and pain shots and filling out charts for ten patients. I really like having to work one to one with a patient that requires a lot of attention." Another nurse said of the low census, "We're all used to a fast pace. This is hard for us."

I asked one nurse why she chose critical care as opposed to another area to work in. She responded by saying, "I think I need the challenge not found on a regular floor: the need to be constantly updating myself with the latest treatments, latest technology, plus filling all the needs of the critically ill patients."

CONCLUSION

Part of the frustration with the low census is the conflict the ICU staff feels with the administration. It is always easy to label and blame a collective, non-individualized "they," which any type of administrative body is faced with. But what is the conflict at Penrose Hospital? For some of the staff there is no conflict. These people see the situation (of low census) in a certain way and accept it. But for all of the Intensive Care Unit staff, there was a general frustration of not having enough control over how they go about doing their job. But why should there be this frustration? Why should there be any conflict if they all have the same fundamental goal of providing the best patient care?

The problem becomes apparent when the means of reaching that common goal are looked at. The ICU might have certain values that the administrators wouldn't need in their sphere of influence. Likewise, the administrators might have things to consider that might not seem relevant to a nurse's concerns in a critical care unit. See Figure 4 for a diagram that illustrates the situation.

There is a need to better understand each other's values, needs, and means of accomplishing a task. I had been told about a program called PIP (for "Pride in Performance"), which is designed to give the nurses some input into the creation and implementation of new ideas. But it is still within the framework of the vertical/lateral organizational tree, and for new ideas to climb up the tree is always slower and more difficult than it is for policies and regulations to slide down.

The conflict is certainly not a new one. But with the advent of DRGs the conflict has been accentuated and is coming to a head. A hospital at

FIGURE 4

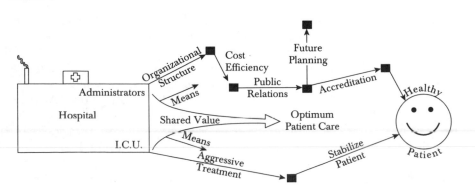

least 50 percent of whose patients are on Medicare has to become cost efficient in order to survive. This ultimately means for the ICU staff that they will probably have to do a lot of adjusting and getting used to changes like lower census and having to float to less specialized floors. The administrators can do their part by making the ICU staff—and other staffs—a more integral part of the decision process in the future. Also, when constructing a model of the hospital's organizational structure, the patient should be included if the model is to be a working one.

I began with a preconception of entering a high-drama, action-packed environment where life and death struggles happened daily. While that element was real—and I observed some of it—it didn't predominate. The ways in which the nurse's role is and will be changing were the predominant elements and what frustrated the nurses the most, especially when the changes are out of their control.

Death is something hard for them to deal with. Even so it is a phenomenon they face often. Some think an internal support group would be beneficial. But they can deal with it. They can know if they have done all that they could, all that is medically and humanly possible, to save a life. Furthermore, death is not necessarily a negative, as one nurse pointed out to me, "Some people deserve to die, Chris. There are a lot of worse things than death, and we see those things here."

GLOSSARY

bag   Verb used to describe artificial respiration by manual use of an airbag. Example: She bagged the patient while he gave chest compressions.

census   Total number of patients in a given unit, floor, or the house, as specified.

chart   Complete set of documents, orders, diagnoses, and history, for a given patient. The information here, as in the doctor's orders, is the legal record for the patient.

code blue   Term given to a patient's condition when he or she is in a life-threatening condition, in cardiac and/or respiratory arrest. The people assigned to code blue on a given shift must respond to whatever part of the house makes the alert. These people are legally responsible to do everything in their power to save the patient. A "no-blue" refers to a patient who has been designated such by the physician, meaning that if the patient enters a life-threatening condition no code will be called, but the assigned nurses will administer predetermined amounts of treatment. If they are unsuccessful the patient will be permitted to expire. Equivalents for code blue: "code," "blue," "Dr. Blue."

crisis nurse   Nurse who is assigned by the on-shift administrative supervisor to whichever area most needs urgent immediate assistance. Also responds to code blues.

defibrillator   Device that uses electric shock to restore a normal heart rhythm when a patient goes into cardiac arrest.

DRGs   Diagnosis Related Groups: a proposed payment system for all Medicare patients. Approximately 400 groupings of diagnoses by the federal government by which hospitals are being required to operate. It means a flat fee will be prorated and will correspond to one of the 400 groups. These price controls award cost efficiency and penalize lack of efficiency.

expire Verb: to die.

extubate Verb: to remove an airway tube from someone's throat.

float Verb: work in an area of the hospital different from normally assigned area. Typically happens when the assigned area is at a low census while another area needs more workers. Example: "She floated to 9th floor tonight; they were shorthanded."

house The hospital complex.

H.P. heart monitor Hewlett-Packard monitoring device that shows the patient's heart rhythm and rate on a green display screen.

hypothermia unit Machine used to regulate patient's body temperature.

infusion pump Machine that controls the rate and amount of a certain intravenous line.

intubate Verb: to insert a plastic tube or airway into the patient's trachea.

IV Intravenous, as in a line for medicine or nutrients.

respirator Machine that breathes for the patient by supplying oxygen at a certain rate and alternating pressure to expand and deflate the lungs. Also called a ventilator.

V-Fib. Ventricular fibrillation: the state in which the heart is no longer beating but is quivering or fibrillating such that there is no cardiac output (blood flow).

V-Tach Ventricular tachycardia: greatly accelerated heart rate at which point cardiac output is greatly reduced, since the blood in the heart cannot continue through because of the too rapid successions of opening and closing valves.

Ethnography of a Greyhound Track: A Study on Social Stratification and Diehards

by Stephanie Smith

Who would have thought that customers at a racetrack (short of Ascot with its Royal Enclosure) would stratify themselves, and be stratified by management, into three distinct categories? Smith says she thought she had found a quick-and-dirty solution to the problem of doing the big ethnography, but seduced herself, instead, into a thoughtful probe of racetrack fans. She handles with a light humorous touch in the first two paragraphs something that characterizes a great deal of ethnography, both amateur and professional: The work is dangerous to prejudices and preconceptions and will always challenge and may change them. Many student papers report the same process, almost always with the same air of surprise. (See, for instance, the next paper on a strip bar.)

Smith makes no attempt to "study" the dogs, the managers, the ownership of the track, or the culture of employees. By sticking to customers she not only keeps her task within the bounds of feasibility, but also produces a well-focused paper that says a good deal about the informants she chose to describe.

She also uses a writing style full of verbs and nouns, chary of adjectives and adverbs; the result is speedy prose that matches her topic. In one respect she is too speedy for her own good: "Diehard" is a central concept, which she uses but never defines. Compare the exhaustive glossaries of White's and Goodwin's papers.

When I thought about taking on the Rocky Mountain Greyhound Park as the subject for my ethnographic study, I had some preconceived notions about what it would be like. I wanted to study the "type" of person who participated in the dog races. I was assuming there was one type of person I could classify and study, no problem. I imagined this seedy place with lots of middle-aged down-and-out loners, placing bets with money they hocked their TV to get. I was convinced I could construct a model of this type and fit all of my informants into the mold.

Then I went out to the track. My first thought was, "Oh S——!" as I looked around at the crowds of senior citizens, young couples, business types, and even families with four children. A two-second look around at the track will clue in any moron to the fact that the crowd is a diverse mishmash of every type of person. I had a lot of work to do.

Along with the physical and age diversity was the difference in intentions. Not everyone goes out there just to bet. Some go for the entertainment with the kids or the food. Some go for the novelty of betting, picking dogs for their names, or look at the minimum $2 bet. Others are more serious, studying the dogs and placing big bets. The more I studied, the more I began to see an underlying social structure. This structure is determined by the three areas from which the public can watch the races. Although the focus of my study is not the actual greyhound race, that is the reason everyone is there. I think it is important to understand what the races, the park, and wagering, are all about.

THE COMMON DENOMINATOR: THE SETTING

The Rocky Mountain Greyhound Park opened in 1949, a few months after the first track in Pueblo started. Located in the north-central part of Colorado Springs, it sits on approximately 25 acres off Nevada Avenue. The elevation is over 6,000 feet, and to this day RMGP remains the highest greyhound park in the world. It is a part of a nationwide system of 57 tracks. Until this year the racing season at RMGP had been three months in the fall. Due to a recent court decision in which the state of Colorado approved tracks to operate live racing six months a year, the season has been changed to April through September. (Although not publicized, gambling or wagering occurs all throughout the year via closed circuit television. People gather at the park and wager on live races broadcast from other parks.)

The RMGP consists of a racing track, spectator stands (indoor and outdoor), an administrative building, and an immense parking lot (see map). Spectators have three areas to choose from: the Grand Stands, the First Turn Tavern, and the Cloud 9 Restaurant. Admission to each area is $1, $2, and $3, respectively. Race programs sell at $1.25. The park and all areas are opened to the public one hour before the program begins. The program is a set of races, usually 13, that take place one or two times a day. Matinees take place at 1 P.M. Wednesday and Saturday; evening performances take place at 7:30 P.M. A typical 13-race program will last three and a half hours. Most of my work was done during the evening programs.

PROCEDURE OF A RACE

Many people arrive as the park opens an hour before the first race. I had even seen a small group waiting for the gates to open one Friday evening.

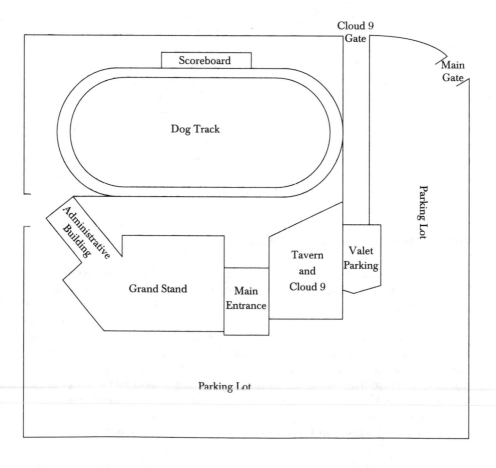

I noticed that the majority of people who arrive at the park early come to figure out their bets, study the night's dog selection, and to view the previous night's replays on the many TVs that cover every nook and cranny of the place.

About fifteen minutes before post time the dogs are paraded before the spectators. There are eight dogs per race, each one wearing a numbered blanket and a muzzle. (The muzzles are worn only to determine the outcome in photo finishes.) They come out single file in numerical order led on a leash by official handlers. Each dog is subject to an inspection; the muzzle and blanket are pulled and tugged. The purpose is to show each dog and its statistics up close on the TV screens. The dogs are paraded up and down the length of the track for all the spectators to see. During this time the people can change or confirm their choices and place a bet. When the scoreboard says "O min to post," the dogs are placed in the gate according to their numbers. At the announcer's last call the handlers leave the gates and the lights are turned out in the spectator areas. An Aldritt mechanical lure they call "Rocky" then pops out of its gate making its way to the dogs' gate. The announcer does a Johnny Carson type "HERERRRRRRRRRR's ROCKYYYYYYYYYYYYYYY" at the end of which the gate to the dogs is opened, and the dogs are off.

The greyhounds take off from the gate chasing the lure, reaching speeds from 25 to 40 mph. The general speed of the race is determined by the class, "A" being best, "E" and "M" being the lowest ranked. The first turn is usually the deciding factor in the race. The best dog can easily trip or be knocked out on the first turn. After the dogs come out of this turn, the leading two or three dogs are apparent. Of course this can always change, which is what people are literally betting on. When the dogs have gone three-quarters of the track, a light shines on the finish line. The dogs pass the line and a picture is taken. If the 1st, 2nd, and 3rd places are obvious then the paybacks are listed on the scoreboard and TVs right away. If there is any doubt, the picture is analyzed and scores held back until the judges reach a conclusion.

Meanwhile the dogs are stopped by a net farther down the track. The dogs are herded into one area and the handlers scramble to get their dogs back on the leash. The dogs once again are led single file in numerical order back to their respective trainers. The next batch of eight dogs take their place in the lineup to be paraded. This exact procedure is followed for every race I saw. It was pulled off smoothly even in inclement weather and as it says at the bottom of the race programs, "strict post time observed."

GRAND STAND AREA

The Grand Stand area holds the largest number of people, 3800, and at $1 is the least expensive to gain entrance to. It is a huge indoor structure with three levels that look out a wall of windows onto the track. The first level is primarily food and betting windows. The entire north wall is dedicated to betting windows (and one information booth), 34 total. There are two bars and concession stands on the south side. The food consists of hot dogs, hamburgers, chips, popcorn, nachos, candy bars, and such. The bars offer beer, wine, and mixed drinks. There are many doors leading to the patio on this side. Scattered all over are TVs. Between the two main stairways are rows of chairs facing large TVs.

The second level is tucked under the main Grand Stand area, above the first level. This is similar to the offerings of the first level. It has 20 windows, one food stand, and one bar. A large-screen floor TV dominates the attention around the tables and rows of chairs. The third level is where most of the seating is. It is just like Grand Stand seating, with reams of seats, one right next to the other, sloped toward the event. Seating right in front of the window is divided into boxes. It costs $2 to sit in a box seat. Box seats offer a better view of the track, cushioned seats with arm rest/drink holder/ash tray, and separation from the general crowd. The range of people that attend the races, especially in the Grand Stand area, is extremely diverse. The dress is casual—jeans and more jeans. I estimate the percent of whites who attend runs about 60 percent. The other 40 percent consist of mostly black, then Hispanics and Asians. There are couples, families, groups, and "solos." The couples range widely in age and race. The elderly couples usually settle in the box seats close to the window. Usually the man gets up and down, presumably to bet, while the woman sits in her seat. Young couples sit in the Grand Stand area toward the window and bet together. Then there are the buddy couples. Quite a few male duos hang out there, of either the same age or father/son type. I saw very few female duos.

I was surprised to find so many families. The families tend to favor the box seating. Many couples bring their children out to the track, and extended family groups, with grandparents, cousins, and so on, are not uncommon. Children under 18 are not allowed to place bets but they can be in certain areas. The next classification, the solos, were the most interesting to me. This is the type I expected to dominate the scene at the track. The solos are people who hang out at the track alone. My own stereotype for a solo is a 40+ male who hangs out in the upper section of the Grand Stand away from other people. He bets on every race using a system he invented. Since this characterization is a stereotype, I found exceptions to it but not many.

One of my informants who frequents the Grand Stand area is "Flamingo," a 35-year-old black man with a granddaughter. He likes to come to the track by himself, claiming "I'm a loner, I cook for a living. I see [enough] people." He plays the dogs every day the track is open but does not consider himself a "diehard." Diehards are "the ones you can't see. They hang out in the Cloud 9 Room. Instead of work, they are here all the time."

Flamingo uses a system of betting that allows him to stay away from the track. He comes up with three numbers and then plays the trifecta (see "wagering") with the same numbers the whole night. He does not know statistics or other information about the dogs like some diehards do; he just plays the numbers. Usually he bets in the future for a whole program. This means he will pick his numbers and place his bets for say a Friday night program on Thursday. This way he does not have to be at the track during the races. "This is not exciting to me! I don't have time for this s——! I look in the paper [the next morning] like a kid at Christmas to see if I won." If he wins he can collect the money the next day.

Flamingo claims to do quite well at the track. He uses the winnings as a supplement to his job income. "I could take a second job, but I take a chance on this." I saw him win with this method. Apparently on one Friday he won $130, Saturday night, $106, and Monday, $480. All of these paybacks were off $2 bets. "I've made about $800 in the last three days out of 48 bucks. I expect more but I settle for this." When Flamingo told me these figures I just kind of nodded my head thinking "yea, RIGHT!" However I saw him win $130 from only $2. Something in his method works.

FIRST TURN TAVERN

The First Turn Tavern is located on the first level in the building west of the Grand Stand area. The tavern has two entrances, one from the main gate and another on the west side of the building. This entrance is exclusively for the tavern and the Cloud 9 Room. Access to the Tavern cost $2 and no one under 18 is allowed. The price includes the use of a table for the duration of the program. The decor of the room is in oak, brass, etched glass, and maroon plastic tabletops.

The Tavern has a capacity of 300. There are four tiered levels of tables and chairs all facing the track. Each table has a small TV that operates for an extra $1.50 and broadcasts network TV as well as the Greyhound information. The Tavern offers food and beverages in a bar-type atmosphere. The foods offered are various appetizers, burritos, deli sandwiches, salads, cakes, and ice cream. The bar serves beer, wine, and mixed and blended drinks. The food and drinks are pricier in the Tavern than the Grand Stand, and everything is served to the tables by a waitperson. The only reason to get up from your table is to bet (or go to the bathroom). The Tavern has 17 betting windows.

The first thing I noticed when I walked into the Tavern was a sign that said,

AVOID INCONVENIENCES
BY REFRAINING FROM EXTREMES
IN CASUAL DRESS

I suppose "extremes" is the operative word in that request because the dress of Tavern patrons is quite casual. As in the Grand Stand area, the main trend is jeans. For men, shirts tend to be short-sleeve Izod types, and button-up cotton shirts, a step above the T-shirt. The women are just as casual in printed shirts and blouses.

Another major difference about the Tavern people is their age. The 18-and-over policy no doubt raises the average age. Interestingly there are more young-to-middle-aged people than anything else. The proportion of whites in the Tavern rises to about 80 percent, the other 15 percent black and 5 percent Hispanics and Asians. The ratio of elderly persons seems low in comparison to the Grand Stand area, and there are no families. The majority of types in the Tavern are groups of three to five. There are mostly men, but women are definitely an active part of the Tavern scene. The solos who do hang out in the Tavern either do so in the very front, where no one else can see them, or in the back standing at the counter.

The social atmosphere is similar to that of a bar. The low ceiling imposes an air of intimacy not found in the Grand Stand area or the Cloud 9 Room. Everyone has a drink at their table. The waiters and waitresses socialize with the customers and know a good many of them on a first-name basis. The table seating arrangement causes people to look at each other and interact more than if they were sitting shoulder to shoulder in rows of seats. By the same token people do not walk around to other tables and mingle as often as in the Grand Stand area. The wagering seems to be taken quite seriously. Many tables are crowded with various racing papers. Reams of notes are being taken and lots of bets are made.

Mark jokingly refers to himself as a "degenerate gambler." He says, "True pros will sit in the Grand Stand." But Mark is a pro; I consider him a diehard. He hangs out in the Tavern just about every night the track is open. He is a white male in his late thirties (his age is a guess because he would not tell me), has a mustache, wears glasses and dresses in short-sleeve polo shirts and jeans. "Professionally I'm a U.S. Merchant Marine. On my time off I play the dogs [to support myself] until I run out of money."

Whenever I see him he is always very friendly and willing to talk to me, but 95 percent of the time his eyes are on the TV screen. He carries around a spiral book of notecards, which he constantly writes on. I have seen the cards a few times, but I cannot make any sense out of his diagrams and figures. Like most diehards he has a method for betting but he is not eager to reveal it to me. I am not sure I could even understand it. I can say it is extremely analytical. Unlike Flamingo, Mark is definitely interested in what the dogs look like, their weight, present and past performance, and other statistics. Unfortunately, he would not give me exact figures on his paybacks, and he placed future bets so that I never saw the amount of money he bet with. But I can only assume, given Mark's serious dedication and attention, that his bets average much more than the $2 minimum.

CLOUD 9 ROOM

The Cloud 9 Room is a restaurant located above the First Turn Tavern. It is structured similarly to the Tavern. The Room has four tiered levels of tables, a full bar and food selection, a capacity of 300, and its own betting windows, 11 total. The decor is dark wood, brass, glass, carpeting, and linen tablecloths and napkins. The ceiling is quite high and every table seems to offer a good view of the track.

The restaurant has its own gate to the park (although it can be easily reached by the main gate) and one entrance to the building. Valet parking is offered at $1 to patrons. Upon entrance to the building you must stop at a hostess booth to pay the $3 cover charge and to confirm your reservation; there is no admittance to the Cloud 9 without one. At the bottom of the escalator that whisks you up to the restaurant is a sign that says,

IMPORTANT NOTICE TO CLOUD NINE PATRONS
Proper attire must be worn for admittance
to the Cloud 9
Body Shirts, frayed jeans, tank tops, shorts
and similar styles are not accepted

At the top of the escalator is another hostess booth. A host in a tuxedo takes your reservation slip, checks it against his records, then leads you to your table. Each table has a number, which is given to you in case you want to request that table again. It is just like the procedure at a fine restaurant. The menu has appetizers, steak, seafood, pasta entrees, ice cream, cheesecake, coffee/tea, and vintage wines. There are many servers around to cater to your needs. The waitpersons are very friendly and attentive. Like the Tavern servers, many of the Cloud 9 servers know their customers by name.

The crowd was about 95 percent Caucasian, 5 percent Asian on the night I went to the Cloud 9 Room. The dress varies from nice casual to dressed up. The standard dress for men is a clean short sleeved polo shirt and slacks. Some wear sport coats, suits, or designer sweat suits. It is similar for the women, who wear mostly slacks and blouses, some dresses and some designer sweat suits. Couples dominate this scene. I took a census at one point and out of 30 occupied tables, all were mixed couples or groups except one. That table had two men.

Socializing is the key theme in the room. It is not the milling and mingling around type of interaction characteristic of the Grand Stand area. Socialization occurs at the tables. It does not take long to figure out it is a highly social atmosphere within the table unit. There is much laughter and conversation in the air. Most people have smiles on their face directed at the person across from them instead of the track below them. There is not a dominant preoccupation with betting that is characteristic of the Tavern and among the Grand Stand diehards.

"This is the only place to be," said Mary, an elderly woman who is a regular with her husband Jim at the Cloud 9 Room. They frequent the dog track circuit, which runs from Pueblo to Denver (Cloverleaf). Although the drive from Canyon City is a pain, Mary and Jim do it every weekend to have dinner and bet on the races. To Mary the Colorado Springs track is her favorite because apparently the other tracks do not offer good dining rooms to hang out in.

Mary does not do any betting; she leaves it up to her husband. "I don't come here for the gambling . . . . I like to watch the dogs run. I'm a ranch girl." Jim has the concentration of a diehard. With pen in hand and eyes on the TV screen, he is constantly scribbling on his program and putting his hand on his forehead to think. He keeps himself much too involved to ever talk to me. I can sense he does not want to tell me anything. Mary is quite happy to converse, since she is just there for the entertainment. When I finally asked Jim about the amount he spent on each bet he muttered, "Oh not much, certainly not much for this room." Then Mary piped in, "Oh pooh. You spend about $20 on each bet; I'd say that was a lot of money." After that Jim told me he usually manages to pay for dinner, traveling expenses—he breaks even.

ANALYSIS/INTERPRETATION

There are so many intricacies at the dog track it is difficult to define the whole "culture" of the place. What makes the culture of the track is the people. The diversity of people is immense and what keeps them coming back is the entertainment, the social opportunity, and of course the wagering, that "$2 dream." At the risk of sounding like a commercial, it truly has something to offer everyone. Because of this the track draws from every social stratum of the city. I found on any given night that the track has a cross section of society in attendance. But the different social classes are not interacting together. The diverse appeal would not be there if everyone were meant to mingle.

A social hierarchy exists, which is staked out quite clearly by the three rooms. The Grand Stand represents the working class, the Tavern is the middle class, and Cloud 9 is the upper class. This structure is supported and perpetuated mainly by the diehards, who maintain myths and preconceived notions about the different sections.

The administration for the dog track has handled this situation quite shrewdly. The Tavern and Cloud 9 Room did not exist until 25 years ago. Before then both the buildings were Grand Stand areas. Stacie Taylor, head of promotions and publicity, acknowledges that there was a need for the type of services that the Tavern and Cloud 9 offer. She says they have served most successfully as facilities for group parties and fund-raiser benefits.

Whatever the intentions of the administration, the different rooms make it possible to separate oneself from others. This is an idea more appealing to the upper class, so it makes sense that the areas reserved to them have restrictions in dress, high prices, and an emphasis on service. It is also no surprise that whites dominate the scene. It is all a reflection of the social hierarchy that exists in the community.

But the nicer areas are not inaccessible to the everyday Joe. It is not like a club where you have to "belong" and be voted on to gain entry. Admittedly, the signs concerning dress code in front on the Tavern and Cloud 9 do have a deterring effect. Any sign indicating some restriction immediately sets off a signal in a person's head that there is some type of assumption about the customers and the atmosphere. I felt some trepidation when I first walked up the ramp toward the hostess booth at the Tavern. Was I dressed OK? Will I stand out too much? But other than fitting in in a superficial sense, I had no worries. If you have the money, entry to the Tavern or Cloud 9 only takes a little planning ahead.

Interestingly, the diehards all have their theories about one another, according to the room. Flamingo told me that the real hard-core diehards were the "ones you can't see" in the Cloud 9 Room. If I were to believe his theory, Cloud 9 would be a place full of solos in suits calmly smoking cigarettes and placing thousand dollar bets. In reality I found the Cloud 9 Room to be a highly social place, with no solos. *[Informants' and ethnographers' perceptions occasionally contradict one another. Contradictions should be highlighted, as Smith has done.]* In fact the crowd would get extremely rowdy during a race, more so than in the Tavern, yelling for their dog to win. My informant Mary, a little old lady going blind in one eye, even started yelling, "Go baby go!" at one point.

The high-rolling diehards that Flamingo imagines *do* exist in the Cloud 9 Room according to Lissa, my waitress one night. I never had the opportunity to speak to them. They either pretended they didn't know what I was talking about, did not want to talk, or really were not diehards. Lissa told me, "I've worked here two years . . . you see a lotta lotta money. I've talked to a couple people here, asked if they had day jobs and they said no. They just follow a winner around [the circuit] and make their money." When I asked her how much a "lotta" money is she told me about $2,000 to $5,000 a bet. Mark thinks that the pros are really in the Grand Stand. I could never quite get to the bottom of his reasoning for this, but he seemed pretty sure about his opinion.

Jane, a cocktail waitress in the Tavern, told me, "There is a different crowd here than at the Grand Stand. They spend money to come in and sit. [People in the Tavern] are willing to spend money in here, there is nicer dress in here. Plus there are no tabs, so I make more in tips. People come in here holding a lot of money."

Crossovers into different areas happen often; the culture does not demand that you stick to one room. But the social stratification between the rooms is so obvious it is hard not to notice it. The mobility among the rooms exist in a downward direction, much more than upward. Nonetheless, the spectrum of intentions from the little old lady who bet $2 on a dog because of the name, to the diehard 30-year-old with reams of notes placing $2,000 bets to pay the rent, all exist at each level. The ratio of the types in each room varies, but they are all in there. The main difference is appearance and bank account. This is obvious from the similarity of offerings in each area. The basics are the same for every room: food, drinks, bathrooms, a view of the track, a place to sit, betting windows, TVs, and people.

I also believe the track is a great service to the people of the community. There are many benefits for the large number of senior citizen patrons: free admission for 60+ and nighttime escorts to cars. Families may bring their children so they do not have to find a babysitter or stay home. On a more subtle social level, as one informant said, "It's a good place to learn about people—lots of weirdos." Perhaps "weirdos" is pushing it, but I think she was right in her assessment of the situation at the Rocky Mountain Dog Track. It is a good place to learn about people and provides a perfect model of how social stratification works. And hopefully make a buck or two in the process.

Women of the Night: An Ethnography of the Women Who Work at Kitty's

by Elizabeth Cunningham and Kathryn Hayes

This ethnography, like Irving and Allen's on the elementary school, shows the advantage of working in teams. It probes discrepancies between informants. It is also a good example of gender-specific strength. Male ethnographers either would have been unable to study a strip bar at all or would have produced quite different results, in which the intimate picture of the dancers would have been replaced by emphasis on the manager, the bartender, or perhaps on the bar as a business. Inventory your special abilities, and work with, not against them.

Names of employees and the name of the bar have been changed. Names of all other individuals in the paper are unchanged.

This paper tells the reader more than most such ethnographies about the moral climate of the city surrounding the scene. A mark of good ethnographic work is to shed light on cultural environments as well as on the micro-cultures described.

Descriptions of the setting (glossary) are good; a floor plan would have been welcome.

The following is a list of company rules to be put into effect *immediately!!!*
- Male employees must wear a dress shirt with tie, dress slacks, no jeans. Hair must be off ears and collar. Be on time for your shift.
- Female employees—costumes will be in good repair at all times. Costumes to include heels or boots also in good condition. Heels or boots to be worn at all times while on the floor of the club. Make-up, hair styling, and nails are important also.
- Girls may not go outside without an escort.
- If you are not scheduled do not hang around club.
- When you are here to work your current husband, boy/girl friend, and/or love interest is not allowed in club!!
- The most important part of being an entertainer is attitude. Before leaving the dressing room please look in the mirror and ask yourself "Would I tip this person?"

We read these rules posted outside of the manager's office while we first waited to speak to the manager about the possibility of researching Kitty's. The rules gave an idea (but not an entirely accurate idea) of the culture we would soon be entering. For the next two weeks we frequented the adult club called Kitty's, and our stereotype of strip bars radically changed. We visited at various times of the day and evening and spent the majority of the time in the dressing room talking to the dancers and observing the activities of the back room. Life at Kitty's centered around the dancers, and consequently we centered our research on the dancers and their relationships with the rest of the employees.

THE ORDINANCE

The manager appeared very concerned with a new city ordinance in Colorado Springs. The ordinance drastically hurt business, and employees were very eager to talk about it. It states that adult bookstores, clubs, and theaters cannot stay open all night, owners must remove doors from bookstore viewing booths, dancers must stay on a stage, customers must stay at least 3 feet away from the stage, and management must provide tip boxes for employees so that the customers cannot touch the dancers. Both employees and customers must be 21. The city says that the purpose of the ordinance is to regulate the industry to prevent increases in crime, especially prostitution; to prevent the transmission of sexually transmitted diseases, especially AIDS; and to prevent the blighting of businesses that adjoin adult-use businesses. This ordinance has affected eleven businesses in Colorado Springs.

Not surprisingly, these businesses are fighting back. The new ordinance allowed the businesses forty-five days to make the necessary changes after it was put into effect. During these days Kitty's hired a lawyer to get an injunction against the ordinance. Dave Odom, the attorney for Kitty's, said that by serving as a regulatory umbrella for all of the various adult use clubs and shops, the city ordinance is "unconstitutionally overbroad. It's going to be challenged on that basis."[1] City attorney James Colvin said that all of the provisions of the ordinance have been taken from laws elsewhere that have been upheld. Bill, the general manager of Kitty's, was involved in an earlier case in Adams County, Colorado, as a police officer (before he began to manage Kitty's). The judge awarded an injunction for Kitty's because not enough time had been spent looking over Kitty's special case. Kitty's does not serve liquor, so the minimum age for customers and employees was 18—not 21 as in other establishments. The establishment has all-nude dancing, not just topless. An older law in Colorado Springs says that if an establishment wants to serve alcohol then only topless dancing is permitted. *[The new city ordinance prevailed after this paper was submitted.]*

Since the injunction was lifted at Kitty's, business has declined rapidly. Bill reported that he lost 58 percent of his business and one-third of his dancers due to the age limit. He once had 80 to 90 employees, reduced now to 25 or 30. His $1,000 a night gross decreased to $400. The owners stated that the law would "essentially kill their business."[2] Air Force Academy cadets and other college students made up much of their business, most of these under the age of 21. Many of their former patrons now frequent Deja-Vu, an adult club on the other side of town. Because it is outside the city limits the law does not affect it, and they still allow customers under 21. "We're just going to run a respectable business,"[3] reasons Albert Gaeke about the unnecessity of the ordinance.

Before the ordinance went into effect, the required distance between dancer and customer was 12 inches. "Twelve inches is 12 inches but still there is a really big difference between 12 inches and 3 feet," says Bill. Because of this distance and the prohibition of physical contact between dancer and customer, customers tend to give less money. As Bill says, "Now a guy can't give her a kiss or hand her a dollar."

---

[1]"Council O.K.'s Rule for Adult Use Spots," *Colorado Springs Gazette Telegraph* (Dec. 9, 1992).

[2]Kathryn Sosbe, "Adult-use business law upheld," *Colorado Springs Gazette Telegraph* (Mar. 5, 1993), p. B1.

[3]Jim Buynak, "Judge blocks enforcement of new law at nude dance club," *Colorado Springs Gazette Telegraph* (Feb. 3, 1993), p. B5.

The dancers have different reactions to the effects of the ordinance. The majority of the dancers believe it has made work much harder: Because of the lack of dancers, each dancer must be on stage longer and more often in a night. "You have to be in good shape," Marlene says. Often they make less money even though they spend a longer time on stage—there aren't as many men to tip them anymore. However, Colette, another dancer, likes the new ordinance. She thinks she can still make the same amount of money in tips with her dance skill, and she appreciates the effect the ordinance had on how often the men grabbed at her. "I can see the men more and I know if they are going to try and grab me." Patrons find it more difficult to reach over a space of 3 feet than 1 foot, and the dancers can see the action of the customer and get out of the way before the situation gets uncomfortable.

THE DAILY ROUTINE

Every day at work the dancers run through approximately the same routine. They come in, stop to talk and joke around with the other employees, and proceed to the back room to begin to prepare for the evening. The average shift is from seven to nine hours long. However, some dancers may work for as many as ten or twelve hours at a time. They come in at noon and may stay until midnight or 2 A.M. because other dancers don't show up for their shifts. The dancers relax in various states of undress and smoke while they apply makeup and fix their hair, then decide on a costume to wear.

Usually within fifteen minutes of arriving, the DJ puts them on rotation and they are dancing. The girls stay in this order and dance in turn all evening. Since the ordinance passed, usually only one dancer is on stage at a time. When the club gets busy, a second stage opens up and two women dance. They dance in sets of three songs each. At the end of the set the dancers collect the money from the tip bowls on the stage floor, exit the stage, give the money to a manager for safekeeping, and prepare for the next set. The entire process is then repeated. At the end of the evening, the dancers perform the platter dance. They all dance on stage together and the men tip their favorite dancers.

When the women aren't dancing or getting ready, they spend much of their time pushing fantasy dances. Fantasy dances are one-on-one dances done just for a customer. The dancer takes him aside and dances for him. Customers are expected to spend a lot of money at the club. The cover charge alone is $6 and customers are required to purchase one nonalcoholic drink. The dancers usually charge $5 for a fantasy dance but some charge as much as $15 or $20 per dance. This is one way they make extra money. However, the women are never forced to push fantasy dances for money. This is not the case at all clubs. Some other clubs expect women to hustle the men and make as much money as possible. Many women prefer to work in the more laid-back atmosphere of Kitty's.

At the end of her shift a dancer must take out 15 percent of her tips to give to the DJ, bartender, waitress, and doorman. They usually pay the DJ the most because "he can really screw you over on your songs if he don't like you," Marlene says. They give the next largest amount of money to the bartender. The doorman is tipped because he is there to protect the dancers from the men. But one girl says that she doesn't tip him much because "our doormen suck!" They give the remaining money to the waitress, and go home. If the club is busy the dancer leaves through the side door; if it isn't she leaves through the front—always with a male escort.

COSTUMES

Costumes help create and set the mood of the dance and enhance its seductive quality. The dancers usually change between every set to give both themselves and the customers something new and exciting. As Colette says, "I hate wearing the same thing—I like to show wild sides, sensual sides, funny sides." "All of my outfits have to coordinate." She doesn't feel complete on stage without a matching, mood-enhancing outfit. Some dancers use different stage names to create different moods. One dancer says that it is "like different outfits." Bid does a lot of characterization in her dances using hats and other clothing to assume the role of military, nurse, or Wild West. Every dancer owns her own costumes—they only trade among friends. If a new dancer comes in and has no money for costumes they may loan her something for a dance. Usually, however, even new dancers have an article of lingerie or a short skirt that they can wear.

There is no typical costume, but most dancers wear T-bar underwear under their other clothing. The dancers assured us it is very comfortable, as long as the strap in back isn't too wide. All dancers wear 3-inch high-heeled boots or 4- to 5-inch high-heeled shoes, and they often share the thigh-high boots. To Colette, a pair of 1½ inch high boots are "flats." The costumes depend largely on how much money the dancer wants to spend. A new costume from erotic dancewear "costume ladies" costs around $80, but a used costume generally costs $10 or less. Many dancer's costumes consist of lingerie, skirts, tank tops, and slips bought at regular department stores. Some create and sew elaborate costumes. Managers believe that denim is unattractive and instruct the dancers not to wear it. At topless bars, dancers must cover their butts, but here they both dance and talk to customers off stage in only T-bar underwear and a shirt.

Makeup depends, again, on the dancer. Everyone wears at least a moderate amount, highlighting their eyes and lips. The red light in the dressing room corresponds to the red light of the stage, softening lines and creating a sultry atmosphere. Dancers put on perfume quickly between every set and renew makeup to appear fresh for the next dance. Many dancers feel that keeping a tan is part of the appearance upkeep. As Susan says, "If I'm not tan I feel really s——ty."

Handling clothing plays a large part in the dance. The dancer usually dances the first song with her entire costume on (covering at least her breasts and pubic area). During the second song most dancers take off their tops, but some, such as Marlene, choose to remove their bottoms first. In the third song everything comes off except for the boots or heels and they dance the rest of the set naked. Their methods of removing the clothing are important in the dance; the more seductive or provocative, the larger the tips.

Accessories include, at times, whips, chains, and handcuffs. Depending on the dancer's taste and the types of customers, the dancer may choose to do an "S & M set." "They either love it or they hate it!" says Colette. Once a customer tipped her $10 every time she whipped him.

When asked what dance moves are the most provocative and therefore bring in the most money, each dancer replied differently. Maggie "looks straight at their eyes, gets in their faces, and smiles." Colette uses her flexibility to put her leg behind her head, along with sliding down the pole and hanging upside down from it. She does many back handsprings and other gymnastics on stage. Bid says she still "believes in the old-fashioned striptease."

STAGE NAMES

Very few of the dancers use their real names at work; they take on an entirely different persona. The only name that both customers and other employees call them is their stage name. "It lets you be whoever you want to be" (Colette). The dancers choose their own stage names. "I chose Colette because it was exotic and I have always loved the name," said Colette. Bid chose her name easily—made up from her initials, B.I.D. She has Bid written on everything that she owns. Only one dancer goes by her real name. Whatever the name, the dancers have them for a reason—to escape from reality into the theatrical world of dancing. These names serve a practical purpose as well. The customers find it much harder to look up dancers with stage names. This usually prevents stalking, although one dancer has been followed to her home.

CUSTOMERS

We were not able to study the customers personally, but instead researched how they relate to the dancers and what the dancers think of them. Since the ordinance passed, a large percentage of the customers have been older, married men. Most of the dancers stress that they come in mostly to talk and have some female company. "They don't just come here to look at girls—they come to talk, play pool" (Colette). Maggie even says that "a lot of guys don't look at you as a sexual object." They like to talk about their wives and families or even how their day went. They often show the dancers pictures of their families. As Marlene says, "Maybe his wife's a bitch and he just wanted someone to talk to." The dancers make more money and establish regulars when they talk to customers, which they do both on and off stage. "You make money a lot better when you get to talk to the customer. That's where the money comes from" (Colette).

The actions of the men depend somewhat on their age and state of coherence. Dancers often cater to the older customers because they have more money to spend. Younger men sometimes come and sit and watch for hours without tipping the dancers—a "free look." Also, the younger guys are usually more judgmental about body type and dancing ability of the girls. However, according to Marlene, the "oldest men are perverts." "If it weren't for masturbation they would never get off," adds Dominick, the bartender. All of the customers, whatever their age, are rudest when drunk, although they tend to tip more. Because Kitty's serves no alcohol, many men, especially groups of younger men, get drunk before they go to the club. Intoxicated men grab or yell rude comments more often than sober customers.

Depending on the DJ (who incites enthusiasm) and the dancer, men will hoot and catcall during a dance (which is beneficial to the dancers because they get more tips when the customers are enthusiastic). Since the ordinance, men give the dancers tips by throwing money on stage or putting it in tip bowls, not sticking it in their G-strings. If a customer appears to like the dancer and tips a lot, the dancer will ask him if he wants a fantasy dance while she is on stage. Most of the time the customers say no, but selling even one fantasy dance means another $5 to $10, so the dancer keeps asking.

The customers are usually not rude and follow the rules; they just watch the dancers. Occasionally, however, they yell lewd comments, such as, "Let me eat your p——!" or "Can we f——?!" to which the dancers usually reply with something cutting. They "don't put up with it." Since the ordinance, customers grab for the dancers less often because they are farther away. Dancers' instinctual reaction when a customer "grabs for your p——" is to slap or kick him, but this may result in the customer suing the club, so the dancers are taught to just walk offstage, bringing embarrassment to the rude patron and vindicating herself. Most of the dancers have few overt complaints against men, but Susan kept repeating, "Men are pigs. I hate them!"

When talking and socializing with the customers both dancing and offstage, dancers "learn to lie a lot." Customers often ask questions such as "what is your real name?" to which Maggie would reply, "My name in here is Maggie—that's all you need to know." Maggie has a personal policy of not going out with any customers, although some dancers do. When they ask a dancer for her phone number she will often reply, "I don't have a phone," or "call me here" and gives them a Kitty's business card with her stage name on the back. Many times customers will take them up on that offer and call them at work to chat or to see when they are dancing. Dancers make a lot of their money from these regular customers. Once in a while a dancer will take the number of a customer and call him.

Customers rarely interact with each other. They "act like they are in a dirty bookstore—they don't talk," says Susan. They ignore the presence of other men around. Their purpose there does not include socializing with other men. There are hardly any fights between customers on the floor. Very few fondle themselves or masturbate while watching the dancers; it is not allowed in the club.

MONEY

More than anything else, Kitty's is a business. The women dance to make money. One woman says "I'm an exhibitionist—I like showing off." But, as Maggie says, "It's all about money." They usually make $100 to $120 a night, and $500 to $700 a week. Most of this money is tips. They only make $2.13 an hour in wages—less than minimum wage. One dancer even refuses this pay because she doesn't want to file W-2 forms for the little she gets. She works for tips. Each dancer's opinion of the job changes according to the tips made that night. Melody, who had just told us of her dislike of the job, walked back from a set with $30 in tips declaring, "Now I like working here." Maggie stays dancing even though she hates it because she is "making money." As any dancer may say, "Made me some kick-ass money that night."

Many start dancing because they are low on cash and need money very badly. Marlene says that when she got kicked out of her house during the second semester of her senior year in high school and had to live in a hotel, she went to apply for a waitressing job at Deja-Vu. As she was filling out the application, the manager walked back from dancing with a lot of cash from tips and Marlene, desperate for cash, started dancing that day. Because many dancers are single parents or are putting their boyfriends, husbands, or themselves through school, they need a job that gets them a lot of cash with few hours. However, not all of the dancers use their money in such constructive ways. As Susan says, "It's a good job to party with." The ready cash is easily spent on alcohol, drugs, and eating out.

Even the bartender, DJ, and waitress make a lot of money. The DJ and bartender are tipped by the dancers, and when the dancers have a good night they may be tipped as much as $50. Sometimes when a customer requests a song he will tip the DJ also. Dominick uses his extra money to travel and take his son on vacations. The waitress often makes as much if not more in tips than the dancers if she hustles for tips.

Even though their purpose is to make money, dancers must disguise this if they want to make any. "If you're going in for money, you probably won't make any." They must go on stage with the attitude of an entertainer; a dancer "must perform." If they go on stage with the need for money foremost in their minds, customers can tell and they don't tip.

Tips depend entirely on the customers and the dancers. Some nights just one or two customers may tip dancers $20 bills all night, and a large group may tip nothing. On any particular night one dancer may get $50 in tips and another $9 because of the taste of the customers, and the next night different customers will tip exactly the opposite. The club's busiest time as well as the time they make the most money is on the first and fifteenth of every month (and the weekends right after) when the GIs get paid.

Customers also differ in what they tip. The usual fare consists of $1s, $5s, and occasionally $20s. But one dancer recalls being tipped a $100 bill. She says it was "a rush—an ego trip. But I couldn't understand it. I couldn't understand why they would tip me that much." Some customers give things other than money. A certain patron gives dancers jewelry and earrings, another one gives candy bars every time he comes, in addition to money. Dancers have been tipped sets of keys and business cards to get discounts on products.

They have an information network in the back to find out which customers have money and therefore whom they should concentrate on in their dances. One dancer will ask another, "Do they have money?" "Ask Betty, she serves the drinks." Those who have the opportunity to see the customers' wallets report to the dancers what they see. Susan says, "When you get here you can tell within an hour how your money goes." Nights tend to run in trends; if a dancer is having a bad evening then this will usually continue all night, but if she is having good luck with tips, this streak will usually last. This is due to both the customers that come in that night and the dancer's attitude and energy. If a dancer makes a lot of money one set, she will be enthusiastic for the next set and customers will like her.

DRUGS AND ALCOHOL

There are two very different sides to the drug and alcohol policy of Kitty's. Bill, the general manager, tells us, "This place—no drugs, no alcohol—we see it, watch for it." Bill and Dominick both say that there are as much drugs and prostitution at a grocery store or bank as at Kitty's. We were given this version of the drug and alcohol policy on our very first visit. In reality, this "official" policy does not hold up. There is an enormous discrepancy between what the public relations man says happens and what actually occurs in the back room between sets.

Employees consumed large amounts of alcohol on at least one occasion, and many other times at least one dancer swiped drinks from a bottle in her locker. As one dancer says, "There are lots of drugs here but by far the most common abuse is alcohol." Only one of the women we talked to did not drink on a regular basis. On one night the dancers slammed drinks from the moment we arrived until our departure three hours later. The drink of the evening was spiced rum and Coke. The waitress (from whose bottle they were drinking) brought back Cokes in the small glasses used at the bar. The dancers threw half of the Coke in the garbage can and then filled the glass with spiced rum. Two or three girls stuck their swizzle straws in the drink and at the count of three they "slammed it." The drinking took maybe five seconds. Then the waitress refilled the glasses and the dancers and waitress did it again. All of the dancers except one did this numerous times during the evening.

On several other occasions we watched a dancer take small drinks out of a bottle in her locker. These drinks were much more discreet than the open drinking of the other night. It appeared as if the girls knew that they weren't supposed to be drinking but that it didn't matter as long as they hid it.

We did not see any open use of drugs while we were at Kitty's. The dancers assured us that many used drugs but that they themselves "didn't use them." Only one dancer admitted, "If I could afford to be an addict I probably would." She did not use hard-core drugs; she only smoked a little marijuana. The attitude about drugs is nonchalant. "Yeah, some girls just go into the bathroom and get high. They know where the managers are and when it's safe." "But I would never do it," commonly responded our informants. One dancer said that if someone came in and did a drug test the place would get shut down.

By far the most common substance abuse was cigarettes. Everyone is a chain smoker. The most frequent complaint in the dressing room was "S——, I forgot my smokes," or "Does anyone have a light?" or "I really need a cigarette." Between every set the dancers came backstage and smoked while they prepared for the next set. The managers also constantly smoked in the back rooms as did the DJ, bartenders, and waitress. We do not know if they smoked in front of customers, but smoking in front of customers isn't considered good public relations.

MOTIVATION

Drugs and alcohol are not the only discrepancies between what the managers say and what the dancers say. Bill says that many of the girls have very low self-esteem and confidence. Many of the dancers disagree with this. "I used to be very shy and never talk. Dancing has helped my confidence a lot. I'm a lot more outgoing than I used to be," says Marlene. This appears to be true in many cases. Dancing has made the women more outgoing and more satisfied with their bodies. The women agree that when a man pays her to dance for him it definitely helps boost her self-confidence. But this confidence in their bodies does not always reflect in the rest of their lives. Bill believes that 90 percent of the dancers come from broken homes and that 80 percent have been sexually abused. Susan, a sociology major, reiterates this point by saying that the majority of dancers come from dysfunctional families. They are also often involved in abusive relationships with their husbands or boyfriends. "Lots of girls are hardened by the job. They lie and cheat and steal. It's a hard life but for me it's only a game," says Maggie.

A lot of the dancers are single, young mothers. "You know how that is" (Dominick). When dancers are pregnant they get their doctors' permission to continue dancing. Many of the women wear panties with a high, wide waistline to help disguise the show of pregnancy as long as possible. The women continue to dance until the strain of dancing hurts them or else the pregnancy begins to show—whichever comes first. Another problem the dancers face is what to do while menstruating. They can't stop working for an entire week. The women solve this problem by placing their tampon strings inside of them. Then the women check every two sets or so to make sure that the string is still in there.

The dancers have different opinions on dancing. Some women really love their jobs and some can't stand it and only do it for money. Colette loves her job because of her skill at it: "When I get out there I entertain." Maggie, on the other hand, hates her job: "I do it for the money." Marlene loves her job but still says that "it's a s——ty job. Everyone f——s you over every chance they get. At first you have to pretend like you are dancing for your boyfriend. You smile and pretend like you like it. But now I love it! It's very addicting." Many women agree with Marlene. They stumbled onto the job because they needed quick cash, hated it at first, and now they love it and are addicted. As Colette says, "There's bad parts about it but it's great. It's what I do well."

One of the largest draws to the dancing profession is its lack of structure, especially at Kitty's. The dancers have a schedule but they never rigidly follow it. The women come and go as they please. When a dancer doesn't show up for work the others complain a little but forgive and forget by the next evening. A no-show gives the girls a chance to dance more and make more money. As Marlene says, "This is the most laid-back funnest club I ever danced at." Many of the other girls agree. The job gives them most of their afternoons off to be with their children and allows them to miss an evening without getting in trouble.

When necessary, the dancers and other employees carry the responsibilities of the entire club. In the informal atmosphere of the club, most of the employees know how to do all of the jobs. For instance, when the manager, waitress, DJ, and one of the dancers had to leave, three dancers, the doorman, and the bartender assumed the responsibilities of all of these jobs. The dancers waitressed and DJed for each other.

The dancers all agree that a woman gets really banged up on stage. "It's hard on her knees and back." Now that the club bought a new dance pole it should get easier. The job keeps a woman flexible. "I like it because it keeps me in shape," says Susan.

However, all of the dancers agree that dancing is not what they want to do for life. Their career goals range from receptionist, flight attendant, teacher, graphic designer, to attending law school and becoming involved in entertainment law. Melody, who used to be a circuit-board maker, has plans to start working soon for AT&T. Colette thinks that she will continue to dance when she gets another job because she loves entertaining. But even Colette says that she will only dance until she is 25. All of the women consider dancing just a temporary job. Everyone agrees with Maggie who emphatically states that dancing is *"not a career!"*

EDUCATION

A large number of the employees are educated past high school. One of the women has her B.A., one her M.A. in sociology, one is a year from graduating from college, and several, like Colette, are currently attending school. One of the dancers was a dental hygienist. Most of them have plans to continue school or to go back and further their education. Susan intends to get her doctorate (with a thesis on strip bars) and teach. Even the bartender has a bachelor's degree in history. However, a few women didn't like school and do not plan to go back. (We have a somewhat biased view because the more educated women tended to talk to us more. Some of the women did not talk to us at all and were very resistant to questions.) As to why the educated women dance instead of working in their profession, they usually reply money or even boredom in a routine job. They can often make more money strip dancing than in a typical college-level job.

RELATIONSHIPS

The relationships among employees at Kitty's are one of the main defining elements of their subculture. Because they are in direct competition with each other for men's attention, and therefore money, the dancers rarely establish strong bonds of friendship. In contrast, most of the dancers seem to be fairly close friends with Betty, the waitress, because she does not compete with them. However, because they are involved in such an isolated, scorned subculture, they must share the common bond of their experience.

They often have personality conflicts. When one dancer makes more money than another and brags about it, tensions rise. However, the tension manifests itself in unrelated ways. Although the dancers are jealous of anyone who makes more money, they never mention their jealously outright. The dancers verbalize their opinions about everybody and everything except for the important issue of competition and jealousy. They will, for instance, yell at each other for showing up late even though this should not be a cause for argument in the casual atmosphere of the club. The dancers will also slander each other behind their backs.

An example of this is the fight between Maggie and Melody. Maggie had been working since noon, making less money than usual. It was close to ten and the club was busy when Melody finally showed up for work. Melody had not been scheduled that night and showed up only at the urging of the managers. It took Melody half an hour to make it to the dressing room to get ready. While she was in the hall Maggie yelled out that she was being a "bitch, lollygagging around." Melody confronted Maggie with her accusations and they yelled at each other about lateness and bitchiness. Five minutes later Melody and Maggie joined each other at the makeup mirror to talk about the customers. The argument had already been forgotten. Later that night Maggie told us that they really do like each other and that she had just been in a bad mood, presumably from lack of money. Melody went on that night to make a large amount of money in tips while Maggie still barely made anything.

In general, the dancers do not trust each other with their possessions. They always lock their lockers whenever they leave the back room and they rarely loan clothing or money. As Colette says, "you lock your s—— up!" We witnessed dancers checking and double-checking their locks to make sure they were closed before leaving for even a 12-minute set. On one occasion we witnessed two girls fighting about money.

A strong camaraderie holds the dancers together. Even though, and perhaps because, the dancers release their frustrations on each other, they closely bond together in the back room sharing their life experiences and opinions along with makeup, cigarettes, and tampons. Most of the dancers believe that they are friends with everyone despite frequent quarrels. As one dancer said, "We don't come here to make friends. We come to make money. But we do end up making friends here." When the dancers are having a rough evening or just want to complain, someone always listens and sympathizes because they have gone through the same problems. Maggie says she likes to "let things out" to the other dancers; they support one another. Their frequent joking and bantering adds humor to the back room: "We just like to f—— around."

However, these friendships rarely go beyond the club doors. Although the dancers occasionally go to a bar after or during work together, they seldom hang out when they aren't working.

The dancers we talked to were either in their very early twenties or in their early thirties. We encountered no dancers of in-between ages. The older ones appeared more educated and somewhat separated themselves from the younger dancers. They were not as anxious to miss work and go to bars. They weren't as interested in forming friendships and relationships within the club. To them it was just a job.

RELATIONS WITH THE MANAGEMENT

The relationship between dancers and managers is very complicated. Some of the women date managers, others hate them. Whichever is the case, their relationships are strained. The managers do not seem to know the dancers on the same kind of personal level that the rest of the employees know them. All of the managers are male.

In general, the dancers and other employees have little respect for their managers. They considered a manager on at least two occasions to be a "typical f——in' male." A manager called an employee up on the phone to ask him to hurry up and get on the floor. When he hung up the phone he yelled "F—— you," while a dancer joked with us, "The management's a little shaky." It becomes obvious that the management does not know the dancers when there are such discrepancies between what Bill says about the dancers and what they say about their own lives. When we called the first time for an interview, Bill told us that he doubted that any of the women would talk to us, which proved to be false.

Zeroes say the most about the manager's relation to the dancers. The managers rarely appear in the back room to socialize with the dancers. They stay out on the floor or in their office. They do not seem to want to stoop to the dancer's level. They wear suits and ties while the dancers wear only strip outfits or nothing. They have distanced themselves from the dancers.

Marlene is dating a manager, Erik. She is now "officially" working elsewhere because she had so many problems working under her boyfriend. However, three times we have been in the club Marlene has been working. "I hate it (working with my boyfriend) more than anything in the world." On one occasion they got in a fight that appeared extremely abusive to us—we heard screams, cries, thuds, and crashes in the room next door. The other dancers reassured us that this happens all the time and that no one was being physically abused. (We still think differently.) This occurrence seemed normal to the dancers in the back room and they paid no attention to it. "Between couples in here it happens." They referred to the similarity of their own previous relationships within the club.

RELATIONS WITH THE DJ

The duties of the DJ include, along with playing music, listing the dancers and the order in which they dance and backing up the doorman in case of trouble. Frank says he "does not have much of a problem with rowdy customers—usually I have to excite them because they haven't been drinking and are self-conscious." The DJ has authority over the dancers.

The dancers usually get along with the DJ, depending on who the DJ is and how the evening is going. (There are three DJs but we only had the opportunity to talk to Frank, who works five nights per week.) Frank is one of the dancers' favorite DJs because he cares about them. Frank bothers to learn what type of music the women prefer to dance to or lets them pick their own sets. "Some dancers let me pick, it just depends on how picky they are," he says. Because of this, the dancers usually tip Frank a lot at the end of the evening. However, when a dancer makes little money, or thinks she dances less than the others, she blames the DJ for not getting the customers enthused. "I quit. F——in' DJ, no enthusiasm," says Maggie.

RELATIONS WITH THE BARTENDER

Dominick, the one bartender we talked to, and Frank relate to the dancers in a similar manner. Dominick and the dancers joke around, hang out in the back, and share good times together. In his relations with the girls he says that he is not a "f—— me and I'll give you a job" kind of guy. Dominick says that the nudity of the back room no longer affects him. This seems to be the case with the other male employees as well. Nudity rather than clothing becomes normal to the employees. The women also appear to be perfectly comfortable sitting around and talking to the male employees while nude.

OUTSIDE RELATIONSHIPS

Because of their particular profession, dancers sometimes have a hard time relating to people "outside" who stereotype and do not understand. When meeting new people, Maggie says she does not tell people what she does for a living until she knows they will not be judgmental. Depending on their background, some dancers do not even tell their parents. Maggie's mother knows only that she is working in a bar, not what kind of bar. Those from middle-class backgrounds tend not to tell their parents, fearing their judgment and that they would be hurt. Usually lower-class parents care less about their daughters' career choices. In some cases they have kicked their children out and do not care at all.

Many of the dancers date within the business because outside boyfriends sometimes have problems with jealousy. "Boyfriends love to hate it," says Susan. "It's easier to date someone in the business because they don't get jealous" (Frank). However, most boyfriends, husbands, and fiancés know that "it is only a job" and restrain their jealousy. Some even hang out at the club to watch the women and spend time with their girlfriends or wives. A few of the women, such as Maggie, dance to send their boyfriends or husbands through college. Some of the married women have husbands in jail. For instance, one woman is currently thinking of getting a divorce from her husband (whom she married out of high school) because he has been sentenced to seventy-eight years.

Those with children usually hire babysitters for their shifts, but because of the hours of dancing they still spend a lot of time with their kids. Colette, whose children are 3, 4, and 6, sometimes even takes them to the club if she can't find an appropriate babysitter or if she wants to spend time with them. She did not appear to have doubts about having her children in the atmosphere of a strip bar. Dominick says he works this job to be able to spend as much time as possible with his 2-year-old son. Most of the parents we talked to were single parents. They appeared to care a lot for their children and sometimes chose this job for the sake of their kids.

CONCLUSION

Marlene was upset at another dancer and so she referred to her as a "typical female dancer," reinforcing the general public's image of a dancer. They use societal stereotypes at their convenience to put down other dancers, unconsciously hurting themselves as well. Although they profess not to believe in these images, the dancers are well aware of society's general beliefs about strip dancing and the low image that it carries. We think that subconsciously the dancers sometimes do view themselves in this manner. Society's opinion of the dancers is an obvious undercurrent even in the exclusive society of the back room, and it may play a bigger part in the dancer's lives when they are outside of Kitty's. When we first began researching the women, Marlene asked us our opinion, as women, of strip dancing in general. Our opinion of strip clubs has changed radically since beginning research, and as Susan says, working (or researching, we might add) in a strip bar "desensitizes one to cultural norms—the abnormal becomes the normal."

The dancers' language always includes "four-letter words," and many dancers (including the educated ones) use poor grammar (double negatives, for example). Part of this stems from the fulfillment of the lower-class image that society gives them, as well as the infusion of less educated women into the dancing society. They also refer to themselves as "dancers" rather than "strippers," which is a term the outside society usually uses to describe them. This gives them some amount of dignity and self-respect. However, the management refers to them as girls, rather than women or dancers, further stratifying their society.

We entered Kitty's with the preconception of a low-class, sleazy, dirty strip joint. We left the establishment with respect for the club as a business and the employees as real people. We found in the back room a close-knit community that supports each member along with creating drama in each person's life. Colette captures the atmosphere of the club saying, "You only live once in your life; when it's gone, it's gone."

EPILOGUE

After Elizabeth did her oral report on postmodern reflexivity (when we had already submitted the first draft of this paper), we realized we had changed and reinterpreted our information to suit our needs. We also realized that our questions were influenced by our ulterior motives (mainly writing an interesting paper). We used the contemplative approach to writing an ethnography because we did not consider the interaction between ourselves and the dancers to be important. Although for the most part we let the dancers talk and did not ask many leading questions, our very presence in the room caused the conversation among the dancers to go in certain directions. On one occasion the dancers talked about education, specifically calculus—not a normal back room dancer conversation. We tried to be as objective as possible, but we are aware that our subjectivity influenced this paper.

GLOSSARY

Floor   The floor consists of three round stages surrounded by 3-foot-wide tables and chairs for the customers. The bar lines the back of the establishment. Next to the bar is the door into the back room. On the left-hand side as one enters the building is the DJ's sound system surrounded by a 4-foot wall. Within are shelves filled with records, CDs, tapes, an elaborate sound system, and a mike. On the right-hand side, one step up, are pool tables and video games. Against the walls are several tables and booths. The doorman's "podium" stands just to the left of the door. Here he charges customers and checks their IDs as they come in.

Back Room   The first door to the left in the hallway going back is the manager's office, where dancers spend a great deal of time. It has one desk and some shelves. There is a door to the right leading to the women's bathroom, then another door to a private room with a couple of chairs and tables used for interviews. The hallway opens up at the end into the back room, which is lined with 6-foot brown lockers. The carpet is light brown and in bad condition, as if a lot of hair spray, perfume, food, and drinks has been spilled on it over the years. A mirror and dressing table line half of the inner wall, and along that same wall is the bathroom.

T-Bar Underwear   Also know as thong underwear. The back of the garment consists of two narrow straps—one across the top of the buttocks and one down the center. The front of T-bar underwear is styled like ordinary women's panties.

The Dale House: Finding a Family in the System

by Jennifer Sands

What makes this paper notable is almost the flip slide of some of the other student papers. Although Jen Sands shares with Chris Goodwin and Andy Lewis a manic approach to her fieldwork, she never asks which definition of culture best fits her data—nor does she distinguish between social organization and the "fabric of meaning," which Jeff White and Chris Goodwin make so prominent. Instead, she shows us how to choose an ethnographic topic so it reinforces the rest of one's intellectual and emotional education and enriches both.

After graduating from Colorado College in political science in 1995, Sands won a fellowship at the Eagleton Institute of Practical Politics, Rutgers University, is headed toward a career in government, and continues acting and volunteer service. Staff names in her paper are real: resident names are changed.

> "[A]nd everyone looked so down and I couldn't help thinking, Christ are we even moving?" Darlene, *Balm in Gilead*, by Langford Wilson.

It is this kind of sentiment in the play *Balm in Gilead* that would never let me forget the residents of the Dale House for very long. I have never in my life become so involved with one idea that it touched and colored every event, conversation, and thought that occurred every waking moment of every day for almost a month. How strange to be thinking all the time of the loneliness and pain of people who for so long have been simply fictitious characters. Just mix the right elements in your head and there they are to be used for a while and then forgotten about—but then suddenly such people and such a world become very real. It is disturbing to be faced with an ugly reality when one is so awfully busy with a somewhat rose-colored way of life. These reservations may not have much point to those who do not know what the Dale House is, or why Balm in Gilead is related to it. I am starting in the middle of the end rather than the beginning. I suppose that the end always seems more important than the beginning while one is in it, but I shall attempt to make the very personal end of this project understandable in some way by proceeding now to start from the beginning.

Before beginning the ethnography, I was cast in the play *Balm in Gilead* as a homeless young woman with a hard attitude and a pretty mean right hook. The rehearsal time put a strain on my schedule, and I was faced with choosing something to do an ethnography on that would fit my limited hours. The thought process began. I wanted originally to work with runaway teenagers, but Colorado Springs has no home for such kids; however, the police gave me the name of two projects for teens that are affiliated with the Department of Social Services: Chinsup and The Dale House Project. I chose Dale House for two reasons: It did not sound like a generic national organization, and it was only a few blocks away from the college campus. I wanted to experience a world I had not been exposed to; I wanted to understand what this unfortunately large section of American culture was all about. I thought that the experience would help me understand the attitudes and feelings that were being found in the characters of the play. I could research my character in the play and do my anthropology project in one fell swoop.

THE METHOD

I was at first unsure how I would go about actually studying these people. I knew they would not react well to the constant presence of a pen and paper, much less a tape recorder. I would not be able to interview the residents, really, and there was only so much to be gotten from formal interviews with the staff. It seemed to me that the Dale House was much more than what the rules and guidelines could ever tell. It was even more than where all of the staff and residents came from. The more I went to the Dale House, the more I came to understand that what the Dale House is all about cannot be told or expressed in an interview. The Dale House must be lived. I did almost all of my fieldwork just "hanging out" at any time I could. I stopped asking questions and started listening and watching. It was only at this point that I began to realize the Dale House is not about the pasts of the residents, but about their futures. It is about gaining a family in a bunch of people who know where you are coming from. It is not about religious beliefs or interviews or case workers or government agencies. It is about life—living it day by day—and learning to deal with people. It is about learning to trust and love. These are not things that are easy to express in words on paper. They just are. When it came to writing them down I was, still am, and probably always will be, a slight bit lost. I expressed these feelings to a resident of the Dale House and she told me, "Dale House is the people who are in it, not anything else. You should write about how we make you feel and then you'll know what it's all about. Just be blunt . . . and cheer up, Jen."

My initial contact was with Beverly Henry, one of the two social workers on the permanent staff of Dale House. She agreed to let me do a paper on the house and gave me a very thorough interview in which she explained to me the background of the house and told me about the general rules and the activities residents participate in.

The Dale House was founded in 1971 by the current director, George Sheffer, III, and his father, with help from family and friends. In 1976 it was licensed as a residential child-care home. The Dale House is a private institution, affiliated with Young Life, a Christian organization, and funded with federal dollars. The Dale House has contracts with the Department of Social Services and the Department of Youth Services of Colorado Springs. When someone comes to live at Dale House they must have an interview and sign a contract saying that they will attend mandatory activities, abide by the rules, and go to school and/or work. Their money must be turned into "bank à la George" from which they will be given an allowance on which to live. They must attend the two "family night" dinners, one on Sunday and one on Wednesday, and participate in the evening activities that follow. They cannot skip school, work, or appointments. If they do, they will face restriction and be given hours of work crew during which they do maintenance or cleaning around the three houses owned by the project, and mandatory studying. All of their time must be accounted for and they can be "checked up on" at any time. Whenever they are missing for an hour or more, it must be reported to whichever department of services they are affiliated with.

THE LOCATION

The Dale House Project owns four lots of property in the block bordered by Cascade Ave., Dale St., Tejon St., and Cache la Poudre. One lot faces Cascade Ave., two are next to each other facing Dale St., and one is on the corner of Dale St. and Tejon St. The lots are connected by an alley in the middle of the block. The houses on Dale St. are painted different shades of blue. (This was actually a mistake. One just recently painted was supposed to be gray, but it turned out to be blue.) All three are two-story wood houses with raised porches outside and hardwood floors inside. The house on Cascade is cream-colored stucco with green trim. It also has a raised porch. The Cascade house contains the offices of permanent staff members and also meeting rooms. The other houses are residential for staff and residents. All of the yards are well kept with short grass, no weeds, well-trimmed bushes, and newly blooming flowers. There is a picnic table behind one of the houses and there are two garages off the alley that have been converted into a weight room and a pool room for the use of the residents.

THE STAFF

The staff of the Dale House consists of three permanent and eight nonpermanent members. The three permanent members are the director and two social workers. The eight nonpermanent members are students doing graduate work in theology. They come from different areas of the country, and most come from small religiously affiliated institutions such as Hope College and Wheaton College. It is interesting to note that they do not dress in particularly trendy clothes, and the women do not wear very much makeup or hair spray. The only noticeable jewelry are a few small crosses on necklaces. There are four males and four females divided into two teams of two males and two females each. The teams take turns staying with the residents and looking after them in three-day shifts. Each of these staff members is the "primary" for one or more of the residents. This means they are responsible for keeping track of their resident's progress, writing up the necessary paperwork, and making decisions about what is best for the resident. The resident relies on his or her primary more than on any other staff person. The younger staff are intermediaries between the residents and the permanent staff. Often the staff are seen as friends to the residents rather than as people in charge. They joke around and play with the residents, and seem like older siblings, but there comes a point when they must still exert authority. The residents always remember this after a while and keep a little of their protectiveness up. Authority in its many forms has always been the enemy for them, and it is very hard for them to trust anyone in such a position completely. For their part, the staff works hard at building camaraderie among themselves as well as among the residents. They are always cheerful and willing to talk to the residents, but they are not afraid to punish the residents for doing wrong things either. They work hard to understand the residents. Their job is extremely demanding emotionally and physically (in that they have to keep up with fourteen kids), and they are all strong people.

THE RESIDENTS

The residents can number up to sixteen at one time. The current number is fourteen. They range in age from 16 to 18 and are all involved in "the system." Some come from families with abusive or otherwise unfit parents and have been taken out of or left their homes, others have been picked up for crimes by the police and have been put in Dale House instead of detention. They dress in the normal manner for people their age, except they do not wear a lot of jewelry. The girls all wear heavy makeup and lots of hair spray with the exception of one. All of them wear athletic shoes. All are on their way to emancipation—freedom to live on their own. There are currently eight males and six females at the house, in various stages of emancipation. They all have different problems. Some see therapists, some are still in contact with their families, some aren't. They have different defense mechanisms such as short tempers, bad attitudes, emotional abuse of friends, in order to gain attention. Many are loud and somewhat obnoxious and some are walking comedy routines. All of these things serve to hide the pain or other feelings inside. They have tough shells, but every once in a while they let a glimpse of softness or insecurity show through. They are basically good kids who have been dealt a really bad hand and have to adopt a strong poker face in order to survive.

THE RELIGION

Religion has an interesting role at the Dale House. The project itself is affiliated with the Christian organization Young Life, and all of the staff are Christian, yet religion is not as prominent as I at first had thought it might be. Residents are not made to do anything religious such as going to church or Sunday school. The only thing they must do that has a religious connotation is attend the Sunday night family night sing-along and sermon. Religion is not forced on the residents, but they often do get curious and ask questions about it because it is such a large part of the lives of the staff. Some of the residents even requested their own Bible study sessions. It is not formalized Christian religion that is stressed and carried over into the lives of the residents, but it is the Christian values of family togetherness, support, and unconditional love that the staff members live their lives by and teach the residents to live by.

THE STORIES

All of the preceding information is dry and pointless without relating certain incidents that occurred during the course of my fieldwork. What follows are things which I consider to have been turning points and/or keys to my understanding of how many things work at Dale House and why they work that way. Some are more personal than others; all are important.

I left my dorm room at 5:50 on a Sunday night, apprehensive. I was about to encounter the residents of the Dale House for the first time. I wondered how they would react to a person so close to their age, with an obvious number of advantages they did not have, coming into their turf to "study" them.

I entered the building that houses the eating area and the kitchen of the Dale House at 5:55 and went directly to the kitchen, where some staff I had already met were just finishing dinner preparations. They greeted me as a friend, and that recognition put me somewhat at ease. Two male residents wandered into the kitchen and one of the staff introduced me. The two said their respective "hello's" and moved into the dining room. One of the staff called everyone for dinner as I helped put food on the table. Everyone began to gather around the large table in a noisy procession. I was making my way into the room when one of the female residents saw me, looked me up and down, turned to a staff member and asked loudly, "Who the hell is she?" making sure that I did not miss it. The staff member ignored the question and introduced me in a very polite fashion. The resident looked me up and down again and moved away.

The rest of the evening brought mixed reactions to me throughout dinner and "hang out" time. Two females introduced themselves with incorrect names. Two of the males ignored my presence completely. Two males spoke with me, one quite openly about anything and everything, one in a friendly manner, as if I were just another resident or staff person. All of them looked at me and watched how I spoke to those who were speaking to me. Many of them asked me a few guarded questions. Others simply ignored my existence. One girl came late, as she had been working, and she was the only nonstaff female to speak to me all evening.

At about 8 o'clock we all left the Dale House to go to the home of Marti Sheffer. I drove the two friendly male residents to the house on Tejon Street on the other side of the Colorado College campus. We entered the house and one of the staff members introduced me to Marti. We all crowded into a large living room and a staff member handed me a small brown book of songs and some pieces of paper bound together at the top. When everyone was settled, a female resident, a female staff member, and a bearded man walked in at the front of the room and sat in the three chairs we were all facing. The resident and the man were holding guitars. The staff member introduced all of the guests present, myself included, and every one clapped after every introduction. The two guitars began to play and everyone sang for about half an hour—some religious songs and some not. I sang along and looked around the room watching people. As we sang, the faces of the residents began to soften. There were smiles on faces that had not been there earlier.

"You and I can climb every mountain/ cross every sea and drink from every fountain/ in His name . . ."

One of the female residents who had been rude earlier caught my eye and smiled.

When the singing was finished, I left to go to play rehearsal and missed the talk by George Sheffer. I began to feel confident that studying the Dale House would turn out well.

*   *   *

At 9:25 the Monday morning after family night, I found myself walking once again in the direction of the Dale House. This time, however, I went to the house that holds the offices of the permanent staff members and serves as a meeting place for the weekly staff meetings. These meetings actually begin at 9 o'clock with some sort of religious observance, but I was told to come at 9:30 for the regular meeting. When I entered they greeted me in a friendly way and showed me the correct chair to sit in. (Although there are no assigned seats, everyone seems to like his or her own special spot and it was important that I not upset anyone by taking his or her seat.) I sat and there was general talking and socializing among all of the staff as they waited for George to come into the room. The mood was jovial, and people seemed well bonded.

George entered, and the meeting began. After general comments and announcements, one staff member, an ex-cop, warned the others to watch out for a certain teenager, known to be a criminal and a tough guy, who had been seen in the neighborhood lately, looking to cause trouble with two of the residents over some rumor on the street. Everyone paid very close attention as evidenced by the forward-leaning positions of their bodies and the focus of their eyes on his face.

After these items of business, the staff members were each asked to give a specific report on their primary resident(s). Some of the reports were brief and some were very long. The reports included schedules for the week, problems from the last week and their solutions, concerns about reaching emancipation, court cases going on, requests for money for contact lenses, positive occurrences, and finally personal problems in dealing with residents and/or handling the personalities.

At one point in the reporting, one of the staff members nearly burst into tears. Her resident was giving her the emotional runaround and it was wearing on her. She had reached the point at which she could no longer cope. She was tired. She did not know what to do. It was here that the support network became evident. The staff member next to her hugged her and everyone consoled her. They understood how draining it could be. They offered solutions and ways of dealing. The social workers gave psychological reasons and explained how to deal with certain personalities. They were working as a team. It was an amazing thing to be in the middle of as an outsider. I could almost see the web that bound them all together and skipped me.

I left as quietly as I had come, reflecting on the difference between the staff as I had seen them Sunday with the residents and as I now saw them among themselves. I realized for the first time that the residents were not the only ones with a guard up. The staff all had to keep up a certain manner and appearance while they were around the residents. Their façade is just as complicated as that of the residents, and just as important to them.

*   *   *

One afternoon sitting on the porch steps I was talking to a few of the residents, just hanging out while they all smoked cigarettes. I was asking a few questions, but basically just shooting the breeze about nothing and listening to them talk among themselves. One of the boys turned to me and said, "Are you a nice person?" He was wondering if I was reporting to the staff, but the phrasing of the question really got to me. How could I be a "nice person" in their eyes and still maintain my own identity?

One evening sitting in the television room of the house eating dinner, a female resident said, "This is my family, man. It's like we've all grown up together in the system. Me and Chris and Sue and Debby were all in Chins together. And me and Jason and Sarah were in Zeb Pike [state-operated detention center]. Yeah you could say we been a family for a while. It tripped me out to come here and see everyone, but it was cool, you know. Hey Sue, you remember when we were in Chins and couldn't wait to come here? We couldn't wait, man. Funny, huh? It trips me out."

They have grown up together. They are children of the system. Their roots are somewhere in DSS (Department of Social Services) or DYS (Department of Youth Services). They only have themselves and each other.

*   *   *

Another evening in the same television room, a former resident who was visiting asked me how I had found the Dale House, and when I told her she said, "You're glad you did the Dale House. Chins is like a zoo for kids. Dale House is good place to be. I like it here."

*   *   *

One afternoon behind the house, I was sitting at the picnic table and one of the residents was telling me about her home life and how she had come to the Dale House. She spoke of an ongoing courtroom battle with her mother. "Me and my two brothers, we're all in the system. She's a bad mother." "I just wish she wouldn't fight me, you know. I'm trying to get my life straight and I'm doing good. She just keep telling lies about me in court. She says I'm on drugs. She's lyin'."

*   *   *

Two of the boys sat down and started to tell their stories. "My mom says the dumbest things, man. She's always tellin' me to steal all my money out of here and come home. F—— that, man, it's stupid. She's stupid."

"Yeah every time he's on the phone with his mom he be yellin' at her and s——, man, every time."

"That's cause she's stupid that'all."

* * *

In the television room one day with a resident and her friend:

"I don't wanna do nothin' else to my hair, man. I like it."

"It's flat, though. Maybe you outta get a perm or somethin'."

"I don't want no perm, man. The last time I got one of those they had to cut off all my hair, man." (to me) "They cut it all off, man. I was on the run and dyed my hair and me and my boyfriend and his friend and his friend's girlfriend we were all in Alaska—man, it was pretty—and I went to get my hair permed and it killed my hair, fried it. It was gross. And they started to cut if off and I told 'em not to cause I figured I could just use lots of conditioner and it would be okay, but they cut it off anyway. It was down to my butt and they cut it all off man, shorter than Megan's and I cried, man."

* * *

At this point I found myself in the middle of some intense rehearsals of *Balm in Gilead*, character-developing sessions and discussions about the theme of the play. We spoke about having no family, or none to speak of, and of the way one's personality develops as a result of abuse and/or loneliness. There was a lot of talk about trust and the lack thereof. There was also talk about the intense human need for companionship.

As I thought about these things in connection with the character I was playing, my thoughts flew back to some of the residents of the Dale House. I began to understand the wary looks and the tough attitudes. They were protecting themselves from everyone. I then began to notice the subtle difference between residents who had been there longer and the newcomers. The older residents' guard was down more. They were easier to talk to than the others. They were not as threatened by my presence.

* * *

I began to watch the body language of the older residents as they spoke with each other and hung out on the front steps, smoking. They stood straight and firmly grounded. They looked each other and the staff members in the eyes while they were communicating. However tough this stance made them appear, their caring was shown in occasional smiles and looks of concern as they spoke. There was also a lot of physicality among both residents and staff in the form of hugs and a little friendly roughhousing, much as one would see in a functional family.

*   *   *

On the porch one evening, two male residents nearing emancipation spoke of their plans for the future:

"I'm gonna get a good job and go to college. Probably at night. Do they let you do that—have class at night? I heard they do. That's what I wanna do."

"I might go to college too. I want to do art. Or maybe I could be a tattoo artist. I've done lots of them and I heard if you take pictures of one hundred tattoos that you do and send them in you can get your license."

"Yeah. I guess so. I wanna work in a radio station or somethin' maybe."

"I'm gonna have a job, then I'm gonna do art."

They smile at each other.

"Yeah."

*   *   *

Playing guitar on the porch with one of the female residents:

"I play when I'm feeling bad, you know. I like it. At first I was afraid to play in front of people and stuff, but now I'm not really. I like to play the songs that we played on Sunday. I want to help people like me, you know, go into youth ministry. Do you think that's stupid?"

*   *   *

Sitting with a resident during the middle of an argument between another resident and a staff member:

"F—— you. Man, I didn't do it. I told you what I did, I didn't do anything else they say. F—— you."

"I hope she don't do nothin crazy. She'd hit her, man. She would. I hope she just walks away. Walks away and goes inside."

*   *   *

Talking with a staff member in the television room:
"I really like it here. It's hard sometimes, but it can be really rewarding. Sometimes I get frustrated and don't know what to do, but most of them are good people. You just have to keep up."

*   *   *

On "girls' night out" walking to Josh and John's for ice cream with two residents:
"If I were in the Philippines I would be in college right now instead of high school. I'd be in my second year of college. It's different over there."
"Jen, are you coming back here after you go home?"
"Yes."
"When?"
"In August, near the end."
"Oh, I'll still be here. So will Linda."
"Are you glad you came with us?"
"Yes."
"Oh."
The two girls smile at me. I am surprised. They are two that usually do not speak to me at all in friendly ways around the others. We enter the store and join other customers.

*   *   *

A female "crasher," someone who has been placed in the Dale House temporarily, who has been around for a few days, needs to get ready for a meeting with her mother and a case worker. She asks one of the toughest girls if she will help her fix her hair and get ready. The resident agrees. As I watch the scene, I become aware of a tenderness that I have not seen before in the resident. She takes her time and seems really concerned with the girl's appearance. While she does the crasher's hair she talks to her about the upcoming meeting and comforts her, telling her that things will work out and it will be okay. The crasher pours her heart out. She says that she wants to stay at Dale House. The resident tells her that maybe they will let her stay, but even if they don't that she can always visit. At some point the resident catches me watching her and, instead of hardening as she usually does, she smiles at me— a little shaky at first. I smile back and her smile becomes more confident.

"If they let you come back, I'll do your hair tomorrow too. Good luck."

"Thanks."

*   *   *

On the steps one afternoon with a resident, another resident arrives "home" from a day in court:

"How'd it go?"

"Well . . . I won! I beat her and Tom said he saw her crying but I didn't care. I just didn't. And you would have been proud of me too, I kept my cool. All day she was trying to make me mad, but I didn't let her. I've never been so happy in my life ever!"

"That makes my day. I'm so happy for you. The system worked, man, that's awesome! I'm so happy for you. Congratulations."

They hug and I hug her too. I've been following the battle and hoping for her. Suddenly I am smiling. Any troubles I have had are suddenly no longer important.

"Look, Jen is smiling. Man, you made her day too. She was all mopin' around and I was tryin' to cheer her up all day."

*   *   *

Somehow, I had without knowing it become part of the support network that I had been trying to study. They had become important to me and I had become important to them. I was amazed at the change that had taken place in just a few short weeks. I had gone from being a threatening outsider to a "nice person." It was a good feeling.

*   *   *

In the closing days of my time to study the Dale House I went by a few times and tried to follow up on all of the stories going on. I also gave the

Dale House some tickets to my play. I hoped that they would see how lucky they were to have a family and to have a future. A couple of them came to see it and I spoke with them backstage after the performance. They were congratulatory and hugged me. We chatted for a few seconds and then they turned to leave. One of the female residents hung back and winked at me, whispering "I'm glad I came—I understand." I realized then that they did not need to see the world of *Balm in Gilead* to feel lucky. They had already been there. They know how lucky they are. I was the one who needed to see *Balm in Gilead* and the Dale House. I was the one who needed to understand the reality of the world I could only play at, and I also needed to understand that there is hope in that reality. It was an emotional journey indeed.

The night after the Sunday matinee performance, I went to my last family night at the Dale House. After the introductions, I stood up and thanked everyone for allowing me to enter their lives, and wished them all the luck in the world with whatever might come their way. They clapped for me and a few of them got up to hug me. They thanked me and told me to come back and visit them next year if I could ever find the time. "Some of us won't be here, but some of us will."

LAST THOUGHTS

What began as an objective "get the assignment done as quickly and efficiently as possible" kind of ethnography turned into a personal journey somewhere along the way. I began to look forward to going to the Dale House every day and was disappointed when I couldn't find the time to do so. I went to the Dale House when I had no real purpose as far as the paper was concerned. I went to be with the people, to hear their stories, to feel a part of the web of support. I began to wish that my character in *Balm in Gilead* could find a place like the Dale House to ease her pain and give her a sense of togetherness with other people. It is that support, that togetherness, that we are all looking for. For some of the lucky people it comes naturally in the family, but the residents of Dale House and the characters in *Balm in Gilead* are not so lucky at all. They have built up defenses against the world and its evils. They have become tough, seemingly immune to the harshness others can deliver. The difference comes in the fact that the residents of the Dale House have found a place where they get support, not only from the staff but also from each other. They still have the defenses, but they are becoming softer. Every day they are moving away from the characters of *Balm in Gilead*. Every day brings a new breakthrough or a new step. Sometimes there are backward moves when rules are broken and sometimes the defenses come back as hard as ever, but at least they are moving. The world of *Balm in Gilead* is behind them, still visible but not as sharp as before. The Dale House succeeds in doing what it sets out to do. It gives a sense of family to those who need it most.

Bijou House

by Andrew D. Lewis

Lewis was a freshman when he wrote this paper. He approached everything—even complaining—with exuberance that year. He was encountering the world outside of his home community for the first time, just as many students in this course are, and expressed wonder at what he saw in both literal and metaphorical exclamation points.

This paper, which is condensed here because it was so long, started him on a path that led to a senior honors thesis in anthropology on homeless young men in Manhattan and Westchester County, which won first place in a national contest for undergraduate papers in anthropology, publication of that thesis (Schlig, 1989–90), and winning a competitive internship in New York City government.

Note that although Lewis describes freely (and at times melodramatically) his re-action to the people who are his informants and teachers, he does not let those reactions dominate the paper, but strikes a balance.

My heart raced with excitement as I slipped on an old ripped-up pair of blue jeans, shredded T-shirt, and a secondhand army jacket. I left the safety and security of my dorm with just $2 and identification, and rode my bike to the 7-11 across the street from campus. I bought a pack of Marlboros in the hope that it would help me gain information later, as well as get me into the right "frame of mind." How awkward it felt to be dressed as a "street bum," yet riding a $500 bicycle! With only 80 cents on my person, I pulled out of the 7-11 parking lot and headed down Tejon Street.

The farther downtown I rode, the fewer the street lights became. The farther downtown I rode, the tighter my stomach became—tight with the anxiety of what lay ahead. The farther downtown I rode, the more I felt I was leaving a familiar world and entering a world of the unknown—a hid-den, "underground" culture that the first world knows very little about.

After a fifteen-minute ride, I came to the designated area where I was to leave my bicycle behind and become "one with the street." After locking my bicycle, I lit a cigarette and headed down a pitch-black street. By that point I was trying with limited success to block out conscious memories of my "past life" of a quarter of an hour earlier. I was alone—with no past and no future. My worldly possessions consisted of a pack of cigarettes, 80 cents, identification, and myself. I finally reached the entrance to the Red Cross Shelter. It was 9:45 P.M. All I needed to do to gain entrance was present some identification (a New York state driver's license) and to sign a form stating that I was carrying no weapons. With those formalities out of the way, I was officially in "the heart of poverty." My one night spent at the shelter will never be forgotten.

It was a warehouse—a warehouse for what one informant called the "leftovers of society." The head count for that particular night was about 150. Until 11 P.M. (lights-out), I mixed, mingled and observed as many persons as time allowed. A good part of this time was spent in the TV room. By watching some commercials, I realized how little of the "outside" larger culture of the United States pertained to these people. "Use Dove Soap for just seven days and your face will look and feel softer." "Those f——ing whores never wash themselves—they never wash their hands, their faces, or their goddamn p———. They wake up the next day, put more makeup on, and do whatever it is that they do." "That's right, in just five low monthly payments, you too, can own this beautiful sofa and coffee table." "If I ever catch the asshole who stole my boot, I'll cut both of his legs off with this knife!" "Sign up now and get your first month's membership to U.S. Swim and Fitness at half the normal price." "Yeah, at age 18 I was involved in an alcohol-related car accident in Pennsylvania. When our car hit the telephone pole, I was thrown through the windshield and run over by a car traveling in the opposite direction. My skull and spinal cord were severely damaged. My left hand and knee were crushed. My jaw was broken in seventeen places. And I sustained serious brain damage from two weeks in a coma, causing blindness in one eye, slurred speech, partial retardation, and seizures. My mother's an alcoholic. She couldn't take care of me. We had no money so I'm on the road looking for work."

Everyone has their own story, but they share many things in common; the most prominent is poverty. I didn't sleep much that night. My mind was racing with sorrow, pity, and disgust. Conditions were filthy, overcrowded, and violent. Parents with little children were actually using these wretched facilities. I clung to my few possessions and waited for morning.

Why did I spend the night at the shelter? I have learned that there is no better way of learning about a condition than by experiencing it. My research project is centered around the Bijou House, an establishment designed to house twelve homeless persons. Conditions at the Bijou House are much better than at the Red Cross Shelter. I felt it was worth my while to investigate the shelter to better understand where the Bijou residents are coming from (many Bijou residents come from the Red Cross Shelter) and what conditions Bijou staff members are battling in Colorado Springs. It was a valuable experience that helped put many things into perspective—mainly, just how valuable the Bijou House is for the poor and homeless.

More explicitly, this paper focuses on the Bijou House's system of operation and on the binding force between members of the staff, the majority of whom have altered and devoted their lives to helping. My main methods of data gathering were formal and informal interview sessions with staff and residents, and simple observation. My definition of observation is to have open, unassuming, nonjudgmental eyes and ears.

Before I describe the Bijou House's system of operation, it is necessary to understand the staff members and how most of them choose to live out their lives. There are eleven supervisors, ranging in age from 24 to 45. Seven of the eleven are members of one or two communities: the Bijou Community and the Tejon Community. The other four people are affiliated with these communities but, for varying reasons, at this time they choose to remain separate.

What are these communities and how do they operate? The Bijou and Tejon communities are groups of people: Tejon has seven adults and two children and the Bijou has seven adults and one child who choose to live a life of simplicity, where all of their earnings are pooled and the wealth is distributed evenly among the adult members. They live as a family, bonded by common ideals, working toward justice for the poor and peace for all realms of life. Approximately two years ago, the Bijou community split, budding off the Tejon. This did not occur because of strife but rather they wanted to maintain close personal ties, which was difficult with such high numbers. One member of the Tejon community said it was getting to the point where nobody knew what was going on in anybody else's life. Members of the Bijou community are spread out in four different locations: 411 E. Bijou, 235 E. Fountain, 14 W. Bijou, and 217 S. 13th Street. Members of the Tejon community are located under one roof at 817 S. Tejon. They all live as a "a family of friends" bonded by common ideals encompassing how they live their lives. What are these common ideals and how did they originate?

Approximately sixteen years ago, two Roman Catholic priests left the luxury of the parish because they felt that their lives were too separated from the people. Their decision to live a simpler life caused a disagreement with church officials. So Steve Handin (one of the two) left the priesthood entirely.

Fifteen years ago, at the height of the Vietnam War, Mary Lynn Handin (not yet married to Steve) found her way to Steve, who had already started to take in the homeless on a very small level. She, like many others, was a conscientious objector.

Mary Lynn, Steve, and other objectors started what they called the Colorado Inner City Assistance Agency. They needed to call it something in order to get selective service support (this would take the place of cleaning bedpans). Its function was to aid the poor and homeless in Colorado Springs. In the beginning, this agency was a haven for people who "CO'd" out of the military (became conscientious objectors), as well as those who were heavily involved in draft resistance. The agency offered assistance through food and shelter for the homeless. From the very beginning its members pooled whatever income they had and evenly distributed it. They found that if they worked together they could help the homeless. Slowly, the community began to help people who lacked food, clothing, and shelter. The number of poor increased during these early years. Mary Lynn attributed and still attributes this to the military: "The military is the cause of poverty and poverty feeds back into the military." As demands increased, buildings were rented for shelter and a soup kitchen was established.

For the past fifteen years, the community system has expanded. Community members sharing common beliefs supervising the shelters and soup kitchen are "the family." The poor and homeless using the facilities are also considered community members, and are "the extended family." Members of the Bijou and Tejon community voluntarily operate the Bijou House, the Vermijo House, the Marion House, the soup kitchen, and the drop-in center. Although the poor people using the facilities are considered community members, the supervisors do not "push" their personal religious, political, and social philosophies. In fact, most supervisors and residents live in different dwellings. Residents and supervisors make up two separate parts of the community.

As I mentioned, community-member supervisors are tied by common beliefs. What are these beliefs?

To begin, by becoming a member one has decided to live out a simple lifestyle. Supervisors work part-time jobs where they earn less than the taxable income. What they earn is pooled in a community "chest." Although the Bijou and Tejon Communities are closely related, each has its own community chest. After all monthly expenditures have been taken care of, each adult is allotted $25 for the month as spending money. They live simply for two central reasons: By earning below the taxable income, they are not contributing to the military. By living a life of abstinence they become more in tune with poverty and human suffering, hence more in tune with themselves. The only way of truly understanding the poor is by living among them.

One supervisor said, "We are no better than anybody who does not have an education. We have a responsibility to our fellow man—to help people live out *their* ideals within their personal limits." Another supervisor used to be involved with a public social service department. She found there was too much red tape involved in helping people. When she came to the Bijou Community in September 1982, she found it more satisfying because of its direct contact with the poor. A third supervisor told me that we are all explicitly interconnected. The fact that other people are starving does us psychological damage. "The more in touch we become with human suffering, the more we are in touch with ourselves." A noncommunity-member supervisor said, "In order to help these people, workers must feel an inner simplicity. It is simply not good enough to "throw money at the problem," hoping that will "get them [the poor] out of the way." Head supervisor Mary Lynn recognizes the necessity of charity. "We would not exist without it." But for her and for other supervisors that is simply not good enough. The "poor are swept under the bridge" so the rest of society does not have to deal with or even see them. All community-member supervisors feel that working among the poor is the best way of helping them and countering the neglect of poverty. Another noncommunity-member supervisor said, "I have never witnessed as high a level of devotion."

To conclude this summary of beliefs, generally the higher one is on the economic scale (more accumulated wealth), the more there is to protect. The more there is to protect, the less open one is to helping the less fortunate. Mary Lynn explains that Christ is calling for a life of nonacquisition. With acquisition you need protection so you cannot be available to everyone.

Community-member supervisors devote the least of their time to paying jobs. They earn only the bare minimum for essentials. The rest of their time is devoted to community promotion of justice for the poor and worldwide peace. Although the Bijou House and the city's poor are the center of their attention, just about every family community member (but not residents) is involved in justice and peace issues. These include the environment, nuclear threats, and large-scale poverty. Most are actively involved in the Pikes Peak Justice and Peace Commission, whose main focus is to educate the public on issues and present sides not presented by the media. To varying degrees they also participate in nonviolent protest. Issues usually pertain to U.S. policy in Central America and the arms race. One supervisor is presently serving prison time for a protest-related offense. Other supervisors jokingly told me that the community members "take turns" serving prison sentences. One supervisor told me that last year several supervisors were imprisoned at the same time, making it very difficult to cover all of the shifts at the Bijou House.

Where do these people come from? Why? What are their goals? One of the supervisors I talked with recently graduated from Notre Dame and found this community while in a one-year Holy Cross Associates program. I asked him how difficult the transitional period was from a "normal" existence to a simplified one. He pointed out that he was not coming straight from the security of home. Dorm life already prepared him for the reduction in privacy, the budgeting of money, and so on. Also, no one instantly became a community member. They spent time as noncommunity-member supervisors, becoming familiar with the community system. They knew what they were getting themselves into. "The transition period is ongoing, but I enjoy it," said one of the Notre Dame graduates. "Nothing is ever the same." Other community supervisors came from middle-class families with high-paying jobs, and after some time found that the ideals of the community matched their own. After talking to these people, I realized that it truly is "a personal call." The adjustment could not be made if an individual didn't agree with the community system and its ideology. The adjustment could not be made without a strong sense of caring, selflessness, insight, and devotion to its cause. However, if a person does possess these traits, the transition is possible from any wealth status. To be a member involves a material sacrifice as well as a sacrifice of a familiar and secure way of life.

[The author discusses goals and roles of community and noncommunity supervisors.]

The Bijou House is a white three-story house located at 411 West Bijou Street. I define the establishment as a sort of "place of transition"—transition from the streets toward a goal set by the individual. Resident goals usually take the form of finding a job and earning enough money to find a place of his or her own. There is space for twelve occupants at a time. Length of stay depends entirely on individual circumstance; sometimes the stay is two weeks (until a person finds work), other times (although less often) it has been two years and longer. Basically, the house serves as a place to eat, sleep, interact, and pursue personal goals. Residents have the freedom to come and go within the confines of some structure—structure (supplied by supervisors and house rules) that helps each individual resident pursue their own goals, within their own personal limits.

How does one get into Bijou House? First of all, people either get referred from doctors, authorities, or most commonly, from the Red Cross shelters. If the individual is interested, he or she will go to the house for a short interview. He or she will always be openly welcomed with no "opening prejudices" on the part of the supervisor on duty. The supervisor will explain the rules, how the home operates, and what is expected of the residents. At this time, the supervisor will question and observe the individual in order to best understand his or her particular problems, needs, and goals. Standard procedure is to allow two weeks for the person to find a job and an additional two weeks for the first paycheck. If, after the first two weeks, the resident has not found work, the supervisor will sit down with the individual and figure out the trouble. There is no standard procedure for this dilemma. Every situation is handled on an individual basis.

Once prospective residents have been informed of the rules and agree to abide by them, they are put on a waiting list. They are then expected to check back daily to see if there are openings. The list changes frequently as people are taken in and others move out. People who check in daily are given priority over those who only check in every week or so. I was told by one informant that in a way the waiting list is "a bunch of bull——." Priority is given to people who know one of the supervisors, to previous residents, and to people getting out of prison. (Often a prisoner will not be released without a place to stay.)

What is expected of residents? Supervisors want residents to feel comfortably at home, but to treat the property with the respect that a guest should show. These simple rules and procedures are expected to be followed:

1. People are expected to help with chores around the house in order to keep down expenses.
2. Any problems should be brought to the supervisor's attention.
3. Absolutely no drunkenness will be allowed. When cases arise, again, they are handled individually. Sometimes a resident will be kicked out, other times a severe warning is issued.
4. Alcohol, drugs, and weapons are forbidden on the premises.
5. Cigarettes may only be smoked outside.
6. The Bijou House is locked at 10:30 P.M. Anybody still out after this time is usually not let in.
7. Finally, rent is $180 per month. People are expected to pay what they can. Nobody will be evicted for lack of money. However, if it is known that a person is making money but not contributing, he or she will be confronted and dealt with individually.

Where do the finances to support the Bijou House come from? No assistance is accepted from religious institutions. This is the community's personal protest against established religion. Their main source of income is through cash and/or food donation. Hewlett Packard, which employs 2,000 people locally, donates unused cafeteria food. Food drives can raise thousands of cans and packages of food. My impression was that Bijou House depends the least on a steady income from monthly rent paid by residents. Mary Lynn said that rent is the last of their concerns. The best way of covering house expenses is by keeping expenses low. Most food that has not been donated is bought from the food bank. This is a branch of Care and Share that sells bulk food (usually by the pound) that is near its date of expiration. Most items sell for 12 cents a pound. Finally, they do all maintenance and repair work themselves. In fact, there is a community-member supervisor whose main responsibilities are house maintenance and building bikes for residents out of scrap.

Although the turnover may be relatively fast, the types of people using the facilities generally remain the same. There are three main categories: the mentally ill, substance abusers, and people just down on their luck. The second and third often, but not always, overlap each other.

Schizophrenics account for many of the mentally ill. Unlike other brain diseases, in most cases it can be controlled by medication. The term *controlled* means they don't pose a threat to society. The schizophrenic man I observed at the Bijou House posed no threat, but was certainly unable to work.

A comparison of community housing to institutionalized mental health care is a tremendous study within itself. I feel it is worthwhile to at least touch on the issue. I was fortunate enough to speak with a noncommunity supervisor who is being trained as a psychiatric nurse. She has "seen both sides" and assured me, in reference to the schizophrenic staying at the Bijou House, "this milieu is the perfect psychiatric setting. Mary Lynn has such a natural insight into how to nurture and support these people." In comparison to the Cedar Springs Psychiatric Hospital (one of the best in the city), "this [The Bijou House] is the same milieu for which people pay thousands of dollars. One can exert his independence and autonomy within the confines of some structure. It's like a baby touching Mom, just to know she's there." In a crisis situation, a mental hospital would be the best setting, but not for a stabilized patient. "He couldn't grow in an inpatient psychiatric center." In Colorado, mental health centers also take in the second category of Bijou House residents: substance abusers. This psychiatric nurse assured me that the same holds true for stabilized alcohol and drug abusers: They are much better off in an environment comparable to the Bijou House.

Not all professionals agree with this opinion. Marsha Schlig *[the author's mother]*, a certified social worker who has had experience in mental health facilities, feels these people need round-the-clock professional care to assure the best possible results. She believes that although Bijou House may not do harm, they cannot bring about the best results. Schlig's limited experience with community living makes me leery of whether she is qualified to make such a judgment. Perhaps the community housing situations she is familiar with are not nearly as adequate as the Bijou House.

[A list of cooperating agencies, a list of supervisors' duties, and a discussion of staff meetings follow.]

I have learned a great deal from both residents and staff—information known and truly understood only by members of the Bijou culture. The evening before I was to write this paper, a resident, David, who had never spoken a word to me before this point, sat me down and told me about himself, giving me a lecture that made an indelible impression. He told me, "Don't ever forget that everyone is an individual. Everyone has their own story, their own desires, their own limitations." He reprimanded me for my continual generalizations and categorizations. I thought very intently about what he told me. His words made me aware of my deeply ingrained biases, prejudices, and stereotypes.—how often I take my economic position as "the desired position." He pointed out to me that not everybody wants the same things out of life. Not everybody has the same goals, the same limitations. Because of his lecture, the importance of relativity and individuality are intertwined throughout this paper.

My personal opinions, beliefs, and ideologies matched those of the community-member supervisors very closely. I am a "lefty" on the political spectrum. My mother is a social worker, so I have been brought up in a socially conscious environment. And I am very concerned over the same justice and peace issues that members are actively involved in. Because of this, the research project has been a grand success. In fact, it has inspired me to dream up a long list of social reforms. But as David put it, I've "got a lot to learn."

Both residents and supervisors taught me that not all of the poor are looking for superheros. Not all are looking for people to show them "the better life." Mary Lynn told me, "We are here not to elevate the poor and change their lives. You can't know what is good for rich or poor. We are here to offer services, but we can't tell someone how to live." Dave pointed out that the only way to understand the poor is to become one of them. The only way to conceptualize all of the different needs, desires, and feelings of the poor is to talk with them. Until then, don't make judgments. My conversation with David opened my eyes to what I feel are the inadequacies of overcategorization and overgeneralization. I have begun to wonder whether anthropology relies too heavily on such classification procedures.

From Mary Lynn I learned that everyone has their own needs and also has different ways of solving these needs. She looks at any person as somebody

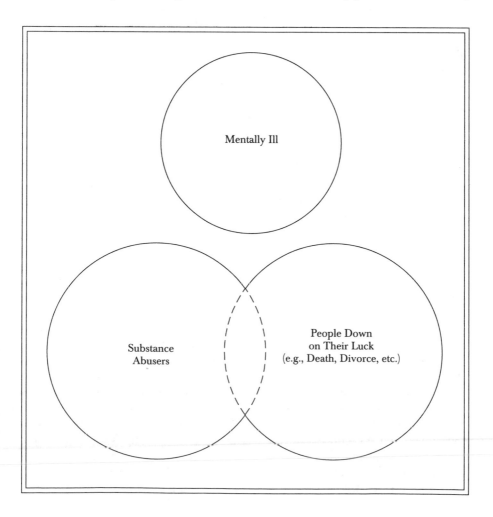

with certain needs. We are here to help people pursue their individual goals through routes most suitable for their specific situations. "I look at myself the same way," she said. She told me that in order to help a person who wants a job in Colorado Springs, we need to categorize him as "high functioning" or "low functioning." These terms are relative to Colorado Springs. Somebody who functions well here might be low functioning on a small farm, and vice versa. Everything is relative to a particular setting. A banker's wealth may be reduced from $5 million to $100,000 "overnight." This person probably cannot function with just $100,000 and might go so far as to kill himself. A bum is hit over the head and robbed of his last 10 cents. He'll be back the next day. Everything is relative. This is an integral part of the Bijou House's philosophy.

Mary Lynn (staff) and David (resident) are very closely tuned to each other's philosophies on the best methods to help the poor. Residents who choose to live at the Bijou House and use the affiliated facilities are usually in pursuit of something—their own goals. The Bijou House is much more of a home than an institution. "The importance of the home can never be overestimated," said one supervisor. The balance of freedom and structure is the perfect environment for individual residents to pursue their own aspirations without pressure from an "authority."

On a personal note, I greatly admire the volunteers involved with the Bijou House. They are rare individuals who have purposely immersed themselves into a realm of our society that so many others try so desperately to ignore.

The author appends several charts, one of which is reproduced on page 190. He told the class that, after this fieldwork was completed, he invited a schizophrenic resident of Bijou House (perhaps it was David) to visit the CC campus with him, and the view of the home campus through strange eyes astonished him.

Denny's: A Discovery of the Night People

by Jack Denman

Not every good ethnography produces an epiphany for the author. This description of an all-night fast-food restaurant is similar in conception to the undergraduate ethnographies in Spradley and McCurdy's pioneer work. It competently describes a working scene and its shared understandings, weaving into that description something of the author's reaction to the world that works when he is usually asleep.

As an indication that good work in the course is not limited to embryonic social scientists, it is worth noting that Denman majored in geology, doing so well that he was hired as a department paraprofessional the year after he graduated.

INTRODUCTION

It's a slow night on the town, all the parties have died down, the movies are all closed, you don't have much money left, and you don't want to go home yet. You are too young for the bars and you don't have any hope of getting lucky with the girl you're with. To top it off, you're also a bit on the hungry side.

OR

It's 2 A.M. The bar is closing. You're still wired from the drinks and music of the night. You have to drive across town to get home. Just before you reach I-25, the more intoxicated passengers in your car spot a large yellow sign in the sky and you steer toward it to grab a late night snack.

OR

It's 4:15 A.M. on the night watch in the crime-infested streets of the city. You've spent the night chasing imaginary burglars and drunks all over town. You are in desperate need of a break and the company of people besides your partner in the police department.

OR

You have just awakened from a deep slumber. You're dressed for work before the sun comes up and you need a cup of Jo' to keep you from dozing back to sleep, but there's no point in making a whole pot of coffee just for yourself. You'll just stop somewhere on the drive to work and grab one.

OR

It's a little cold to be sleeping outside tonight, besides, you can sleep all day if you're really tired. You have nothing else you have to do. You reach into your pocket and find some loose change you picked up at the bus station and start walking, looking forward to a hot drink.

What do all of these situations have in common with each other? Their subjects end up at the Denny's restaurant on West Bijou at some time of the night. Each of these characters shows up at the door to be seated by one of the hearty souls at the restaurant famous for being "Always Open." Those working the graveyard shift see each one of these characters every night they work. Those who choose to work this shift, for whatever reason, have their share of experiences with these "customers of the night." Although they were all trained by similar methods and have worked with each other for various amounts of time, all the people working the graveyard shift at Denny's are members of a society like no other. They bring with them a variety of backgrounds and philosophies that help them to cope with the stresses of the late-night shift. The differences in how each of the waiters or waitresses works with customers, from the regulars to the strangers, appear to reflect some aspect of their background.

This ethnography concentrates on the interactions of two waiters and a waitress I talked with over the course of my visits. I discuss the differences in their work habits and methods of dealing with clients as well as their reactions to each other. It is by no means a comprehensive view of the entire life of a server at Denny's, but a short insight into the late-night world that many come into contact with but few have the time to understand.

BRIEF DESCRIPTION

Denny's Restaurant is a "family eating place" that is open 24 hours a day. It is a nationally franchised restaurant that has locations all over the country. Most of the Denny's across the country look alike—a green decor on the inside, a large yellow sign that is often placed on a high pole so it can be seen for some distance. The advantage of Denny's restaurants over other restaurants is both that they are open all the time, except for Christmas Day, and the fact that they serve breakfast, the meal they are famous for, any time of the day or night.

The Denny's on West Bijou Street in Colorado Springs is located next to one of the main exits off I-25. Because there is a bend in the highway from the exit north creating a long line of sight, the large yellow sign is clearly visible from far down the highway. Thus many cars turn off the highway at all times of the night to come in and get something to eat.

The restaurant has a parking lot on the east side that holds fourteen cars. This wraps around to the service entrance in the rear of the building where there is extra parking.

There are two handicapped parking places and four newspaper vending machines just outside the front door. There is also a new Total gas station across the street.

To the west of the restaurant is mainly a residential district with duplexes and small houses. Behind the restaurant is a fence that stands between the service entrance and another set of apartments.

Inside Denny's, there are stickers on the windows that advertise their ALL YOU CAN EAT 'GRAND SLAM' BREAKFAST FOR ONLY $3.99. A cigarette machine sits in the front area where customers wait to be seated. Customers are seated at tables and booths (see chart). They can also seat themselves at a bar that runs along the outside of the server area. All the sections are smoking with the exception of the western section that has nine of the twenty-

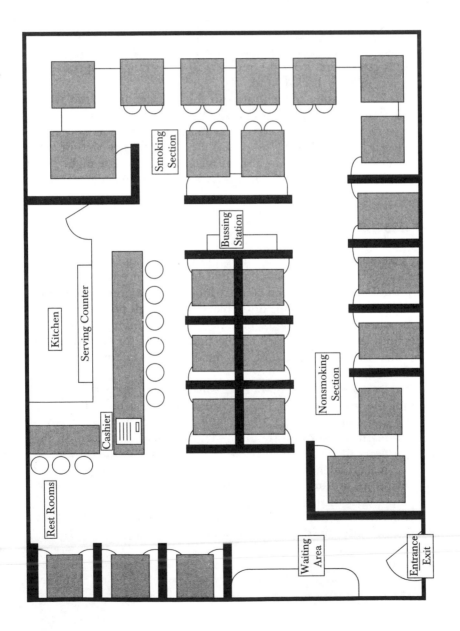

four tables. Some of the round booths have tables that fold out to connect with the booth next to it in order to seat more people. The bar can seat fourteen people on swivel chairs. The tables at the booths are all made higher than most other tables. The tops of them are at least 3 feet off the ground, but the seats sink very low, so one can almost set one's head on the table and shovel food directly into one's mouth without lifting a fork. The tables are equipped with salt and pepper shakers, an ashtray, and a folded pamphlet of the new dishes they have at the time.

INFORMANTS

My principal informants were three servers*—Ellen, Brendan, and Rob. I didn't choose them as my informants but rather they were working most often when I would come to do my fieldwork. I also talked to the manager, the busboy, and the cook, but most of my information comes from the three servers. There were others working some of the nights that I chose to study the shift, but they weren't as accessible as those I had already talked to, although I did include them in my study.

Ellen is 30 years old, but looks much younger. She is just divorced from her "asshole ex-husband" of fifteen years, "who refuses to pay child support." She has five children—two boys, whom her ex-husband has, and three girls whom she takes care of. She works up to two shifts at Denny's and a third shift at Western Omelet on weekends. Although she is struggling to make ends meet, she doesn't believe in welfare. The biggest problem she has with such a full schedule is the trouble of finding a reliable babysitter. She has been through three already. The first night that I talked to her, she had been awake for almost three full days because one of her daughters had an asthma attack two days earlier and had to go to the hospital. She was in high but very tired spirits that night.

Brendan is 20 years old and grew up just east of downtown. He graduated from Palmer High School and has been working at Denny's for about a year and a half. He has thought about going to college and has amassed a large savings account in preparation for it, but doesn't know what he would want to study. He puts it off so as not to waste his hard-earned money. He enjoys jazz music at work, but rock and roll at home. He and Rob play a semi-noncontact form of medieval sword fighting with broomsticks and ax handles on the rocks in the Garden of the Gods.

Brendan is engrossed in the aura that surrounds everything about the Middle Ages. He has been to the Renaissance Festival in Northern Colorado

---

*I use the term *server* instead of *waiter* and *waitress* throughout this ethnography, not as a politically correct term, but as a convenience. It would get complicated to refer to them by their gender-specific terms.

for the past two or three years, where he gets dressed up and talks with an accent in order to sound like he works there. "It's a way to get free beer from the 'tourists,'" he claims. His mother is a psychiatric nurse at the regional mental health center.

Rob is a lot taller than Brendan, but they are the same age. They went to high school together, and the two have been friends since eighth grade. Rob has been working at Denny's for only about four months and doesn't foresee himself staying much longer. He is anxious to get back to college and party. Rob went to the University of Arizona for a year where he played football, but he is back in Colorado to earn some more money.

Tom is a manager in training. He is from Colorado Springs and has been working at Denny's for a little more than a year. He started as busboy and is working up the ladder in hopes of becoming a full manager. He is in his 30s and is married and has two daughters. He is looking to stay with Denny's for a while.

The other informants I talked to include Sarah and Karen, both servers, Larry, the busboy and dishwasher, and the cook, Kurt. Each of these people provided me with an extra glimpse into what life is like on the graveyard shift.

NIGHT HAPPENINGS

The Denny's graveyard shift begins at 10 P.M. and lasts until 6:30 the next morning. The restaurant is usually quite crowded in the early hours of the shift, but the numbers taper off as the night wears on.

The early part of the shift, from 10 o'clock until 12 or 1, is filled with the younger crowd—high school, college, and men and women who appear to be under 30 years old. They are usually killing time after a full day, taking a study break, or just getting out for a night with some friends. There are usually three servers, a manager, a busboy/dishwasher, and one cook working at the start of the graveyard shift. By 1 A.M., the initial night crowd has tapered off and there is a brief lull in the activity, a time for the cook to take a needed break, the servers catch up on their cleaning, and the busboy to restock the dishes. Around 2 A.M., the place starts to pick up as the nine bars within a 9-mile radius start to close, and the bars' clients head home. The activity in the restaurant increases markedly when the people from the bars show up. The workers all put up with them as a part of their business, but vary in their reactions to the various types of drunk people, some gay, some homeless, and others of all ages and backgrounds. I discuss the reactions to the customers later. The people from the bars stay any length of time, but generally leave between 3 and 4:30 A.M. After the bar rush, the manager and one of the servers leave for the night. This is usually about 3 o'clock.

The cook, the busboy, and two servers are left to fend for themselves until 6:00, when the day crew comes in. From 3 until about 4:15 is usually a very dead time with the number of customers ranging from a hectic twenty to a peaceful three. If there is a large rush at this time, the servers are constantly on call and are extremely busy taking care of all the tables. If the number of clients is at the lower end of the scale, the servers and cook can be much more relaxed and take a break.

Smoking seems to be the activity of choice during breaks, which are taken either in the back, behind the door to the kitchen at a table specifically for the purpose, or at the counter in the main part of the restaurant. Breaks are also a time to grab a bite to eat and a cup of coffee to stay awake. The busboy usually doesn't take a break at the same time as the servers because he has his work to do while there are fewer customers.

About 4 A.M., the servers begin to clean the counters in preparation for the morning crowd. They clean the tables, the food counters, and the juice and coffee machines. They restock the tables with sugar, salt and pepper, and refill the ketchup bottles. They also put most of the salad food away and restock food items in the cabinets in the front with food from the storeroom in the back.

At 4:30, the menus are changed from the "late-night menus" to the larger "day menus" that have almost twice the food. There are more cooks during the day. By the time the cleaning is finished, the morning customers have started to trickle in. The graveyard cook is usually done about 5:30, at which time the two to three day cooks come in.

NIGHT DUTIES

There are three different types of jobs at Denny's during the graveyard shift. Each one has a specific uniform that distinguishes their wearers from the others. The servers wear striped green shirts with a cloth apron, the busboy wears a solid green shirt and rubber apron. The cook wears a white uniform with a tall white hat. The cook must always wear his hat and a green Denny's scarf around his neck. Each position has its own training. The servers start with a three- to four-week training period, followed by a four- to five-day on-the-job training period in addition to a written test. The length of the training depends on the amount of experience. Once they become qualified servers they start working the graveyard shift, where they train further, and with seniority can apply for a different shift when a position opens. They serve as hosts, take the orders, deliver the food, work the cash register, and clean up customers' tables as well as keeping all the areas clean.

When a customer first comes in, the servers take turns seating them. The server asks whether they want smoking or nonsmoking while she or he picks up the appropriate number of menus and silverware sets wrapped up in paper napkins. After showing the customers to their seats, they ask if they would like something to drink, regardless of who their actual server is. The host leaves, getting the drinks, and returns with them to let the customers look over the menu. A few minutes later, the server in charge of the table arrives and takes their order. The server then takes the customer's order and goes to one of the three computers located throughout the dining area and types the order in under a heading that keeps track of the server's name and the table number. The order is then printed up in the kitchen on a printer at eye level where the cook tears the slip off and tacks it up on a board and starts to prepare the food. While the main part of the meal is prepared in the kitchen, the server gets any additional parts of the meal ready, such as the salad and dressing, butter and syrup, or the ketchup and steak sauce, all the while taking care of other tables in their sections. All the food for the table is then put on any one of five sizes of tray and taken to the table. The server checks on customers any time that they are in the area, refilling drinks or getting more food. When customers are done with their meals, the server gives them a printout of their order and leaves them to fig-ure their bill out. The customers pay their bill at the cashier computer near the only door before exiting. After they have left, the server picks up the tip and cleans the table off, putting the dirty dishes in one of the bins for the busboy to pick up to take into the washroom. The table is wiped off and is ready for the next customer.

The busboy needs the least amount of training. He doesn't really bus the tables, but does most of the cleaning work at the restaurant. He is in charge of making sure that all the dirty dish bins are emptied and the clean dish trays are filled. He is constantly bringing out new trays of coffee mugs and taking the dirty bins into the back. He also does the vacuuming when there are few customers.

The cook remains in the kitchen most of the night except for breaks. While meals are cooking, he cleans the kitchen area.

The manager has the position with the most responsibility, hence is the one who requires the most training. The manager must be able to wait ta-bles, cook, manage the food stock and work schedules, control unruly cus-tomers, and calm the tempers of complaining ones—all of this while making sure that everything will run smoothly after he or she leaves for the night. The managers weren't working a majority of the time that I did my research, but I was able to talk with one, Tom, who was in the latter part of training.

NIGHT CUSTOMERS

A wide variety of people come to Denny's at all times of the night. The early part of the night has an assortment of different customers, whereas the later it gets, the more homogeneous the customers get. Some late nighters come every night; others who are not "regulars" usually fall into a certain type. I realized through my own observations and talking with the servers that there are certain general types of people that come at specific times of the night.

The earlier part of the late night shift sees a variety of old and young customers who come to eat a late-night meal or grab some dessert. The variety of the customers is as wide as the menu at this time of night. Large burly men and women (some of the men with beards), wearing Harley-Davidson attire, come in force as well as younger, cleaner, high school and college-age men and women wearing jeans and T-shirts or sweatshirts.

The late-night customers usually consist of three types of people. There are first the drunks and second the "weirdos," who constitute a majority of the people who frequent the late-night hours. The third type of customers are the traveling businesspeople who are on their way to or from work or are taking a break during work for a cup of coffee. The drunks come from any of the nearby bars, and the weirdos and workers come from everyplace else. Each category of customers promotes a different degree of receptiveness by the servers, which is usually based on the conduct of the customer.

As midnight rolls around, the earlier crowd starts to filter out and a sporadic assortment of characters lingers until the bar rush, which comes about 2 A.M.. The majority of the people that I saw come before the bar rush were much more disheveled than those still around from earlier in the evening. They were dirty, had clothes that hadn't been washed in a long time, and their hair was in a heightened state of uncleanliness and disarray. Most of the people that fit this description would come alone and sit at the counter, often just ordering a cup of coffee. Some would try to get a cigarette from one of the servers, who knew a few of the "regulars" by name. The financial problems of some of these people can be quite severe; I witnessed one instance in which a man, who appeared to be very hungry and was obviously known by the servers, got a free salad late one night. This is not always the case, however, because, on the same night, another man was forced to pay and leave with the help of a police officer. Many of the people who pose such problems for the servers and the customers at Denny's are not a part of the regular crowd.

The condition of the "weirdos" varies widely from a drunken, incoherent state to that of a very friendly, talkative one. But regardless of their condition, all of them are treated as the same customers from the start. The extent to which service is provided to them depends on their conduct with both the servers and with others in the restaurant. Some are met with hostility by the servers because of previous confrontations; others are met with a certain amount of friendliness and welcome. One regular, "Fred," fits the description of a hobo, but no one really knows his story. He came in on a Tuesday night and sat right down at the bar. Sarah, the server at the bar, asked him how he was doing and immediately got him a cup of coffee and kept up a conversation with him. When another man who was dressed similar to "Fred" came in and sat down, Rob, the other server that night, got him the cup of coffee that he asked for, but ceased any form of conversation with him because of his incessant complaints about the service. The second man ended up being escorted out of the restaurant by Rob and Tom, the manager, because he was getting loud and obnoxious with two ladies sitting in a booth. A major problem with many of the strange late-night customers is that they have any number of mental as well as social and economic problems. Brendan told me that his mother is a psychiatrist at the mental health center and joked, "I don't want to hear about her work, because most of her patients are probably here every night they aren't over there." The mental health of the customers is beyond the control of the servers, but customers must be served until they cause large disruptions or endanger others. When things do get rowdy on the weekends, it is not unusual for someone to be escorted out by either a number of servers or the police. Regardless of the mental condition of the customer, their conduct can largely determine how well they are taken care of by the servers.

The bar rush brings a different type of customer from bars closing at 2 until as late as 4:30 A.M. They range from slightly buzzed and friendly to passing out in the handicapped parking place outside. They are usually rowdy and loud and can be both threatening and dangerous to the servers as well as other, sober customers.

The third group of clients who frequent the late night Denny's scene are those who are traveling to, from, or are taking a break from, work. This includes taxi drivers between calls, businesspeople on their way to work and, the best represented, the police. The cops on the night shift can be considered a class of regulars in themselves because they are there almost every night of the week. They come around 3:30 to 4:30 in the morning and gradually fill the back section of the restaurant as the night wears on. Most know each other by their first names and are on very good terms with each other. Their ages are between 25 and 35 years old, and they work in the central and western parts of the city. The servers welcome them with open arms, not just because they are assured that they won't cause any trouble, but because they are also lifesavers at times. With the violence and disruptions during the odd hours of the night when only four to five people are running the establishment, the help an officer can provide with an unruly customer is invaluable. "I'd gladly give them free food so they show up immediately," says Brendan, "The faster they come, the safer we are." Evidently, whenever a call goes out that help is needed at Denny's, three to four squad cars arrive almost in a matter of seconds. Brendan explains that they all know they will get free coffee if they show up, a big incentive at 3 A.M.

Certain nights are known for their different clientele: Wednesday night is known as "gay night" because of the crowd that comes from the Hide and Seek Bar a few blocks away. There are usually around fifteen men who come from the bar each Wednesday night. Although they all come from the bar together, they don't always sit together. They tend to sit in groups of three to five, with some saving places for friends. The men eat and talk just like all the other customers, but they also hug and occasionally kiss one another. They flirt with both the male and female servers. The females are flirted with a little more jokingly, whereas there is a noticeably different tone in the flirtations toward the male servers. The trouble with these customers comes when they sit in a group larger than three. Ellen complained that they get extremely rowdy and almost unmanageable when they get in groups that large because they all get cocky and very forward with everyone even though some know the servers fairly well.

NIGHT PROBLEMS

Violence is prevalent during the night shift. No major disputes occurred during my fieldwork, but smaller ones that needed the aid of police and removal of a customer did happen. The police came and convinced one to pay and leave, and another was removed by Rob and Tom—both small skirmishes compared with the large brawl that erupted just two nights before I made my initial contact which needed ten cops to quell. I found out that this is almost the norm at some times. "I have been hurt more on the job trying to break up regular barroom brawls than I have sword and staff fighting with my friends on my own," claims Brendan. One weekend, I am told, a woman even pulled a knife on her husband in an argument. Things are far from dull on the night shift. One doesn't know who will come or what someone will do from one minute to the next because the condition of the customers worsens as the night wears on.

Logistical problems that erupt during the night can also wreak havoc in the workings of the restaurant. Often, toward the end of the week, the food for certain dishes runs out and the servers have to cope. This inconvenience can turn to trouble when trying to explain to an intoxicated customer why he or she can't have the food that they want.

*   *   *

VIOLENCE AT NIGHT

The frustrations of the violence at work also comes out in the actions of the workers. Brendan and Rob are stressed by the possibility of violence. Both have been involved in breaking up scores of fights and have gotten hit by drunks quite a number of times. Their frustration shows in what they say as well as in their body language. Rob's clenched fists when he had to remove the rowdy customer show that his temper was very high and was on the verge of getting physical. When the situation was over, he shook his head and rolled his eyes and sighed through his still clenched teeth as he walked past me into the back where he could let out his anger in private. A confrontation was avoided this time, but when one does occur, the frustration is compounded when one of the servers gets hit and isn't allowed to hit back because he is wearing his uniform and, "It would look bad on the corporation . . . they could end up suing us," explains Rob with a note of sarcasm in his voice.

The threat of violence among the customers is a unifying factor that enables the servers to unite against a common enemy. The body language that has developed through this unity is phenomenal. All a server has to do is to glance or nod to another, and they understand that they could use some help.

STAYING AWAKE

The different servers have various methods of enabling themselves to stay awake. Some of these methods help the others on the shift to stay alert as well; others do not. Brendan, for instance, says that you have to stay laughing the entire time. The minute you stop laughing, is the moment you border on going crazy in the confusion. Kurt, the cook, agrees with this philosophy and tries his best to crack jokes about everything that happens to anyone, regardless of the cruelty of the joke. Most of the conversations that are held at the late times of the night seem to center around a popular subject: sex. I asked Brendan about this and he said that just about every conversation in the place revolves around sex at one point or another. "It's something you can always laugh about, and that's what keeps me going," he says.

The fact that work time is always interesting and exciting, not knowing what will happen next, is a major factor in keeping Ellen and Rob awake and on their toes.

The servers also depend a great deal on Kurt. He is isolated from the stresses of dealing with the customers and talks only with the servers, who come to him to laugh or complain about their tables.

SEX AT NIGHT

"Sexual harassment is part of the job, and if some 'superfeminist' came in here, we'd all be in jail." This wraps up Brendan's view on the flirting aspect. He says that it is a part of the job that no one can refuse to bypass. It is essential to flirt with everyone, regardless of their age or looks in order to get good tips. It is what gets the tips, keeps you awake, and sometimes even gets you a date. Both male and female workers take part in the sexual innuendo games played at night. There are no rules, no holds barred; surprisingly, the women were a little more creative.

The abundance of the talk about sex could be a defense mechanism to help them deal with the fact that they have to work during the hours that most sexual activity takes place. They might feel that since they can't take part, they might as well talk about it. Rob relates this to a perk that the job offers: the ability to stay up longer than your girlfriend when you have a night off.

NIGHT ACTIONS

The differences in the actions of the workers also affects what happens during the course of the night. What one worker does can have a profound affect on what the other workers do. One night, Sarah, the oldest of the four still working, made herself a sandwich for her break. It was very slow at this point, so she came out to sit at the counter to eat it. Once she sat down, both Brendan and Kurt came out to talk, joke around, and ease their anxieties. The conversation centered on sex and different ways to have it.

The atmosphere isn't always this calm, warm, and supportive. For instance on a separate night, Karen cleaned the tables and the counters, which is normal, but she did it without stop from 3:00 till almost 5:00! This was the deadest time of the entire evening when I would usually sit with the servers and Kurt at the counter shooting the bull about all sorts of different things while the servers kept an eye on the customers and did a bit of cleaning here and there. What was fascinating about Karen's cleaning was she was so incredibly meticulous, opening the juice machine to clean it as well as packing down the butter in the butter carton like ice cream. I asked her if she was like this at home too and she said that she was, if not worse. The consequence of her continuous cleaning was that the other server there at the time and Kurt both seemed to feel obligated to clean as well. The other server, Mary, spent the time restacking the coffee filters in a new stack from the one they were shipped in—an efficient idea, but one that could be done socially instead of standing at the back counter as she was. Kurt totally changed his character at this time as well. He had previously been a very relaxed, carefree person, not overly concerned with cleanliness or authority. When the manager would leave at 3:00, he would discard his hat and scarf. But this night, instead of taking the lull in the customers' area to grab a smoke and chill out as he had before, he spent the time meticulously cleaning the kitchen. He usually cleans up while orders were cooking (something he could do while still watching the food), but he scraped, scrubbed, and washed the area down more than I had ever seen him do. He also swept and mopped the floor, something I have never seen done at a time that he would have normally grabbed a smoke. It was obvious that Karen's constant cleaning, which bordered on compulsive, had an effect on the actions of the others working that Sunday night.

SOCIAL LIFE

Not many of the people who work graveyard really hang out together apart from their job. Brendan and Rob do, but that is because they were friends before working together. When one person has a party, they invite the others, but they don't solely hang out with the others while on their days off. The conversation, I am told, usually turns to shop talk. One night, however, I noticed that Brendan had come in at the end of a night at a bar with some friends. It was a form of role reversal in a sense, but he knew everyone who was working as well as a majority of the regular customers. I asked why he was here. It was because he knew the people who would be here and wanted to hang out for a while. He came with a bunch of friends who all seemed to know the people working as well. In some ways, the workers act as liaisons for their friends to meet other people they would not normally come into contact with.

WHY NIGHT?

Each of the people who work the graveyard shift have their own reason for staying with the odd schedule in addition for the need for money. Rob stays mainly because he can live at home and work. He claims to be a night person and this gives him the days and evenings free. Brendan stays because it has the highest pay-to-work ratio of any shift. Although the day shifts make much more in the way of tips, they also work at least twice as hard. Ellen stays mainly because she needs to support her three daughters and this is the only time that she can have away from them and not worry about their safety. Tom stays because he hopes to move up to full-time manager and this is the only way to do so. He also finds the night life exciting and interesting. They all seem to agree that the graveyard is the most exciting time to work at Denny's and is never boring.

In addition to the reasons that I heard for working at Denny's, I also started to understand the differences in the attitudes that each of the servers had toward the work. Each attitude appeared to be a reflection of what the individual thought of working there. The servers essentially were lackadaisical toward their work—an "I don't really care" attitude. Tom reiterated this view but stuck up for them by adding that they could put aside their feelings about the job and get work done when the place got hectic. I believe this statement is a defense mechanism against the pressures that are forced on them at unpredictable times.

JOB SATISFACTION

The differences in job satisfaction among the different workers varies with their positions and their approach. Most of the servers regard their work as at most a prolonged temporary job. The manager's view, on the other hand, is one of permanence. He sees himself staying with the company long after the servers have found other employment. The variation in satisfaction that each one gets with his or her job directly relates to their view of their job. Consistent with a study done by Lynn Shore and Harry Martin (1989), shorter term workers rely on more immediate measures of their performance than do those who seek the longer, more permanent position with the company: Servers gauge job satisfaction by the amount of tips they receive, which they consider an immediate review of job quality. The better job they do the more tips they receive; the more tips the more they enjoy their job. The manager, on the other hand, doesn't receive tips, just headaches, and Tom complained about that as a drawback to his job. His satisfaction is directly related to long-term commitment and advancement in the corporation.

REALIZATIONS (ETHNOGRAPHER'S AND INFORMANTS')

I see the uniform the servers wear as a cloak they can put on to change out of their old self into a façade they wear with it. Both Brendan and Rob realized while I was talking to them that they were vastly different outside of their work. They realized in their own ways that their personalities changed from when they are at home among friends to when they are at work. Brendan realized that he is actually a very shy person outside of his workplace. He is very shy at home, not generally one to walk up to strangers and start a conversation with them. Rob, on the other hand, says he is much more outgoing outside than he is at work. He generally enjoys the excitement of meeting new people at parties, but rarely starts up conversations with his customers. The previous example of Tom, who has to accept the lifestyle of the gays that he does not believe in at all, is yet another way in which the work at Denny's changes the personalities of the people.

CONCLUDING THOUGHTS

The more familiar they became with me and the more they knew what I was doing, the more I became a neutral party to whom they could let out a sigh or take a break and complain about a table they had.

In conclusion, the night watch at Denny's is exciting. I had no idea that so much actually happened during the times I am usually asleep. The people who work this shift have formed their own support group in order to make it through the late night hours. They bring with them a variety of different backgrounds with different ideas and habits, all of which reflect in the ways that they work with each other as well as serving their customers. No two servers serve people the same, and their personalities are the mechanisms that determine their behavior. Although some plan to be employed by the corporation longer than others, they all have their own methods of gaining enough satisfaction to get them to come back each night. The people who frequent the restaurant are as diverse as the people who work there, and all of them are interdependent.

BIBLIOGRAPHY

ABU-LUGHOD, LILA. 1991. "Writing Against Culture," pp. 137–62 in Richard G. Fox (ed.), *Recapturing Anthropology*. Santa Fe: School of American Research Press.

AIRASIAN, PETER W., and MARY E. WALSH. 1997. "Constructivist Cautions." *Phi Delta Kappan*, 78:444–49.

ANGELL, J.W. (ed.). 1950. *The Thomas Mann Reader*. New York: Knopf.

BAKHTIN, MIKHAIL. 1968. *Rabelais and His World* (trans. Helene Iswolsky). Cambridge, MA: MIT Press.

BENEDICT, RUTH. 1934. *Patterns of Culture*. Boston: Houghton Mifflin.

———. 1946. *The Chrysanthemum and the Sword*. Boston: Houghton Mifflin.

BERNARD, H. RUSSELL. 1994. *Research Methods in Cultural Anthropology* (2nd ed.). Thousand Oaks, CA: Sage.

BIRDWHISTELL, RAY L. 1952. *Introduction to Kinesics*. Louisville: University of Louisville.

———. 1970. *Kinesics and Context*. Philadelphia: University of Pennsylvania Press.

BLOUNT, BEN G. (ed.). 1995. *Language, Culture, and Society* (2nd ed.). Prospect Heights, IL: Waveland Press.

BRENNEIS, DONALD, and RONALD H.S. MACAULAY (eds.). 1996. *The Matrix of Language: Contemporary Linguistic Anthropology*. Boulder, CO: Westview Press.

BROOKS, JACQUELINE GRENNON, and MARTIN G. BROOKS. 1993. *In Search of Understanding: The Case for Constructivist Classrooms*. Alexandria, VA: Association for Supervision and Curriculum Development.

BURLING, ROBBINS. 1964. "Cognition and Componential Analysis: God's Truth or Hocus-Pocus?" *American Anthropologist*, 66:20–28.

CRANE, JULIA, and MICHAEL ANGROSINO. 1974. *Field Projects in Anthropology*. Morristown, NJ: General Learning Press.

EDGERTON, ROBERT, and L.L. LANGNESS. 1974. *Methods and Styles in the Study of Culture.* San Francisco: Chandler & Sharp.

FETTERMAN, DAVID. 1989. *Ethnography Step by Step.* Newbury Park, CA: Sage.

FOUNTAIN STREET CHURCH. 1992. *Seeds: A Family Resource for Liberal Religion.* Grand Rapids: Author.

GEERTZ, CLIFFORD. 1973. *The Interpretation of Cultures.* New York: Basic Books.

———. 1988. *Works and Lives: The Anthropologist as Author.* Stanford: Stanford University Press.

GOODENOUGH, WARD H. 1991. "Reply to James Donovan," *American Anthropologist,* 93:691–92.

HALL, EDWARD T. 1959. *The Silent Language.* Greenwich, CT: Fawcett.

———. 1966. *The Hidden Dimension.* Garden City, NY: Doubleday.

———. 1974. *Handbook for Proxemic Research.* Philadelphia: Society for the Anthropology of Visual Communication.

———. 1976. *Beyond Culture.* New York: Anchor Press.

———. 1983. *The Dance of Life: The Other Dimension of Time.* Garden City, NY: Anchor Press/Doubleday.

HALL, JUDITH A. 1984. *Nonverbal Sex Differences.* Baltimore: Johns Hopkins University Press.

HONIGMANN, JOHN J. 1959. *The World of Man.* New York: Harper & Bros.

KEISER, R. LINCOLN. 1979. *The Vice Lords.* New York: Holt, Rinehart and Winston.

KOTTAK, CONRAD. 1982. *Researching American Culture.* Ann Arbor: University of Michigan Press.

KROEBER, ALFRED LOUIS. 1939. *Cultural and Natural Areas of Native North America.* Berkeley: University of California Press.

KROEBER, THEODORA. 1961. *Ishi in Two Worlds: A Biography of the Last Wild Indian in North America.* Berkeley: University of California Press.

KUTSCHE, PAUL, and JOHN R. VAN NESS. 1981. *Cañones: Values, Crisis, and Survival in a Northern New Mexico Village.* Albuquerque: University of New Mexico Press. (Reprinted by Sheffield Publishing, Salem, WI)

LANCASTER, ROGER N. 1988. *Thanks to God and the Revolution: Popular Religion and Class Consciousness in the New Nicaragua.* New York: Columbia University Press.

LANGNESS, L.L. 1974. *The Study of Culture.* San Francisco: Chandler & Sharp.

LEACH, EDMUND R. 1968. "Ritual." *International Encyclopedia of the Social Sciences.* New York: Macmillan.

LÉVI-STRAUSS, CLAUDE. 1953. "Social Structure," pp. 524–53 in Alfred L. Kroeber (ed.), *Anthropology Today.* Chicago: University of Chicago Press.

LOWELL, AMY. 1916. *Men, Women and Ghosts.* Boston: Houghton Mifflin.

MARTIN, JUDITH. 1982. *Miss Manners' Guide to Excruciatingly Correct Behavior.* New York: Warner Books.

MAYO, CLARA and NANCY M. HENLEY (eds.). 1981. *Gender and Nonverbal Behavior.* New York: Springer-Verlag.

MILLS, GEORGE T. 1959. *Navajo Art and Culture.* Colorado Springs: Taylor Museum of the Fine Arts Center.

MINER, HORACE. 1956. "Body Ritual among the Nacirema," *American Anthropologist,* 58:503–07.

MURPHY, YOLANDA, and ROBERT F. MURPHY. 1985. *Women of the Forest* (2nd ed.). New York: Columbia University Press.

MURRAY, STEPHEN O. 1996. "Male Homosexuality in Guatemala: Possible Insights and Certain Confusions from Sleeping with the Natives," pp. 236–60 in Ellen Lewin and William Leap (eds.), *Out in the Field.* Urbana: University of Illinois Press.

MYERHOFF, BARBARA. 1978. *Number Our Days.* New York: Simon & Schuster.

NETTING, ROBERT McC. 1977. *Cultural Ecology.* Menlo Park, CA: Cummings.

PEHRSON, ROBERT. 1966. *The Social Organization of the Marri Baluch* (compiled and analyzed from his notes by F. Barth). (Viking Fund Publications in Anthropology No. 43.) Chicago: Aldine.

PELTO, PERTTI J. 1970. *Anthropological Research.* New York: Harper & Row.

RABINOW, PAUL. 1977. *Reflections on Fieldwork in Morocco.* Berkeley: University of California Press.

REICH, ALICE. 1993a. "Anthropology as Oxymoron," Paper delivered at Colorado College.

———. 1993b. "Women and Spirituality," pp. 427–40 in J. Wetzel, M.L. Espenlaub, M.A. Hagen, A.B. McElhiney, and C.B. Williams (eds.), *Women's Studies Thinking Women.* Dubuque, IA: Kendall Hunt.

ROSALDO, RENATO. 1989. *Culture and Truth.* Boston: Beacon Press.

SCHLIG, ANDREW D. (ANDREW D. LEWIS). 1989–90. "Marginality: Urban and Suburban Homeless Men," *Journal of the Steward Anthropological Society*, 19:77–161.

SHORE, LYNN MCFARLANE, and HARRY J. MARTIN 1989. "Job Satisfaction and Organizational Commitment in Relation to Work Performance and Turnover Intentions," *Human Relations*, 42: 625–38.

SPRADLEY, JAMES. 1979. *The Ethnographic Interview.* New York: Holt, Rinehart and Winston.

———. 1980. *Participant Observation.* Chicago: Holt, Rinehart and Winston.

SPRADLEY, JAMES, and DAVID MCCURDY. 1972. *The Cultural Experience.* Chicago: Science Research Associates.

STEWARD, JULIAN H. 1955. *Theory of Culture Change: The Methodology of Multilinear Evolution.* Urbana: University of Illinois Press.

TURNER, VICTOR W. 1968. "Myth and Symbol." *International Encyclopedia of the Social Sciences.* New York: Macmillan.

TYLOR, SIR EDWARD BURNETT. 1871 (1958). *The Origins of Culture* (Chapters 1–9 of *Primitive Culture*). New York: Harper & Bros.

VAN GENNEP, ARNOLD. 1909 (1960). *The Rites of Passage.* London: Routledge.

VAN MAANEN, JOHN. 1988. *Tales of the Field: On Writing Ethnography.* Chicago: University of Chicago Press.

WALLACE, ANTHONY F.C. 1970. *Culture and Personality* (2nd ed.). New York: Random House.

WERNER, OSWALD, and G. MARK SCHOEPFLE. 1987. *Systematic Fieldwork* (2 vols.). Newbury Park, CA: Sage.

WISSLER, CLARK. 1900. *The Relation of Nature to Man in Aboriginal America.* London: Oxford University Press.

WOLCOTT, HARRY F. 1995. *The Art of Fieldwork.* Walnut Creek, CA: Altamira Press.

WRIGHT, THOMAS. 1906. *The Life of Sir Richard Burton* (vol. 2). New York: G.P. Putnam's Sons.